Pharaoh's Workers

Also by Leonard H. Lesko

The Ancient Egyptian Book of Two Ways

A Dictionary of Late Egyptian, 5 vols. (editor)

Egyptological Studies in Honor of Richard A. Parker (editor)

An Index of the Spells on Egyptian Middle Kingdom Coffins and Related Documents

King Tut's Wine Cellar

Religion in Ancient Egypt:
Gods, Myths, and Personal Practice
(with Byron E. Shafer, John Baines, and David P. Silverman)

PHARAOH'S WORKERS

The Villagers of Deir el Medina

Edited by
Leonard H. Lesko

CORNELL UNIVERSITY PRESS
Ithaca and London

Cornell University Press gratefully acknowledges a subvention
from Brown University which aided in the publication of this book.

First published 1994 by Cornell University Press.

Printed in the United States of America

Library of Congress Cataloging-in-Publication Data

Pharaoh's workers : the villagers of Deir el Medina / edited by
Leonard H. Lesko.
p.   cm.
Includes bibliographical references and index.
ISBN 0-8014-2915-3 (cloth) — ISBN 0-8014-8143-0 (paper)
1. Dayr al-Madīnah Site (Egypt) 2. Working class—Egypt—Dayr al-
Madīnah Site. I. Lesko, Leonard H.
DT73.D47P47   1994
932—dc20   93-45650

Contents

Contents

List of Illustrations

List of Illustrations

Color Plates
following page 86

Pharaoh's Workers

Introduction

Enough of the ancient Egyptian workers' output still survives to astound all who visit the Nile Valley. The masses of huge blocks moved to construct the pyramids, the soaring granite obelisks, the mighty figures carved from cliff faces, the elaborate decoration of wall surfaces in the chambers and corridors of tombs that penetrate deep underground—all these lead us to ask, who were the people who carried out such works and did so with what we would call primitive tools? Are they not even more interesting than the kings who ruled them; are they not more impressive for the challenges they accepted and overcame? The ancient Egyptian workmen—whether they built vast temples or manufactured intricate gold chains, cut and finished straight walls in the cramped interior of a stone sarcophagus or gave hard stone vessels the thinnest of walls—inspire both awe and admiration.

But who were these people? How did they live and what did they believe? Were they well rewarded for their skilled work, or were they exploited? Were they anonymous, or were they acclaimed during their lives? In order to answer such questions we need contemporary written texts, preferably texts written by and for the ancient workers themselves. Only such documentation can reveal their economic, legal, and social activities and bring the working-class community into focus. So far, in very few archaeological sites have any such documents been found. But fortunately, one has yielded a substantial, well-preserved archive. This is the village of Deir el Medina, the settlement for the workers who hewed and decorated the tombs of the pharaohs of Egypt's brilliant Age of Empire, the New Kingdom.

Consequently, Deir el Medina is among the most thoroughly documented and best-known communities from the ancient world. In this village—located west of modern Luxor on the left (west) bank of the Nile about half a mile beyond the cultivated land bordering the river, and between the Valley of the Kings and the Valley of the Queens—lived a number of the civil servants, stonecutters, and draftsmen/artists who prepared the tombs of their kings and queens. The village occupied the southern part of the Theban necropolis in a valley behind Gurnet Murai hill. Its southern entrance looked out toward the Medinet Habu area, where a small temple was built during the Eighteenth Dynasty and the much larger structure of Ramses III during the Twentieth. The workmen would have used this opening to go around to the southwest when their work lay in the Valley of the Queens. The northern opening of the valley provided the Deir el Medina inhabitants their most direct access to the cultivation, eastward around Gurnet Murai hill and down to the area where the temple called the Ramesseum was built by Ramses II in the Nineteenth Dynasty. Or, heading straight north, they could follow the base of the high, steep cliffs to Deir el Bahri with its Eleventh and Eighteenth Dynasty temples, notably that of Queen Hatshepsut. The major path from the village, however, proceeded north from its western foothills along the top of those same cliffs that surround Deir el Bahri to a spot where the workmen made another small settlement for themselves before the path descended to their most important work area—the Valley of the Kings.

The walled village, conforming in general shape to the narrow valley in which it was situated, could not have provided a pleasant environment. The barren hillsides that surround it reflect the heat of the desert sun on it, and the hill of Gurnet Murai effectively cuts off some of the prevailing north breeze and much of the view of the verdant river valley below. The site had no trees, and all water had to be carried in from at least half a mile away. Nevertheless, these workmen and their families left a record of village life at Deir el Medina that spans almost four hundred years and parallels much of the history of the Egyptian New Kingdom or Empire. The surviving records shed little light on the major events of the time, however. Rather, they inform us about everyday life in ancient Egypt: the

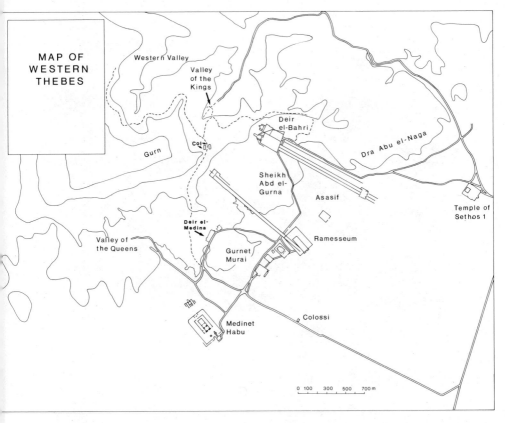

MAP OF
WESTERN
THEBES

Western Valley

Valley
of the
Kings

Deir
el-Bahri

Dra Abu el-Naga

Gurn

Col

Sheikh
Abd el-
Gurna

Asasif

Temple of
Sethos 1

Deir el-
Medina

Valley of
the Queens

Gurnet
Murai

Ramesseum

Medinet
Habu

Colossi

0 100   300   500   700 m

Map of Western Thebes. Drawn by Mary Winkes.

[3]

The Village of Deir el Medina, from the north looking south. Photo by L. H. Lesko.

Deir el Medina from the south looking north. Photo by L. H. Lesko.

Overview of Deir el Bahri from the Gurn. Workmen's settlement is in the foreground with path leading to the Valley of the Kings. Photo by L. H. Lesko.

Overview of the Valley of the Kings (right) and the Western Valley (left). Photo by L. H. Lesko.

The central portion of the Valley of the Kings. Photo by L. H. Lesko.

One section of the corridor descending to the burial chamber of the tomb of Ramses VI (Twentieth Dynasty). Photo by L. H. Lesko.

[6]

organization of work, the economy, society, education, legal and religious concerns, and some factors that are difficult to categorize.

The ancient name of the site was Set Maat, "the Place of Truth," and the workmen were "servants" in the Place of Truth. The community seems to have been established near the beginning of the Eighteenth Dynasty, at least by the reign of Thutmose I (c. 1500 B.C.)—whose name has been found on some bricks in the walls surrounding the village—or perhaps a few years earlier, since the villagers through many generations held Amenhotep I and his mother, Queen Ahmose Nefertari, in special esteem, possibly as patrons of the workmens' community.

The Eighteenth Dynasty occupation of the site is not well documented, however, and it would have been abandoned anyway during the so-called Amarna interlude (1367–50 B.C.), when Akhenaton moved his royal residence and had his tomb prepared at Tell el Amarna. Essentially, then, our story begins at the very end of the Eighteenth Dynasty, with the reestablishment of the royal work gangs in western Thebes under Horemhab in his seventh year. Since the community at Deir el Medina thrived during the Nineteenth and Twentieth Dynasties and continued to be administered from nearby Medinet Habu to the beginning of the Twenty-First Dynasty, we are speaking now of some 230 years, roughly 1310–1080 B.C. Obviously, in the few centuries when the village was inhabited and the work on the many royal tombs progressed, the material remains of the earlier generations of workers would have been displaced by those of the later; and in the several millennia since, much would have been lost to invaders, nearby villagers, monks who settled in the valley, serious tomb robbers, and tourists. Even what survives after all this, however, has much to teach us.

A major find of papyri was made near the village in the 1840s, and throughout the last century objects continued to be taken from the area. Serious scientific excavation of the site of Deir el Medina from 1905 to 1909 by the Italian archaeologist Ernesto Schiaperelli added considerably to the Egyptian Museum at Turin, and its collection of papyri and ostraca (the broken potsherds and limestone flakes used as cheap writing material) grew enormously. A French mission began working at Deir el Medina in 1917 and under Bernard Bruyère's direction between 1922 and 1951 excavated the entire site—village, cemetery, and dump—providing a very substantial base of documented material. From it, we now know many of the people who belonged to the community through the years, often where they lived, where they were buried, what they owned, and even in a few cases their handwriting and artistic peculiarities. With this base much that was removed in the almost free-for-all plunder of the previous century can now be reassociated. Many pieces from the extensive nineteenth-century collections made by Henry Salt and Bernardino Drovetti and now enhancing the British Museum in London, the Egyptian Museum in Turin, the Louvre, the Ägyptisches Museum Berlin, and even the Museo Nacional of Rio de Janeiro are evidently from Deir el Medina, including hundreds of stelae, statues, and papyri.

Bruyère's seasons of work were followed by prompt publication of preliminary reports, though the full publication of the tombs and finds continues at a very slow pace. Unfortunately, Bruyère apparently did not have sufficient control over his dig; it now seems that about half the papyri excavated from the site during the 1920s were removed surreptitiously while the excavations were going on. The large pit used as a town dump, perhaps at a later period, was probably his most rewarding discovery, since it contained thousands of ostraca with texts both literary and nonliterary. Bruyère was particularly fortunate to have had as his philologist the great Czech Egyptologist Jaroslav Černý, who later become professor of Egyptology at Oxford's Queens College. His decipherment and publication of many of the nonliterary ostraca have formed the basis for much of the information that has already been published about the community and the foundation upon which his students and the rest of us are attempting to build.

The sales documents that survive provide important data on prices and exchange in the ancient economy. Private letters reveal details of social relations, parenting, and marriage. Charms and prayers say much of these people's approach to the divine, their beliefs and fears. Egyptologists seeking facts about the history of law and jurisprudence, early medicine and public health, or labor relations naturally turn to the records from Deir el Medina and their wealth of detail. Through popular books and even a television series, millions around the world have been introduced to some of the inhabitants of the village and gained a general understanding of what life was like three thousand years ago in this fascinating artists' colony. There are still myriad details to recover and puzzles to solve, however, and the interpretive work continues. It is the goal of the contributors to this volume to reveal still more about the lives of Pharaoh's workers.

PART I

Social and Economic Concerns

Embellish your place which is in the desert,
the pit that will hide your corpse.
Set it before you as your business,
which is as important in your eyes,
as it is to the great elders,
who rest in their store-chambers.
                              —Maxims of Ani

The workmen who lived at Deir el Medina included the quarrymen or stonecutters who excavated the royal tombs in the limestone hills and cliffs of the Valley of the Kings and Valley of the Queens, and also the sculptors, draftsmen, and painters who decorated the excavated tombs. Although the limestone is generally soft and not difficult to work, the extent of the excavations—often hundreds of feet into the cliffs or the valley floors—and the fine finish of the delicate low-relief carving demonstrate the considerable extent of each undertaking as well as the high quality of the sculptor's work. The quarrymen and sculptors were generally the same individuals, apparently. The decoration was guided by accomplished draftsmen who laid out the designs and enlarged them from gridline drawings to fit the space available, carefully checking and frequently correcting the guidelines on the walls. The painters' confident lines and careful brush strokes indicate their high skill, and the wide variety of pigments available to them permitted feathering, shading, and remarkable detail in the representation of textiles.

The size of the tomb work force varied from about thirty in the slow period during the middle of the long reign of Ramses II to 120 in the reign of Ramses IV; fifty to sixty men would have been the norm. In addition to the artisans, the village generally housed some administrators —specifically, the foremen of the two separate gangs that shared the work, and at least one scribe in the Nineteenth and two or more in the

Twentieth Dynasty. The community included the workmens' wives, children and other dependents as well, and was served by a few resident coppersmiths, carpenters, potters, basket-makers, and even a part-time physician. Support staff who resided not in the Place of Truth but nearby—woodcutters, water carriers, fishermen, gardeners, washermen, and flour grinders—were likewise paid by the state and supervised by local officials. Although some newcomers periodically joined the community, particularly when the work force was increased in size, the population was generally fairly stable, and fathers could be succeeded by sons through many generations. Still, there would not have been enough vacancies for apprentices to provide jobs for all the children of the workmen, and with occasional decreases in the size of the work force, many would have been laid off or forced to accept more menial jobs.

From what we know of the income and status of the workmen, they would have to be considered in modern terms as middle class. They certainly had no royal or noble family connections, and much of their work, such as quarrying the tombs, was difficult and unglamorous. They were not slaves, however, but salaried state employees whose individual wages—paid in the form of rations—were perhaps three times those of a fieldhand. In addition, "moonlighting"—making furniture, stelae, or other funerary equipment for their neighbors—was a widespread practice that helped some achieve an even more comfortable standard of living. When on occasion their pay rations were long overdue, they did not hesitate to go out on strike. In one such instance, on the authority of the vizier (second in command to pharaoh, and the official more or less directly in overall charge of their work), the temple storerooms across the river at Karnak were opened to pay them.

When they were not moonlighting, the sculptors busied themselves in preparing their own tombs and burial equipment, probably making use of the valuable copper tools provided for their use in the royal tombs, even though these would have worn down quickly. The painters likewise either were allowed to use or may have appropriated some of the pigments intended for the royal tombs for their own tomb paintings as well as the commissions they carried out for others. Perhaps such perquisites went along with the job.

The villagers established their own cemeteries on the nearby hillsides, just a stone's throw from their homes. The bottom courses of the eastern hill were the site of burials of babies and children, with adults' graves higher up—many of these from the Eighteenth Dynasty, judging from finds there such as scarabs bearing the name of Queen Hatshepsut. In the larger western cemetery, with its pyramidion-topped tomb chapels with solar stelae, some pre-Amarna inhabitants were buried, but this is primarily the Ramesside cemetery. At the end of the Ramesside period the workmen and their families were transferred for their own safety from the village of Deir el Medina to within the mighty walls of the mortuary temple of Ramses III at nearby Medinet Habu.

It is interesting to note that these particular workmen apparently did not toil in the other nearby tombs of officials and priests; at least there is no evidence to indicate that any of them did so. Nor were they responsible for the construction of the huge mortuary temples of the kings—work of quite a different type involving the quarrying and transport of sandstone and the making of mud bricks. And although one might expect that the relief carving and painting of both tomb and temple walls would have been done by a special class of artists, this was not the case with the tomb workers, so it cannot be assumed that the temple work staffs were organized much differently. Since no separate villages of the temple workmen survive, they probably lived closer to the cultivation or at the temple sites in temporary quarters such as those known from earlier times.

The royal necropolis quite logically had guard posts for protection of the royal burials. A similar post at the village itself has led some modern scholars to posit a very restrictive environment akin to confinement for the workmen, but the matter of the villagers' freedom of movement is taken up below by Andrea McDowell. The question of the ethnic backgrounds of many workmen with foreign-sounding names is considered in detail by William A. Ward, whose study of possible foreign connections has provided a new dimension to the community. But first, the village social setting, familial relationships, and some legal contractual and financial matters are examined by Barbara S. Lesko.

ONE

Rank, Roles, and Rights

Barbara S. Lesko

A man is asked about his rank,
a woman about her husband.
—Maxims of Ani

Contrary to popular belief, the pyramids of the pharaohs were not constructed by slaves, nor the richly outfitted tombs in the Valley of the Kings by men who were subsequently put to death in order to protect the hidden royal treasures. Just how much actual freedom and wealth the tomb builders of the New Kingdom enjoyed is a major concern of the scholars engaged in studying Deir el Medina. The ancients themselves left behind many and various records which, taken together, help shape an assessment of their social and financial status and even their freedom of movement. Judging their actual civil liberties, how much they and their fellow countrymen were able to live free of manipulation by others, to pursue a life of their own choosing, is far more difficult, and the final word on this subject will surely not be written for some time to come.

When the workmen's village was reestablished in western Thebes after the Amarna interlude, it was part of a changed world. Thebes was no longer a power center, for Horemhab and the subsequent kings of the Nineteenth Dynasty saw the strategic necessity of again residing in and ruling from the northern regions of the country, besieged as it had been by Asiatics since the last years of Tutankhamun's reign. Nor were the old Theban aristocratic and clerical families any longer in evidence. If the latter had been victims of Akhenaton's monotheistic religious zeal, the former now found themselves outmaneuvered by the rising professional warrior class. The army was the largest and most cohesive group left after the Amarna period—clearly the only institution on which the king could rely to rebuild the country.

The void left in the temples closed by Akhenaton was, under Horemhab, filled by "ordinary priests and lectors from the pick of the army," according to Alan Gardiner.[1] This policy was accelerated under the Ramessides, and similarly, the militarization of the state administration was undertaken in the late Eighteenth and the Nineteenth Dynasty.[2] The most important officials invariably had military backgrounds, and most now chose to be buried in the north close to the centers of power, as in the great Memphite necropolis at Saqqara. It is noteworthy, however, that in Egyptian culture one finds few private monuments celebrating an individual's acts of heroism and no portraits of military men with their arms and armor. The invincible might of the divine king apparently preempted claims of personal valor and power on the part of private persons.

The population of western Thebes was not large and was very likely impoverished when Horemhab turned his attention to it.[3] During the Nineteenth and Twentieth Dynasties most inhabitants were priests and those who worked temple lands or crafted the divine images and implements needed in the temples or the necropolis.[4] Priestly families lived off the landholdings of their temples and the food that was first offered on the altars. Gustave Lefebvre found evidence that the priests of Amon of the Nineteenth Dynasty enjoyed only moderate social prestige, and Ahmed Kadry found "no proper leadership for a renewed struggle for power" among this priestly hierarchy.[5]

It must be remembered, however, that at its highest levels much of the clergy had its roots in the warrior class and was very much controlled by the crown. Kadry argues that the entire economic life of the country was "controlled by the king through an efficient state apparatus composed mainly of the personnel of the new military class."[6] Indeed, at the top of society, just below the royal family, was the aristocracy of chariot-owning knights, who could live in the provinces if they wished and who held much property in the form of land and slaves.[7] In general, courtiers from the warrior class were given land grants large enough to permit them a decent standard of living after taxes were paid to the crown. They and royal family members enjoyed social prestige and influence with pharaoh.

To argue for the military's hand in everything, however, is to overstate the case. It must not be forgotten that another very important and elite group controlled the civil administration. Ever since the Old Kingdom, Egypt had been run by a vast civil service staffed by men whose primary qualifications were intelligence and education. Almost from the beginning of their history, the kings of Egypt required ambitious building projects, and it was the scribal class that did the calculating required for the procurement of building materials and the engineering of the mammoth structures. Government scribes computed the taxes that paid for these projects and drew up the roll calls for the labor corvées that carried out the work. In fact, virtually every aspect of life in this sophisticated nation, from land measurement to time and calendrical calculations, needed a body of educated civil servants proficient in mathematics, particularly geometry, and well-trained in the reading and composition of a very complex writing system. A literary form beginning in the Middle Kingdom extolled the scribe as superior to (even contemptuous of) those in all other careers, and this together with the popularity of portraying any man of stature as a scribe (a tradition since the Old Kingdom) suggests that the attitude of pride and superiority was certainly well established among this class of people. Even more snobbish variations on this theme are found in the literature of the New Kingdom: "Be a scribe, that your limbs may be smooth and your hands languid, that you may go out dressed in white, being exalted so that the courtiers salute you. . . . one who is skilled, he arises step by step until he reaches [the position of] an official."[8]

The recognition that promotions to positions of real power were readily available within their ranks, which were closed to all who were not as well trained and educated, encouraged the air of superiority among scribes, and theirs was indeed an elite class; as the author of a Twentieth Dynasty school text put it, "One calls and a thousand answer" (P. Lansing, *AEL*). Though it took years of patient study to master writing and required a poor family to forgo the labor of one of its sons in order to permit him to advance in the world, the scribe's life was one of relative ease and status. Even military leaders, significant though they were to the real power of the Egyptian empire, emphasized their education by including "scribe" among their official titles, and it was as a scribe, rather than an armed fighting man, that the great army commanders had themselves portrayed in their statuary.

Administrators of the Tomb

The most powerful civil official in New Kingdom Egypt was the king's vizier, who functioned as overseer of the vast civil service and as chief justice of the land. To this trusted official was also given the responsibility of producing the royal tomb. Thus, when the tomb workers sent a gift of two silver chisels to their vizier in the reign of Ramses V, they were expressing their gratitude and loyalty to the official upon whom they were most dependent.[9] It was undoubtedly the high importance of their responsibility and the "classified" nature of their labor that placed the tomb workers under the direct control of the supreme civil administrator. On behalf of the pharaoh the vizier ordered and inspected the project and officially received the completed tomb from the necropolis community. He was ultimately responsible for paying the artisan's wages; the delivery of these and other supplies was one of the concerns of his office in Thebes. Although there were generally two viziers in the Nineteenth and Twentieth Dynasties, even the one for Upper Egypt is believed not to have lived in the south; however, there are records that a vizier personally inspected the royal tomb's progress and even visited the workers village. Knowing that they were working directly for their pharaoh and answerable only to the highest officials in the land must have given the workers on the royal tomb a sense of great prestige and respect in the eyes of their fellow citizens.

In theory, all the artisans of the tomb, and definitely their foremen and scribes, were directly appointed by the vizier. Certainly, when the workers had a serious problem, perhaps a complaint against a foreman, they felt they could appeal to the vizier for aid. Normally, however, the foreman was their leader, representing their interests to the authorities and hearing their complaints. At the time of highest tensions, when the artisans did not receive their wages, one foreman of the time sided with his men against the administration—clearly represented in this instance by the tomb's scribe, who resorted to threats to try to get the strikers back on the job.[10]

The two foremen (one for each of the two crews, called "Right" and "Left," that worked both sides of the royal tomb at once) were supposed to oversee the work on a daily basis. Together with at least one scribe, they were regarded as the administrators (*rwdw*) or chiefs (*ḥryw*) of the tomb workers. This triumvirate was responsible for maintaining order in the workplace and village and on the weekend sat on the local tribunal that heard complaints. It was the foremen who carried out the decisions of the court. If letters needed to be sent to the vizier's office concerning the work, a foreman was often the named correspondent and the recipient of the reply. Even though the foremen probably could read, however, it was more likely the official scribe of the tomb who penned the letters, as he was specially trained in the niceties of official letter writing.

The number of scribes seems to have varied over the years: sometimes there was only one, at other times one for each side. In the late Ramesside period, Jaroslav Černý found, there were four functioning at once. While the foremen's concerns were with the technical work, its progress, and the workers themselves, a scribe's responsibility was for recordkeeping and other administrative paperwork. At the tomb each day, sitting apart, he noted who was absent and recorded occurrences of significance: deliveries to the work force, events in the village (such as visits from officials), and the like. He created a diary of the tomb, first making notations on stone ostraca and later formalizing his notes as entries on his papyrus roll. Excerpts from this diary were sent to the vizier's office. Probably more than anyone, the scribe was the true on-site representative of the government's interests. But his recording skills were not confined strictly to royal tomb concerns. He was on hand in the village, at least on weekends, to write up various documents such as oaths, wills, and deeds of sale. It is not clear whether this would have been regarded as part of his proper responsibilities or whether he charged a fee for such services. A good number of the artisans themselves were able to read and even write; the draftsmen certainly needed to, as they were the ones who wrote the texts on the tomb's walls—and subsequently often referred to themselves as "scribes." Because a communication to a god needed to be stated and written absolutely perfectly, however, the professional scribe of the tomb wrote the questions that were laid before the oracle of the deified Amenhotep I.[11]

Černý believed that the scribe actually received the deliveries of copper tools, lamps, and timber and other raw materials used in the work; after recording such deliveries, he was the one who saw to their deposit in a storeroom and their subsequent distribution to the workers. Because of this (and with typical boastfulness) a tomb's scribes would then assume the title "Overseer of the Treasury in the Place of Truth." It was thus the scribe who actually issued the payday rations to the staff. With such a responsibility, it is not surprising that sometimes he would have to collect foodstuffs from the producers of the countryside to make up for what the government had failed to deliver on time (paydays were supposed to be the twenty-eighth of each month, but often deliveries were late).[12] The porters who carried daily water and food supplies to the village were also under the scribe's authority.

Income among the Tomb Workers

The military influence on New Kingdom society can be seen at Deir el Medina, which under Horemhab was reestablished along military lines. Within the tomb, the artisans were organized into two "crews" (the word used is the same applied in naval contexts: *isw.t*), and originally this was true also for the housing arrangements in the village. It is interesting to note, as Kadry did, that the pay rations for the tomb workers, though adequate, were not as lavish as those for the troops, who received meat; the tomb workers generally received only fish along with their grain and vegetables. As the offerings to the gods would also have included meat, it can be inferred that priestly families too enjoyed a higher standard of living and were among the classes Kadry called "rich," compared with the tomb workers.[13] Jac. J. Janssen, on the other hand, considered the workers collectively "well off."[14]

It would seem logical to examine purchasing power as a guide to wealth rather than diet. Certainly within the workmen's village there were varying incomes, even officially. The two foremen, who had the most direct responsibilities for the completion of the royal tomb, each received 7 1/2 *khar* of grain (5 1/2 of emmer wheat for bread and 2 of barley for beer) as his basic monthly pay, a *khar* being equal to 76.8 liters. In addition, such commodities as oil and vegetables were delivered to him and all the workers of the village. The foreman's deputy, as he was a man of the crew (and often the son of the foreman), earned the same as his mates: 5 1/2 *khar* each (4 of wheat, 1 1/2 of barley). This monthly stipend in grains has been calculated as more than adequate for a family of ten.[15] Thus a family might have surplus grain that could be used like cash to procure other products in this barter economy.

A scribe's wage has been the subject of some dispute. Apparently he was paid only 2 2/3 *khar* of wheat and 1 *khar* of barley; if this is correct, it would be an example of skilled "blue-collar" workers earning better wages than educated "white-collar" workers. Janssen has suggested that this figure may represent his due from only one side of the tomb, so that when there was only one scribe, he would receive twice this amount. If so, of course, when there were two scribes, their salary would still be lower than that of the tomb workers. More likely, perhaps, it may have been officially acknowledged that the salary was intended to repay the scribe only for his responsibilities to the government, leaving him free to earn whatever he wished to charge for all other scribal work performed in the village. This probability is enhanced by our knowing that the physician's official pay (added to that of the worker who played this role for his neighbors) was also minimal, yet we have documented evidence that the local physician was paid very high amounts by his patients (such as twenty-two *deben* of copper). Likewise, the work done by the village scribe in his off-hours sometimes commanded very high sums, as when the scribe of the tomb, Harshire, inscribed three coffins for a songstress of Amon for 329 *deben* of copper. Černý calculated that his profit was 95 *deben,* no mean sum, a *deben* equaling 91 grams of copper.[16]

Like wages, prices recorded in the ostraca are expressed in *deben* of copper or *khar* of grain, and the worker's monthly 5½ *khar* of grain was equivalent to 11 *deben* of copper in purchasing power.[17] Among the tomb workers were men of various skills—carpenters, plasterers, and draftsmen but also men whose job was pounding out the huge aperture in the limestone cliff—surely not as skilled or pleasant a task. Though presumably such less skilled laborers received the same pay as their skilled fellow workers, the latter could more readily add to their income. Carpenters, for instance, could easily find extra work. Sale records from Deir el Medina show that they charged a minimum of 11 *deben* for a simple chair; a bed could run 25 *deben,* and tables 15 *deben.*[18] This represents a good income for the carpenter, but also suggests that the worker's typical monthly wage from the government, even if none of it was consumed as food, would have represented very little in buying power for the average village family.

How, then, could some villagers acquire the land and slaves they are known to have possessed? The foreman Neferhotep had at least five slaves at the time of his death, and the scribe Ramose owned several head of cattle and agricultural fields. One bull was valued from 95 to 120 *deben;* a cow went for 40 to 50; one young servant girl sold for 410 *deben.*[19] Some men of the crews owned significant property—land, donkeys, stables, and storehouses—that they often rented out to others. Groups of artisans are known to have held shares in the labor of a single servant, and some even had their own personal slaves. How did they manage such large investments?

Years ago, Egyptologists were under the impression that the tomb workers in the royal necropolis were totally dependent upon the state for their living and were relatively poor individuals. Scholars such as William Edgerton doubted that private investment and business were known at all, "all worldly success being tied to public service."[20] Deir el Medina ostraca translated and analyzed in recent years, however, reveal that many of the workmen, apparently with no objection from the authorities, were producing salable items and finding a market in the wider world of Thebes.[21] In short, it has become clear that the people in this village made their real wealth working during off-hours. They seem to have been expected to put in only eight-hour days at the tomb, and their official single day off per ten-day work "week" expanded often to two- or three-day weekends—probably with the collusion of the administrators. In addition to charging for the letters and contracts they wrote for others, some scribes decorated coffins and may have produced and sold copies of the Book of the Dead as well. The carpenter who constructed scaffolding in the tomb also built coffins, beds, chairs, boxes, and tables for his neighbors. A man named Bekenwernero received 91 *deben* for one such order and 52 for another.[22] Sculptors and painters hired themselves out to decorate private tombs and shrines and to carve votive and funerary stelae and statues. And some foremen—whose recommendation of worker candidates would doubtless be extremely influential in the vizier's decision—took bribes.[23] Given these various sources of income, and because the government supplied not only housing and grain rations but also firewood, fish and vegetables, water, and oils for cooking, lighting, and anointing themselves, the workers were probably able to save for occasional luxury items and more serious investments.

The hereditary nature of positions on the work force indicates that the jobs were prized and the workers generally satisfied with their lot. Modest though their income and even perhaps their social status may have been, the people of the village came in contact with senior officials, as Barry Kemp has observed, and a taste for affluent living rubbed off on them, elevating the villagers' expectations; Kemp detects a "pretentiousness" among them.[24] Surely their employment by the Crown gave such craftsmen prestige in the eyes of the buying public, and no doubt brought them numerous orders from outside the village, but a workman's actual financial success would have depended directly on his own initiative and ambition to do extra work in his spare time. Wealth was not general; though some artisans were able to own real estate and animals, they were not able to afford professional morticians to care for their dead. An absence from work in order to wrap a deceased family member is often recorded only a day or two after the absence due to that relative's death;[25] thus, full mummification—requiring seventy days and many expensive fluids—must have been a luxury in Ramesside Egypt, beyond the means of most of these workers. Also the monuments—tombs, statutes, and stelae—left by the village families vary considerably in size and refinement, and some individuals known from the ostraca seem not to have left so much as a stela behind them.

Social Status, Influence, and Mobility

Social status did not depend on finances alone; family reputation and connections, education, and personal skills may have been just as significant in this tightly knit colony of talented artisans. The marriages that took place among the children of the village, sometimes between first cousins, sometimes with apparent disregard for the parents' rank, might seem to indicate a democratic blending of all the people in the village. But it should not be overlooked that a powerful clique at the top controlled the judicial process by forming a majority of the local tribunal.[26] These influential townsmen are known to have been capable of showing contempt and cruelty toward their more humble neighbors. Consider, for instance, the case of the man who came to seek their aid against the son of a prominent draftsman when the young man seduced the fiancée of the humbler supplicant: this poorer man himself received a beating at the hands of the tribunal's participants, who were doubtless interested in defending the actions of the elite.[27] The power of foremen and scribes to use the labor of the men of the crew for their own ends is also frequently documented.[28] Thus, beyond financial status, in the labor force itself and the superior knowledge and skills some villagers possessed would have given them greater prestige and influence. Such social ranking may well have been responsible for the restriction to certain families of the position of *wab* (lay) priest in the local cult of Amenhotep I.[29]

Still, there was some social mobility within the village. Neither the famous scribe Ramose nor his successor Ken-her-khepshef were originally from this community. They were promoted to its administration from scribal posts elsewhere (Ramose's former position was at the temple of Thutmose IV in western Thebes). Throughout the 230 years we know best of the history of this community, however, the majority of the scribes were the sons of other scribes of the necropolis or at least had been educated in the village as sons of men of the crews. Ankh, the son of a sculptor, was a scribe, as was Merymose during the middle of Ramses II's reign, although his father was a workman, so the sons of the village were not held back if they had the willingness to stay in school long enough to become skilled at writing and composition. To get a son even into the artisan work force, however, could take influence, often in the form of large bribes.[30] One lad who began life as a young slave in the village ended as a free artisan on the crew, no doubt because he won the confidence and support of his influential master, in this case a foreman.[31] Some foremen had worker origins: Kahi was the son of a chief carpenter; Paneb, who started as a stonemason, was the son of a workman.

It would seem likely that foremen needed to be literate in order to oversee the draftsmen, who definitely were literate. Thus schooling in reading and writing as well as in painting and drafting must have been available to more than just the sons of scribes, and such proficiency could overcome earlier limitations. In the large body of letters surviving from the very end of the community's history, there is reference to the little boys being at school, and numerous student texts have been found at Deir el Medina, but it cannot be known what proportion of the community's youth was actually enrolled in classes. Those who were training to join the gang were termed "children of the tomb." Records show that generally only the eldest surviving son actually followed his father into the work force there. Most younger sons, with little hope of succession, were faced with leaving the community to find employment elsewhere. In fact, however, the small walled community with its cramped houses certainly was neither an attractive nor comfortable place to live (current summer daytime temperatures record at 130° F.). Except for the pay and relative security of position, young people could not have been loathe to escape into the wider and more colorful world of the Nile Valley. During the war between the high priest Piankh and the Kushites, which occurred at the close of our village's history, the teenaged men who stayed on in the community were as liable as their fathers for conscription into the army. Some of these young men, records show, actually took flight across the river to more populous eastern Thebes in hopes of evading this duty into which their fathers had already been pressed.[32]

Women and Children of the Village

Evidence shows that families were large, and with many young people in the village—quite possibly as many as two hundred during periods of highest population—it is not surprising that a number of them were put to work at local chores. Some of their activities are reflected in art and in texts. The illustrated ostraca show both girls and boys tending oxen, and several depict a boy hunting with a tethered ape. Other boys are shown burnishing a pot, so various local craftsmen were probably assisted by the young. The delivery of food supplies to the artisans at work in the Valley of the Kings was assigned to a large team of young men "who were in rotation on duty every day." Although letters indicate that women prepared the food, it was apparently regarded as undesirable for women to deliver it to the gangs of workers. The ostraca pictures show young girls engaged in such leisure activities as swimming, boating, and bird trapping.[33] We do not know at what age the average girl married, though it was doubtless in her teens. Young men were advised to "marry young."[34]

The records of Deir el Medina have provided most of the information we have on women in the New Kingdom. Wives of scribes, foremen, and workers all shared much the same life within this isolated community's confining walls, although the scribes' and foremen's families lived in the largest houses. It seems significant however, that of the women who used a religious rank with their names, the vast majority were married to either scribes or foremen.[35] They served in the harem of the great god Amon-Re^c and held the titles *šm^{c}y.t* (chantress) and even *w^{3}b.t* (lay-priestess) of that god and *šm^{c}y.t* and *ḥsy.t* (singer) for other major deities such as Hathor and Mut—presumably at temples and shrines in their village, though because the scribes, when writing to some of these wom-en, seem to make a point of their religious status, they may well have been on the staffs of more major temples in western Thebes.[36] It is exceptional to find a workman whose wife had a religious title recorded on a funerary or votive monument.[37] Thus, achieving an official connection with a temple would seem to have been difficult unless a woman belonged to the upper echelons of the village, and a clear sense of class distinction based on wealth and husband's (or parents') position can be inferred.

We should mention also the feminine title of *rḫy.t,* the knowing or divining woman, who, as Joris F. Borghouts has concluded from a few mentions in the ostraca, seemingly had the power to predict events and was consulted to explain "manifestations of the god": illnesses, accidents, or divine oracles.[38] Whether such a woman (she is never named) was paid for helping others we do not know. "Wise" women in other cultures often prepare herbal medicines and assist at the sickbed or as midwives, but in this village one of the workmen was paid extra and given time off to practice as a physician.

All the women of the village were alike in that they were not living in self-sustaining households but depended upon the employer, in this case the state. They were directly helped by the employer's provision of a time-shared servant woman who went from house to house to do the arduous grinding of grain. The numbers of these servants available varied over the years; several days of service a month in each household seems to have been the norm.[39]

The title that accompanies each representation of a married woman on tomb and stela is *nb.t pr,* translated as "house mistress" or "lady of the house," which implies a life revolving around cooking, weaving, and child raising: that is, totally domestic, in-house occupations. The Theban tomb paintings themselves show very little of women's activities, preferring to portray the wife seated among her family or praying before her gods. The bias inherent in such paintings has been exposed elsewhere.[40] Nevertheless, it is still startling to read an eyewitness account from the Twenty-First Dynasty, written by the scribe of the necropolis, Butehamon, about his late wife's varied and arduous activities. In a letter (now unfortunately suffering many lacunae) found beside his dead wife's coffin, he reminisces about how the beautiful Ikhtay used to attend to the couple's many fields and cattle, for example, and carry all kinds of heavy loads.[41] When we consider that Ikhtay and Butehamon were, after all, a scribal family and people of property, it comes as a surprise that the wife had such diverse and arduous duties outside of the home. Perhaps this

Deir el Medina from the west. Photo by L. H. Lesko.

A typical house at Deir el Medina. Photo by L. H. Lesko.

Opposite, top: Low-relief sculpture, tomb of King Merneptah (Nineteenth Dynasty). Photo by L. H. Lesko.

Opposite, bottom: Veneration of deceased royalty: King Mentuhotep and Queen Ahmose Nefertari before the "Lady of the West" Hathor, from the Ramesside tomb of Amen-em-one at Gurnet Murai (TT # 277). Photo by L. H. Lesko.

Above: Workmen's settlement at the col. Photo by L. H. Lesko.

Inherkhau and his family (TT # 359). Photo by L. H. Lesko.

Scenes of daily life from the tomb of Ipuy (TT # 217). Photo by L. H. Lesko.

Ostracon with drawing of woman at her oven. Courtesy of Ägyptisches Museum, Leipzig. Photo by L. H. Lesko.

Ostracon with drawing of an unshaven stonemason. Photo courtesy of Fitzwilliam Museum, Cambridge (EGA. 432a-1943).

Wooden statue of the scribe Ramose. Photo courtesy of the Rijksmuseum van Oudheden, Leiden.

was her fate exactly *because* her husband had a full-time job with the government, but it demonstrates that we must not allow ourselves to be blinded by preconceived ideas about what a house mistress did. Egypt was, after all, an agrarian society, and peasant women typically have myriad responsibilities for their families' survival, sharing in the labors of the men. In the artisans' community, families that owned farm land would have had similar responsibilities on top of the work in the necropolis (even if they had hired laborers or slaves to do much of it), and thus women of such households could have assumed control of all phases of family productivity, especially since their men were away from home much of the time.

That the various roles played by women in complex peasant households led to female power in such households has been recently argued for ancient Israel by Carol Meyers.[42] However, the consequent loss of parity that Meyers expects in *non*agrarian households may well have been lessened at Deir el Medina because of the unique situation that it was inhabited almost solely by women and children and a few very old men for most of the time. The overwhelming concern with women's life seen in the decoration of the village houses is surely in keeping with this fact.[43] While the men were away, it seems logical that a lot of decision-making would fall to the village wives and that they would take a strong role in community as well as household management. It is nice to recall that the Maxims of Ani, which were read in this village (as indicated by excerpts found there), recognize that women could be efficient, skilled managers and should be respected for that ability. Indeed Ani's reference to "her house" seems especially apt at Deir el Medina:

> You should not be overbearing with a woman in her house
> When you know that she is efficient.
> Do not say to her "where is it, fetch it for us."
> Let your eye be watchful while you are silent
> that you might perceive her skillfulness.
> Happiness is when your hand is together with hers.[44]

In this community, where the workplaces of almost all the men were quite separate from their homes, men and women had distinct realms. The men, spending most nights of the week a two-hour hike away, were dependent on their wives to send them food. One scribe's note to his wife, addressing her formally by her religious title, asks for beans to accompany his bread, as he does not enjoy bread alone. Another scribe asks for papyri, pens, writing boards, and texts. These and other such notes suggest not only that the female relatives of scribes could read at least simple messages, but that a wife or daughter might be relied upon as something like the scribe's deputy.[45] Indeed, toward the end of our community's history, when the scribe Nesamenopet was out of town, it was his wife Hennutawi who took charge of dispensing the rations on payday.[46]

Marriage and the Economy

Some anthropologists can demonstrate that women who exert influence over household management also have influence over the economic and marital futures of their children. Similarly, one love song found at Deir el Medina presents the mother as the parent who should be addressed by the suitor for the hand of the girl, even though both her parents are mentioned as alive.[47] But the nonliterary ostraca reveal that fathers took an active role in looking after their daughters' welfare should their marriages be less than satisfactory. One father required an oath from his future son-in-law that he would submit himself to one hundred lashes and forfeit all the property he and his wife had accumulated during their marriage if ever he abandoned her. Another father promised his "good daughter" a piece of property to live on should her man ever throw her out.[48]

Fraternization between the sexes before marriage was possible (as indicated by the love songs); social drinking was indulged in by both women and men; and everyone's participation in public celebrations is documented in the ostraca.[49]

Many daughters of the village stayed there by way of marriages with the men of the village (although some may by necessity have married outsiders or those who moved away in search of jobs). As Černý observed, there was no *paterfamilias* in the Egyptian family.[50] Normally, the young married couple did not live with either parental household but struck out on their own, just as the sage Ani advised. It is possible that some marriages (particularly among families of property) were arranged, but just marrying within the small village meant, often, marrying one's cousin. Thus, in anthropologist's jargon, the village wives were not "aliens in the lineages they joined through marriage," and their status and rights and the obligations of the husband to the wife were all the more easily guaranteed by the nearby presence of the woman's own supportive parents.

Little is known about marriage or wedding arrangements. Egyptian commoners were monogamous, but cohabitation may have been just as normal as more formal marriage in ancient Egypt, particularly for older people whose first marriages had ended through divorce or death. There is a record of a workman who took all his belongings to the house of a woman in the hope of moving in with her, but he was refused—twice.[51] Another document from Deir el Medina has a workman stating that he carried a bundle of provisions (bridewealth?) to the house of the workman Payom and "made his daughter my wife."[52] The rarity of marriage documents suggests that most young couples had very little property to warrant legal provisions. Divorce settlements and wills, made after some years of marriage and accumulation of joint property, are better represented.[53] Women could indicate their own last testaments to suit themselves, as the famous example of Naunakhte shows.

Year 3, 4th month of the Inundation Season, day 5 under the Majesty of the King of Upper and Lower Egypt, the Lord of the Two Lands, Usima-re-skheperenre (L.P.H. [may he live, be prosperous, be healthy]), the son of Re^c, the Lord of Appearances like Atum, Ramses-Amunhikhopshef-miamun, given life for ever and ever.

On this day a legal documentation of her property was made by the Citizeness Naunakhte before this tribunal. . . .

She said: As for me, I am an independent woman of the land of pharaoh (L.P.H.). I raised these eight servants of yours and I gave to them furniture,—everything as is usually done for ones like them. But behold, I am grown old, and behold, they are not looking after me, myself. Whoever of them has aided me, to him I will give my property. As for the one who has not given to me, I will not give to him from my property.[54]

This "independent woman" used the title *ʿnḫ.t nt niwt,* which has been translated as "citizeness." How widely used this term was is difficult to say, but at Deir el Medina the women are generally so referred to in administrative and juridical texts, with the further addition "of the necropolis" (*ḥr*), even though they are not believed to have been part of the necropolis work force itself. Naunakhte was surely stressing that she enjoyed the same legal rights as men and was free to dispose of her own property as she liked. Both female and male offspring were among those she named as heirs. Indeed, women in ancient Egypt could buy and sell property, adopt children, and sue quite on their own. The court case of Mose also shows that a woman who was senior to her siblings of either sex could be selected by a court of law to act as executrix for her brothers and sisters.[55]

In any preindustrial society, women's responsibilities at home were numerous and continuous from sunrise to sundown at least. Because many women did not survive to the age of menopause, a married woman probably spent half her lifetime pregnant or nursing young children. Almost all the Deir el Medina families had eight to ten surviving children out of perhaps twice that many pregnancies. The numerous fetal and infant burials at the bottom of the eastern cemetery testify to this attrition.

Fortunately, the government supplied not only servant help for the arduous and time-consuming grinding of the grain but also a laundry service for these housewives who lived miles from the river. Thus the women of this community enjoyed some advantages. Nevertheless, their varied activities were vital to the village economy. One task expected of the women, Dominique Valbelle suggests, was the making of wicks for the many lamps the artisans needed while they worked underground in the tomb.[56] There are records of delivery of rags to the villagers and the collection of the completed wicks made from them.

As everywhere in Egypt, the baking of bread was of primary importance, since this was the staple of the ancient diet. Preparing other foods was no doubt the women's responsibility too. If goats were kept, cheese were doubtless made. Eggs were collected from the hens that some families owned (some women may have sold eggs to their neighbors). Small herds of pigs were kept at the village, not only as a meat supply but as a hygenic measure, and doubtless the women or children would have looked after these and the other animals. The more affluent, such as the scribal families, kept cattle too. The scribe Hori paid two oxen, (plus some clothing), for a set of coffins. These large beasts were probably kept not in the village but near the fields they might plow.[57]

The use of clothing in a sales deal was not unusual. In the sale of a young Syrian girl by a traveling merchant to the citizeness Iry-nefer of western Thebes, in the sixteenth year of Ramses II, the housewife agreed to the price of 41 *kite* of silver, half the value of which was paid in linen garments and small bronze bowls she had purchased from her neighbors (against just such an opportunity of making a major purchase from a traveling merchant who would have wanted easily portable goods in exchange). The clothing, as Alan Gardiner noted, was most likely created by the housewife herself.[58]

It is too often overlooked that a good weaver and seamstress was able to boost her family's purchasing power considerably in this pre-coinage society. As Deir el Medina records show, the government issued some clothing to the men of the work gangs as part of their yearly wages, but it was only a small amount and would have benefited in particular the men who had no wives to make their clothes. Some of the village women may have worked in weaving studios connected with temples, but others surely worked at home.[59] The amount of weaving that went on in Egyptian households can be appreciated when we know that a single mummy of a commoner might have hundreds of square meters of linen for its wrappings.[60] Probably not all families had the means to own a loom, and some women may never have learned the techniques of weaving and sewing well enough to clothe themselves and their family members or to create salable items desired by others. But a woman who was clever enough to do so could be the mainstay of a family, whether or not she had a husband. It was when a society adopted coinage, issued by government mints, that women came to be at a severe disadvantage, economically speaking, although in agricultural or peasant economies home-raised food items would always supplement a woman's or family's income.

The fact that in Ramesside Egypt women in free families were managers of households and creators of family wealth could have contributed to the social equality between the sexes which seems to come through in the literature, matching the actual equality in legal rights confirmed by scholarly research.[61]

Workers' Rights

Among the positive aspects of this artisans' community is the fact that the workers and their families were free citizens to the extent that they had recourse to the justice system. Theoretically, any Egyptian could petition the vizier directly, was entitled to a trial by his peers, and could appeal to the oracle of the god of his town to settle a dispute if the civil tribunal's verdict did not satisfy him. Our workmen, accompanied by their wives, staged the first recorded labor strikes in history when their pay rations were late, or less than expected, and hunger became a problem.[62] Ordinarily they were well paid, but surely Janssen is overly optimistic when he argues that they were "truly well off and exceptional" compared with the mass of the population in Ramesside Egypt. There were problems throughout the 230 years we can best document.

The workmen of the crews may not have been slaves, but they had little recourse against those who chose to abuse them. The scribes and foremen set workmen at jobs for themselves frequently. Men were ordered to move stones for the scribe Ken-her-khepshef even in the noonday heat. The administrators were slow to pay bills presented by the workmen. The foreman Paneb forced himself upon five women in the village, wives and unmarried daughters of workmen; he ordered others to make clothes for him without remuneration and was accused of perpetrating other crimes (including murder and tomb robbery) for a long time before he was brought to justice, protected as he was by others in the administration of the tomb.[63] Surely this arrogance of power is more significant than wage scales. The scribes, as we know from their classroom texts, thought of themselves as superior to others; the foremen, with the power of command and promotion, held the workmen's futures in their hands, often granting advancements only in return for bribes. These men—and their wives, who were often titled temple clergy—were easily middle class. The artisans' wealth came through extra jobs they took on, and their position on the crew (and thus within the village) was much more precarious.

This is made vivid by records of the long-running strikes the tomb workers resorted to during the Twentieth Dynasty when their pay rations failed to be delivered and they and their families were faced with hunger.[64] Ramesside administrative records also reveal drastic swings in the numbers of artisans employed at the royal necropolis. Even during one reign their numbers varied considerably. Consider that by the middle of the long reign of Ramses II there were only forty-eight on the crews and, by the end of his reign, only thirty-two. What happened to the rest of these people? Did they merely get shifted to some other major construction project of this prolific builder after his tomb was completed? Quite possibly their expertise was utilized elsewhere. On the other hand, during the Twentieth Dynasty, after the number of tomb workers had expanded from forty under Ramses III to 120 under Ramses IV (to produce his large tomb), it was suddenly reduced by half. The vizier's order to the foremen survives: "Leave these sixty men here in the gang, any you choose, and send the surplus outside. Give an order that they should become their serfs who carry for you." Thus the foremen had the decision of who would stay and who must leave. Note that he is not told to lay off those hired last; instead, he could choose the men to be immediately given the menial tasks of the conscripted laborers (or serfs, as Černý translated the term *smdt*) who carried deliveries of rations up to their former crew mates—and whose wages, accordingly, would drop drastically.[65] Most likely, too, their families lost the right to stay in the village, as the *smdt* who served the necropolis did not live within its walls. Now it is possible that this cavalier method of treating skilled workers was peculiar to the Twentieth Dynasty, but it reminds us that Egypt was at all times an oriental despotism, wherein a supposedly free man was at the mercy of the whims of the Crown. The workers of New Kingdom Egypt had not organized themselves into guilds, which might have provided solidarity with social and economic safeguards; rather, all the men on the work force belonged to the pharaoh and were essentially powerless before the state.

The great pyramids and towering temples of the land were not built without a significant cost in human life and limb. Egypt bent its back for the greater glory of its rulers, and an ordinary man called up for work gang or military duty had little recourse unless he was wealthy enough or knew someone influential enough to buy off the bailiffs of the state. The tomb workers may have been well provided for by the state because (to use a modern metaphor) their masters knew a machine worked best when it was well oiled. Security considerations would also have played a part: no pharaoh could risk his tomb and treasure with an impoverished and desperate population living close by, privy to the knowledge of plans and location. But job security, civil liberties, and self-determination are modern concepts and were not within the grasp of pharaoh's workers.

TWO

Contact with the Outside World

Andrea G. McDowell

Deir el Medina was different from any other village of its time. The workmen who lived there with their families were better educated and better paid than the vast majority of their contemporaries; they were craftsmen in a land of tenant farmers; and they were administered directly by the office of the vizier. It is precisely because of its distinctive features, particularly its desert location and its inhabitants' very exceptional rate of literacy, that we know so much about this village, but its peculiarities also mean that what we learn from Deir el Medina may not be applicable to the rest of Egypt. One assumes that the tomb builders would not have been entirely different from other Egyptians, despite the exceptional circumstances in which they lived and worked, since they interacted with their contemporaries in the outside world. If they bought and sold in the west Theban markets, intermarried with the Theban population, and visited the Theban temples, then prices, marriage customs, and religious beliefs in Deir el Medina quite probably reflected those of the greater society. Of course, if they had little or no contact with the rest of the population, then the thousands of texts from the workmen's community are much less relevant to our understanding of the New Kingdom in general.

Many scholars who work with the Deir el Medina material do agree, explicitly or implicitly, that the villagers were in daily communication with the outside world.[1] Raphael Ventura, however, in his *Living in a*

City of the Dead, paints a very different picture. He begins with the assumption that the authorities would as a matter of course segregate the workmen from the general population in order to keep secret the site of the royal tomb, and that therefore the workmen and their families were totally isolated from their fellow Egyptians. The wall that enclosed the village kept the "inmates" in and outsiders out; villagers who wished to see their relatives in the outside world would be escorted to the administrative headquarters of the royal necropolis, where the meeting would take place under controlled conditions. Not even the necropolis supply staff could speak freely to the workmen, who were, in short, sealed off completely from their contemporaries.[2]

The isolation of the workmen is a premise of Ventura's rather than a conclusion, although he cites many texts which he sees as corroborating this view. It happens that those who believe the workmen were free to come and go as they pleased have not presented the full argument for their case either,[3] though it seems clear that their position is based on the many examples of contact between villagers and outsiders which these same scholars discuss in other contexts. A thorough examination of all the textual and monumental data bearing on the degree of isolation of the royal necropolis would require a monograph of its own, but I present here some of the evidence suggesting that the workmen were not so restricted in their movements as Ventura has proposed. I have, of course, drawn heavily on the numerous examples of their contacts which are gathered in the works of Jaroslav Černý, Jac. J. Janssen, Dominique Valbelle, and others.[4]

It was in relation to work, naturally enough, that interaction seems to have taken place on the largest scale. When the gang was expanded, new workmen were brought in from elsewhere; and when, as happened more frequently, there were too many boys in the village for all to find employment in the gang, the extras were taken away. We know very little about the process by which workmen were transferred from other projects to the necropolis. New arrivals seem to have been most common in the community's early days, although this impression may be due to the greater number of Nineteenth Dynasty tombs and stelae, which furnish the most useful genealogical information. The new recruits were selected —we do not know how—from a number of different institutions.[5] At least two members of the gang came from Karnak: Pashed was transferred to the village from his position as "servant of the workshop [$b^3k\ n$

šnʿ] of Amon in the Southern City [Thebes] and stonecutter of Amon in Karnak [*Ipt Swt*]," bringing with him his wife, who was the daughter of the captain of one of the barges owned by the temple;[6] and the sculptor Ken was the son of a sculptor working at Karnak.[7] Before the scribe Ramose joined the gang in year 5 of Ramses II, on the other hand, he had held a number of posts in the mortuary temple of Thutmose IV and elsewhere.[8] The scribe Amen-em-opet even seems to have had some connections with Kush, since his father was a *wʿb* priest of Amon, Lord of the Thrones of the Two Lands, in that country, and Amen-em-opet himself claimed to be or have been a priest in the temple of this same manifestation of Amon in Kush.[9] All these recruits lived and worked under Ramses II.[10] After that period the workmen evidently managed to get their own sons appointed to positions as they fell free.[11] When the strength of the gang was increased to an extraordinary 120 workmen under Ramses IV, however, not all the new members can have been recruited from within the village itself. It is not known from where they came, but when the gang was cut back to its original size some years later, the surplus workmen joined the supply staff.[12]

Such a mass shift of personnel from the gang to the outside was probably unique, but on a smaller scale such transfers happened regularly, since in ordinary times there were more boys in the village than openings on the work crew, and many had to leave. Those whose fathers had furnished them with an education presumably managed to do well in the outside world, but the only documented cases of which I know are the sons of the foreman Neferhotep: one became a scribe of the army and a chariot-warrior of his majesty; the other held various posts, including doorkeeper in the Ramesseum.[13]

Sometimes men of the gang would be lent out, as it were, to work on building projects in temples and tombs outside the royal necropolis, and many indeed bore titles connecting them with other institutions.[14] A fragmentary papyrus records moving operations that involved cooperation between various institutions on a very large scale: a total of 450 men—including the full complement of men of the gang (at that date 120 strong), sixty policemen, forty further employees of the Place of Truth, a ship's crew, and others—are said to have been engaged in "dragging" (*ith*);[15] they were apparently employed in the construction of a temple somewhere between that of Ahmose Nefertari and the Ramesseum, not far from the village.[16] At other times, individual workmen or small groups were set to work on outside projects. In a mid–Nineteenth Dynasty text, for instance, the workman Hormose mentions a time when he was "working in the granary of the temple of Maat," which formed part of the huge complex at Karnak.[17] At a later date, members of the gang were "cutting blocks in the House of Hathor" (*pr Ḥwt-Ḥr*), perhaps near Gebelein.[18]

The path between the village and the temples and tombs of Deir el Bahri was particularly well beaten, and there are several references to individuals going there or returning.[19] At least once a party going out met a party coming back: "Year 1, II *ꜣḥt* 13. This day, coming by Aapehty, Khonsu, and the two boys from Deir el Bahri. And they called to Paneb as [he] was going to Deir el Bahri, since pharaoh would not commission them."[20] These men had evidently expected to be set to work in Deir el Bahri, and there are more examples of members of the gang involved in projects there.[21]

The workmen may also have been called out on smaller jobs. When the draftsman Hori began to paint the sacred bark of Osiris (*nšmt*), for instance, it is possible that this article was brought to the village, but perhaps more likely that he went to a temple workshop.[22]

Černý suggested that work on temple projects may account for the title "quarryman" of Amon or Thoth, which several workmen adopted on their hieroglyphic inscriptions. Since these titles are quite specific, and in some cases even name Karnak or Luxor as the temple with which the workman was associated, they may indeed mean that the title holders carried out work in these temples.[23] Černý pointed out that most of these quarrymen lived in the second half of the reign of Ramses II,[24] when there was no work left for them in the Valley of the Kings, and they were evidently employed elsewhere.

It has even been suggested that the workmen were sent on expeditions to the quarries of Wadi Hammamat and Gebel el Silsila to fetch fine stone. The evidence for the presence of members of the gang at the Wadi Hammamat, as collected by Černý, is quite strong.[25] In year 3 of Ramses IV there was at least one expedition to this wadi to quarry graywacke for the Place of Truth, as is recorded by four inscriptions at the site.[26] One of these inscriptions was left by "the Scribe of the Place of Truth, Neferhotep," possibly the scribe Neferhotep who is known at Deir el Medina from the second half of the reign of Ramses III.[27] Moreover, the famous Turin map of the quarries at the Wadi Hammamat was at some time in the hands of a scribe at Deir el Medina (it has on its verso three texts concerning local matters), suggesting at least that someone in the village was interested in the topography of the place.[28] The map may have been drawn up under Ramses IV, in whose reign the expedition took place, since the same papyrus also bears a description of a statue of this king. There is, therefore, strong but not conclusive evidence that one or more members of the gang participated in an expedition to Wadi Hammamat to bring back stone for work in the Theban necropolis. A similar expedition to the quarries of Gebel el Silsila is attested by a broken inscription at the site which mentions something to be brought to Thebes and refers to men of the tomb who will take an object or objects the names of which are now lost.[29] The date was year 2 of Merneptah, month 4 of summer season, day 6. Except for the one inscription by the scribe Neferhotep, the graffiti from the Wadi Hammamat and Gebel el Silsila do not to my knowledge include any by members of the gang.[30] This would not be surprising, however, if the workmen on the expedition were mostly illiterate quarrymen.

In addition to good evidence that members of the gang were assigned to projects outside the royal necropolis, there is some indication—though very little—that outsiders were brought to the Valley of the Kings to assist with last-minute work in the hectic days leading up to a royal funeral. This is apparently what is described in a papyrus recounting that in year 1, month 2 of summer season, day 7, the vizier, the high priest of Amon, and other high-ranking officials came to install shrines in the royal tomb and that among those who performed some last-minute work on these shrines were "the four chief stone masons of alabaster," who were probably not members of the gang. In what reign theses events took place is a matter of some disagreement. Valbelle argues that since the time of year (month 2 of summer season, day 7) accords well with the suggested season of Ramses IV's death in the last month of winter, this work on the shrines may have been part of the hasty preparations for that king's interment.[31]

More routinely, local officials were continually visiting Thebes on business of one sort or another. The doorkeepers were the errand boys of the community, crossing the river repeatedly with messages to or from the vizier's office, including in one case two silver chisels for the vizier himself, which was only too obviously meant as a kickback.[32] We also have a report to the scribe Ramose from someone sent to collect oil for the gang: "I have arrived at the Overseer of the Treasury, and he said to his deputy who is here in the Treasury in Thebes, 'Give 10 jars of sesame-oil to this man.' So he said."[33] The foremen frequently visited the East Bank themselves, whether summoned by their Theban superiors, or on their own initiative.[34]

The workmen, then, had some contact with outsiders as a result of their work, but they had even more private contacts with the population of the plain. Their activities in the marketplace are well known.[35] For example, we can see the market through the villagers' eyes in the decoration of the tomb of Ipuy. On the banks of the river, where the boats are tied up, sailors exchange their pay in the form of grain for cakes, fish, and other foodstuffs. The local traders, all women, sit by baskets containing their wares. A small shelter shades amphorae that are obviously filled with a drink, since one is furnished with a straw.[36] The riverbank was so closely associated with the market by the villagers that they used the same word, *mryt,* for both.[37] Many texts mention goods bought or sold there by the workmen. The most colorful and best known of these is an ostracon recording services performed for an indigent widow who, the writer says, had asked him to trade a *mrw* cloth at the *mryt* for her, but he found it unsalable: "And she gave me a sash, saying 'Offer it at the riverbank, and it will be bought from me for one *oipe*-measure of emmer.' I offered it, but people rejected it, saying, 'It is bad!' And I told her exactly that, saying, 'It has been rejected.' Then she gave it to me, and I let one *ḫ'r*-measure of emmer be brought to her via Hay son of Sa-Wadjyt." The friend therefore bought the rag himself, at four times the price she had asked.[38]

Some workmen were such frequent visitors to the riverbank that they invested in huts and chapels there.[39] We know of one that he kept some foodstuffs in his hut, kyllestis loaves and sesame oil, but this turned out to have been unwise, because they were stolen.[40] Such huts are also named in divisions of property.[41] Like other private structures, they are most often left to women, who might otherwise have no place to live when their fathers or husbands had died and they had to move out of state-owned housing.[42] The *mryt* was the scene of miscellaneous incidents as well. Suspects were taken there for interrogation; the doorkeepers are once said to have slept there; and various other comings and goings are recorded.[43] It was, in other words, a marketplace like any other and much frequented by the workmen.

More surprising is the indication of agricultural activity by the tomb builders.[44] There are two incontrovertible cases, although each is exceptional to some degree. First, it is clear from the Late Ramesside Letters that some workmen were engaged in farming on their own behalf at the end of the Twentieth Dynasty, but by that time the village had been abandoned, and the workmen had moved down to the cultivation.[45] Second, a unique scene of plowing appears in the Nineteenth Dynasty tomb of Ramose, the scribe transferred to the gang from the temple of Thutmose IV. The plow is guided by the scribe's servant Ptah-seankh, a reference to whom on another of Ramose's monuments lends credibility to this scene.[46] It has been suggested, however, that Ramose's case is also unrepresentative, given his previous connections.

We must therefore fall back on much more circumstantial evidence: indications that during the main period of the village's history other workmen owned land, draft animals, farming equipment, and storage facilities. Ownership of land is meagerly attested, but from a text about a dispute over the ownership of a donkey we learn that fields could be bought be members of the community. The woman from whom the donkey was demanded offers fields instead: "I will buy it and I will give you [its] price [from f]ields ($^{\circ}\dot{h}wt$) in Armant." This would not satisfy the other party, who wrote back: "I will not take [. . .] fields. Now give [the] donkey *itself!*"[47] The speaker is unnamed but may well be the workman Nefer-senet, who gives an account of a similar dispute on the recto of this same document. Clearly, although he turned it down, he had the opportunity to acquire fields. Another text lists the fields belonging to a certain Wen-nefer, totaling 17 *aroura* (4.69 hectares).[48] Finally, at least two chiefs of police are known to have had the use of fields in the countryside.[49]

There are, on the other hand, many unambiguous references to cattle and donkeys owned by the workmen, some of which were probably used for agriculture.[50] Several texts refer to "cultivating" (sk°) done with donkeys, mostly by water carriers who had borrowed the animals from the workmen.[51] There is no clear evidence that the workmen themselves used their donkeys for this purpose. It is less clear that cattle were used in farming, although it is difficult to imagine for what other purpose the workmen would have kept such animals, given that almost all the references in our texts are to males,[52] so they were not kept for milk, and there are almost no references to the slaughter of a private ox.[53] In the one text that refers to the loan of an ox, it is explicitly said to be for plowing.[54] Whatever their use, the many cattle owned by workmen cannot have been kept in the village; to feed and tend them the workmen would have had to go down to the cultivation, and indeed several texts concern arrangements made for feeding oxen.[55]

One might not expect to find farming equipment in the village itself, since the workmen who had huts at the riverbank could store that sort of thing there. Nevertheless, Bernard Bruyère found sieves, winnowing baskets, and the teeth of sickles north of the village.[56] A single hoe, found in an Eighteenth Dynasty burial chamber, shows signs of wear indicating that it was an actual work tool; hoes were also used for non-agricultural jobs such as digging foundation trenches, however, so that this is not conclusive evidence of cultivation.[57]

We may conclude, then, that at least some workmen owned land, many owned cattle, and others were engaged in reaping and winnowing. These were all activities that would entail interaction with the outside world, whether or not one is entitled to conclude that the workmen were themselves involved in farming.

As a natural result of these and other contacts made in the course of official and private business, the villagers had many friends and relatives among the inhabitants of Thebes. Workmen who had been recruited from outside left family and friends behind, others had sons who had gone away to work in other institutions, and we may imagine that friendships were formed through work and trade as well. Some such relationships, though not so many as we might have expected, are reflected in tomb scenes. Pashed, himself recruited from outside, had a crowd of relatives painted in his tomb, including his venerable white-haired father Menna, a "servant of Amon," and his gray-haired father-in-law Tjay, the "captain of the barge of Amon."[58] Among the family members shown presenting offerings in the tomb of Neferhotep are the two sons mentioned above, who had left the village.[59]

Very interesting indeed is the appearance of a member of the gang, identified as the draftsman Amen-hotep, in a scene depicting the funeral of a certain Kynebu, prophet in the Temple of Thutmosis IV, in his tomb at Qurna. This would be the draftsman Amen-hotep, son of Amen-nakhte.[60] Kynebu's desire to have the draftsman's image in his tomb among members of his own family is further evidence of family ties or close friendship between a villager and an outsider. It has been suggested

Relatives of Pashed, some from outside Deir el Medina, depicted in Pashed's tomb (TT # 3). A.-P. Zivie, *La tombe de Pached à Deir el-Médineh (No. 3)* (Cairo, 1979), pl. 23; courtesy of l'Institut Français d'Archéologie Orientale.

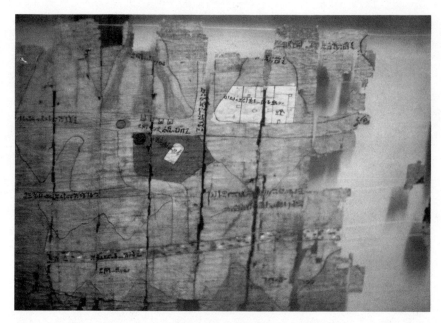

The Turin map of the gold mines. Courtesy of the Museo Egizio di Turino (P. Turin 1879 + 1899 + 1969). Photo by L. H. Lesko.

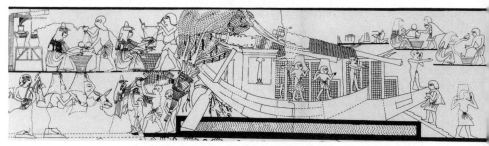

Riverbank scene from the tomb of Ipuy (TT # 217). From Norman de Garis Davies, *Two Ramesside Tombs at Thebes* (New York, 1927), pl. 30 (detail); courtesy of the Metropolitan Museum of Art, New York.

The scribe Amenhotep of the Tomb (second from left) at the funeral of Kyn-bu. From the tomb of Kynbu at Qurna (TT # 113). Sir J. Gardiner Wilkin-son, *Manners and Customs of the Ancient Egyptians,* 2d series, Supplement: Index and Plates (London, 1841), pl. 86 (detail).

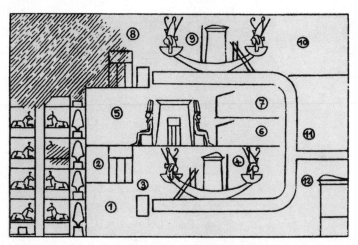

Jaroslav Černý's sketch of the temple of Mut at Karnak from the tomb of Khabekhnet. Černý, *Répertoire Onomastique de Deir el-Médineh* (Cairo, 1949), p. 25; courtesy of l'Institut Français d'Archéologie Orientale.

Ethnic diversity in the New Kingdom: Plaster masks from Tell el Amarna. Courtesy of Ägyptisches Museum, Staatliche Museen zu Berlin. Photo by L. H. Lesko.

on grounds of style that Amen-hotep had had a hand in the decoration of the tomb as well. This same draftsman, together with his son Amen-nakhte (named after his grandfather), also decorated another tomb at Qurna, that of Iy-em-seba (head of the temple scribes of the estate of Amon), who adapted an older monument for his own use in the reign of Ramses IX.[61] The two draftsmen recorded this accomplishment in a graffito of the year 9 of Ramses IX, which they left in the tomb of Ramses VI: "the scribe Amen-hotep came together with his son, the scribe and deputy of the draftsman Amen-nakhte of the Tomb [. . . after] they made (?)[62] the decoration in the tomb-chapel [. . . of the overseer of scribes] of the temple of the estate of Amon, Iy-em-seba."[63] Their claim appears to be confirmed by stylistic similarities between the tomb and other work done by Amen-hotep.[64] This work on two Qurna tombs demonstrates that some workmen got at least this far beyond their village.

More abundant testimonies to family relationships are probably to be found in letters to and from the workmen, but unfortunately, neither a letter's place of origin nor the writer's relationship to the recipient is usually specified. One relatively certain example of correspondence between villagers and outsiders is a letter from a man called Ankhu to his daughter Nebu-em-sau complaining that some cakes had not been sent to him at the riverbank. He tells his daughter to have five cakes sent weekly so that he can give "the boys" a share, "because I give them what I have daily." Although the background to this request is not at all clear, it may be that the woman lived in the village, having left her parental home, but remained in touch with her father.[65] From a legal document we learn that a woman left the village for a full month to go to the country (*shty*); one would imagine she was visiting friends or family. She left an ailing relative behind who cited this instance of neglect as one of the reasons for disinheriting her: "He said, 'As for me, the sickness came to me, and I said to my sister: Do [. . .] for my property. But she went off to the country, and I spend a month dwelling alone."[66] These indications together with those from the tombs, merely confirm what one would have supposed in any case—that family ties were not broken with movement into and out of the village.

The workmen were also in continual correspondence with outside individuals for whom they were making or decorating furniture, and often these clients were also friends. (The fact that the workmen traded so actively with the outside world suggests, incidentally, that the prices in

Deir el Medina and the goods available there would not have been very different from those in the Theban metropolis.) Of the many letters that have been preserved, I can cite only a few.[67] Very interesting is a copy of a message from the scribe Amen-em-opet to a builder of the estate of Amon about a house that the latter had built for him in the street behind the house of the mayor of Thebes, Ha-nefer.[68] At least half a dozen other letters belong to the correspondence of the carpenter Maa-nakhtef, and concern commissions for a bed, decoration of coffins, and other items ordered by various clients.[69] Maa-nakhtef was a son of Naunakhte, who is familiar to legal historians through her last will and testament.[70] His range of correspondents—including a scribe of the temple of Hathor, mistress of Hut-sekhem; a scribe of the vizier; and the vizier Neb-Maat-Ra-nakhte himself, demonstrate the wide and exalted acquaintance that an artisan's talents could win for him. That some of these correspondents were more than mere business contacts is suggested by a letter to Amen-mose, the scribe of the vizier, in which Maa-nakhtef writes, "I wish to hear how you are a thousand times a day. [What means] your failing to come in this year?"[71]

A few letters are from villagers who have gone off to Thebes or even farther and who report back to the family and colleagues at home. Maa-nakhtef himself traveled as far as Diospolis Parva, about fifty km northeast of Thebes by the desert route, or 117 kilometers downstream.[72] From there he wrote back to his brother Ken-her-khepshef to say, "I have arrived at Hut. I will do for myself, Amen-mose, and also the prophet every good thing, consisting of cakes, beer, oil and clothes."[73] The Amen-mose mentioned here is probably the scribe of Hathor, mistress of Hut, from whose correspondence with his "brother" Maa-nakhtef two letters have survived. The writer of another letter, a woman, says, "I am faring downstream to Memphis."[74]

The letter in which the carpenter expressed his well-meant annoyance that his friend, the scribe of the vizier, had not come to see him that year is of particular interest for the suggestion that outsiders might be expected to visit Deir el Medina. Even if this particular writer may not have meant that the scribe should come as far as the village, there are other cases in which outsiders themselves explicitly propose to do just that. The most interesting example occurs in a letter from the scribe Nakht-sobek to the workman Amen-nakhte, another son of Naunakhte and a

brother of Maa-nakhtef (P. DeM 4). Nakht-Sobek elsewhere calls himself
"scribe of the tomb,"[75] but he does not seem to have lived in the village
itself, since he is further known only from a short note recording that he
came to deliver a piece of writing material.[76] I would suggest that Nakht-
Sobek was a scribe of the vizier who dealt with the royal necropolis and
could therefore use the title "scribe of the tomb." It is clear that he is not
in the same place as Amen-nakhte, because he urges the latter to write to
him by the hand of the policeman Bas (r. 7-8; v. 1), but neither can he be
very far away, since he mentions elsewhere that goods sent by Amen-
nakhte (?) arrived within a day.[77] In the letter in question, Nakht-Sobek
complains that Amen-nakhte is offended with him and neglects him in
spite of their friendship of long standing. They are "companions of
eating bread together," he says, and while new things are good, old
friendships are also valuable. Nakht-Sobek proposes to visit Amen-
nakhte, and he will not take no for an answer: "Do not let me be told not
to enter your house, not to make [my] way inside the walls, and to stay
away from the village. And do not [. . .] to me. I will go and enter the
house, and come out again. I will enter my own place."[78] Similar inten-
tions to visit the recipient are expressed in a letter apparently from an
outsider to the guardian Hay, which ends, "I have hastened to reach you
as far as your village."[79] Whether or not the workmen themselves were
free to come and go, one might not have expected outsiders to have had
access to the village,[80] yet these texts suggest that the question should at
least be considered open. They need not imply, however, that outsiders
were allowed deeper into the royal necropolis; in fact, it is noteworthy
that the thousands of graffiti in the western mountains were left almost
exclusively by persons connected with the tomb,[81] including the highest officials—such as the vizier and the high priest of Amon—who naturally visited the necropolis and left both graffiti and more substantial
monuments. An example of the latter is a stela dedicated to Meretseger
by the overseer of the Treasury, Montu-em-tawy, found at the ridge
overlooking the Valley of the Kings; Bruyère suggests that this was made
for him by the draftsman Ken-her-khepshef, but it is not clear to me why
he thought so.[82]

There are, finally, indications of the workmen's involvement in religious life beyond the village, that is, of their participation in the great
Theban religious festivals, visits to outside temples, and devotion to

nonlocal deities. Valbelle has gathered and discussed the material relevant to this subject, which is somewhat more meager than one might have expected.[83] The villagers observed the great national feast days with their own local celebrations; the only nonlocal religious event in which it is certain some workmen participated was the Festival of the Valley, during which the statue of Amon-Re' visited the temples and tombs of western Thebes. A relief of the workman Amen-em-one depicts this procession in two registers.[84] In the lower register, a kneeling figure of Amen-em-one faces the divine bark *User-ḥat* as it arrives on a canal; above, the statue of the god, now transferred to a portable bark, is shown emerging from the pylons of the temple of Seti I. Ramses II offers incense before the god, while the vizier Paser and the scribe Amen-em-ope of the Place of Truth bow reverently behind him. Only one other officiant is identified: the fanbearer, labeled Ipuy—perhaps the sculptor of that name. There is little doubt that Amen-em-one had witnessed the ceremony and that one or even two members of the gang had participated in it. The other references to this festival are less detailed.[85] Similar evidence for participation in the cult of Sokar may not be useful for my purposes because it has been suggested that the procession of Sokar visited a shrine to this god in the necropolis; in other words, the workmen may have been commemorating a local event.[86] Finally, it seems that the scribe Ramose was involved in large-scale preparations for the Opet festival. He wrote to the overseer of the cattle, "The festival of Opet approaches today, but the $ḳ^{3}wt$ boat of the temple of Amon has not yet come to us [. . .] for the festival, and likewise the oxen for slaughtering for the offerings for all the gods."[87] It is not impossible, however, that the supplies he was expecting were for a local celebration of the event.

The evidence that the workmen visited temples outside Deir el Medina is sparse but clear. There is a detailed depiction of the temple of Mut in a local tomb.[88] Even more convincing are stelae left by two workmen in sanctuaries outside the village. The foreman Pashed dedicated a stela to Wadj-mose, a son of Thutmose I, in his chapel near the Ramesseum,[89] while the famous stela of Neb-Re', thanking Amon for saving his son from death, seems to have been found in one of the small brick chapels near the modern German expedition house, directly behind the temple of Thutmosis IV.[90] It is perhaps surprising, however, that the workmen left so few monuments of themselves in the mortuary temples of the kings they served.[91]

Dominique Valbelle and A. I. Sadek point out that the workmen also honored a large number of deities usually associated with other cities, such as Seth of Ombos, Montu of Armant, and even various Asiatic gods.[92] But these cults may have been brought to the village by workmen transferred from other institutions and thus perhaps do not reflect visits to the places of origin of the various dieties.

In short, there is abundant evidence that the workmen were deeply involved in the economic, social, and religious world of the cultivated area. The range of their activities outside the village was even greater than has been suggested above, since there are many references to visits to Thebes which cannot be grouped conveniently under one heading. For instance, in at least one case a dispute between villagers was taken before the court of the Ramesseum.[93] Moreover, the entire population of the village may have moved down to the floodplain at times of particular danger, such as the civil wars in the reign of Amenmesses, and the workmen with their families certainly spent many days and even nights encamped near the great mortuary temples as part of their industrial action during the reign of Ramses III. Other references to trips outside the village, the reasons for which are now lost, include mention of a visit to the temple of one of the pharaohs named Seti.[94] Needless to say, most contacts between the workmen and their Theban neighbors will have gone undocumented and will have far outnumbered the instances discussed above.

However, if the workmen were free to come and go as they pleased, certain other questions arise. Why, for instance, should the village have been built in its valley at all, if not to isolate its inhabitants? The fifteen minutes or so saved in time going to and from work could hardly have justified moving a whole community to the edge of the desert and employing a small army of water carriers to supply it—particularly if it is true that the men stayed near the Valley of the Kings and did not come home at all during the week.[95] To this one can only answer that it was the way of Egyptian building projects to establish a separate walled workmen's village as near as possible to the site, even when this had to be built on the desert's edge.[96] When the situation in the desert became unsafe, the gang did move down to Medinet Habu, without giving up work in the Theban necropolis; there is more than sufficient evidence for participation in the burials of the high priests of Amon after the move took place in the early years of Ramses XI.[97] The isolation of the workmen must therefore not have been considered essential.

Another problem is posed by the *inbwt* or "the five *inbwt*" which, as Ventura has demonstrated, lay between the village and the cultivated area. Ventura accepts Edgerton's interpretation of the *inbwt* as guard houses or fortified gateways and argues that their function was to secure the approach to the village: that is, to prevent unauthorized people from entering or leaving. He suggests that others lay along the path from the village to Medinet Habu.[98] In fact, however, hardly anything can be said about these *inbwt* with confidence; it is not even clear that they were any sort of building. The proposal that they were small fortified structures or watch posts was made very tentatively by Edgerton and accepted by Elizabeth Thomas and Klaus Baer for these particular examples at the necropolis.[99] At other sites, however, *inbwt* appear to have been either enclosures of a much larger area (particularly, for cattle) or even, as Lopez suggests, simply boundaries or limits.[100] Further, there is no evidence that they were manned. Ventura himself says: "We never hear of any active interventions by those whose duty should have been to guard the *inbwt* against trespassers, whether individuals or groups. One gets the impression that either the posts were unguarded, which . . . would render them useless, or that the guard was quite ineffective."[101] As both P. J. Frandsen and Lopez have pointed out, the idea of five watch posts in succession seems inherently unlikely, and Frandsen presents convincing evidence of individual *inbwt* and groups of *inbwt* to the north of the village as well as to the south.[102] Most important, even assuming that they were indeed guard posts, it seems more likely that their purpose would have been to protect the necropolis from intruders than to keep the workmen inside.

Ventura also assigns to the $htm \ n \ p^3 \ hr$, "enclosure of the tomb," the function of controlling contact between the workmen and the outside world. But as I have discussed elsewhere, the htm was the supply depot and administrative headquarters of the community; it does not seem to have performed an isolating role.[103]

In sum, it appears that the workmen shared the lives of their fellow citizens. They bought and sold, farmed and harvested, celebrated and mourned with their friends and families in the cultivated area. This is not to say that Deir el Medina was no different from other Egyptian villages after all; we still do not have sufficient comparative material from other communities to draw a conclusion one way or the other. Though one might still expect Deir el Medina to be significantly different from other Egyptian villages because of its unique function and the relative prosperity of its average inhabitant, we may at least say with confidence that the workmen did not live in a gilded cage. They did not look down from their desert perch to see the real life of Egypt passing them by.

THREE

Foreigners Living in the Village

William A. Ward

The lands of Khor and Kush
and the land of Egypt
You have set every man in his place.
—Hymn to the Aton

It has been recognized since the early years of Egyptology that by New Kingdom times the population of Egypt was liberally sprinkled with families of foreign origin. This phenomenon, however, appeared long before the New Kingdom. During the Middle Kingdom, for example, we know that weavers, dancers, and other professionals from abroad were living in Egypt, and Canaanite merchants founded settlements at Tell ed-Dab'a and related sites in the eastern Delta.[1]

Foreigners came to Egypt primarily for economic reasons, to find work in their various professions or to glean the profits of international trade. By New Kingdom times they were a prominent part of the population, and their presence was further encouraged throughout the centuries of Egyptian control over Nubia and Canaan. Some foreigners may have been forcibly brought to Egypt as prisoners of war, but certainly not in the large numbers that the popular view would suggest; nor did the majority come as slaves (slavery has been vastly overrated as a component in Egyptian society, basically owing to a misunderstanding of Egyptian terminology).[2] Rather, during the centuries that Deir el Medina flourished, there was in the whole ancient world a mobile middle class, people who did not work the land or serve in a local administration and were therefore not tied to a particular place. Weavers, stonemasons, soldiers and sailors, merchants, artists, musicians and dancers, priests— all these moved freely to wherever they could exercise their skills. There were strangers in every town and city from Mycenae to Persia, free agents, moving where they wished and when they wished. Many of them came to the Nile Valley.

A survey of the full extent of foreigners living in New Kingdom Egypt gives the distinct impression that these were largely free people who had come to Egypt of their own volition to find employment and a more stable life than they had had at home. They were already part of the construction industry in the Eighteenth Dynasty, and thereafter we find more and more foreigners in positions of (often considerable) authority. From gardeners and ship captains to army officers and royal servants, foreigners established themselves at all levels of Egyptian life.[3] It is not surprising, therefore, that some inhabitants of Deir el Medina were either recent immigrants or the descendants of families of foreign extraction. Though their presence has long been recognized by the excavators of the site, statements to this effect have been limited to lists of personal names believed (often incorrectly) to be non-Egyptian.[4] And this is the heart of the problem—how to recognize foreign residents by their personal names when there is little more than personal names to go on.

Identifying Foreign Personal Names in Egyptian Texts

There is in the Berlin Museum a small, very crude stela from Tell el-Amarna of a man called *Trr*. He is portrayed as a Canaanite with a Canaanite hair style, beard, and dress.[5] His name is the very common Semitic name *Dalilu*. His wife also has a Semitic name, though she is portrayed as an Egyptian. Here, there is no problem: a foreign name with an excellent Canaanite cognate identifies a portrait of an obviously Canaanite individual. But we rarely have such precise information from Deir el Medina. As far as I know, none of the villagers is *portrayed* as a foreigner with the single exception of a subsidiary figure in one tomb chapel who has two plumes in his hair following the Libyan style (Appendix B, no. 2). It is reported that features of the mummies from certain tombs confirm the presence of foreigners, though no details have been published.[6] Otherwise, the human pictorial and archaeological evidence is silent, and we must rely solely on personal names.

Fortunately, there is every probability that native Egyptians did not give foreign names to their children. Therefore, when we find persons with non-Egyptian personal names, we can generally be sure that either those persons themselves or their recent ancestors were foreign. The practice at Deir el Medina seems to have been that though resident foreigners gave Egyptian names to their children, foreign names often reappeared among the grandchildren as a kind of reminder of the family's origins.

Recognizing foreign names, however, is not always a simple matter. No single method of doing so is totally reliable in itself, but several characteristics—preferably in combination—are useful.

First, a name may have a consonantal structure that is obviously non-Egyptian and for which a readily apparent foreign cognate can be produced. For example, the names *'Irtnn* and *Mrky* can be immediately recognized as Hittite *Aritenna* and Semitic *Milkuya*.[7] Many names that seem foreign at first glance are, however, actually good Egyptian names: *'mk*, thought to represent Hurrian *Ammaku*, turns out to be Egyptian *ᶜ³-mk.t*, meaning something like "great of protection."[8]

Second is the use of the "throwstick" hieroglyph as a determinative. Because scribal practice restricted its use to the names of foreign persons and places, its appearance is an indicator that the name in question is not Egyptian. The problem here is that its absence does not mean the reverse. The throwstick sign is frequently omitted in the spelling of demonstrably foreign names; about half the known foreign names in Egyptian texts are spelled without it, chiefly because of the spelling habits of individual scribes.[9]

Third, when an individual is specifically identified as a foreigner, his name can be reasonably assumed to be foreign. Such are "the Nubian stonemason *Trky*" who plied his trade at Deir el Bahri and "the Canaanite *Basiya*" who worked at Deir el Medina. Yet even these appellations cannot always be taken literally, since such terms as The Canaanite, The Nubian, The Libyan were often used as names by people who were not of immediate foreign origin. The difference is whether such terms are labels ("the Canaanite X") or personal names ("The Canaanite"). The former can be taken as a foreign name; the latter often cannot.[10]

Fourth, there is the use of "group-writing," a method of spelling whereby meaningless weak consonants—*³, y, w*—are inserted into the consonantal structure of a name or word where they do not belong. These insertions have traditionally been thought to represent vowels, and the general belief is that this extended orthography was developed to spell mainly foreign words and names; therefore, its use in spelling a personal name has long been considered a sure sign that the name is foreign. But this is simply not true; group-writing is very common in the spelling of countless native Egyptian words and, especially in the New Kingdom, of countless native Egyptian personal names.[11] Conversely, many obvious foreign names and words are regularly spelled in the normal Egyptian consonantal manner, such as the divine names Baʿal, ʿAnat, and Astarte. It is the use of this orthography in the Deir el Medina texts that has led to the incorrect identification of some Egyptian personal names as Nubian or Libyan.[12]

And fifth, there are frequent cases where a single individual has two names: one is inevitably a good Egyptian name; the other can be either his original foreign name or an Egyptian nickname by which he was presumably known to his family and friends. These may be applied to him separately—say, in different parts of his tomb chapel—or together in the formula "X who is called Y." The difficulty is that Egyptian scribes used this formula reversibly during the New Kingdom. They might give the foreign name or Egyptian nickname, followed by the full Egyptian name: *ʿkbr* (foreign) who is called *Rʿmss-nḫt;*[13] *ʿIpwy* (nickname) who is called *ʿImn-m-ip.t.*[14] Or they might start with the full Egyptian name, followed by the foreign name or Egyptian nickname: *ʿIhꜣ-nfr-ʿImn* who is called *Pꜣ-ḫr* (foreign);[15] *ʿImn-ḥtp* who is called *Ḥy* (nickname).[16] On occasion the same person may be referred to both ways: "Benya who is called Paheqamen" and "Paheqamen who is called Benya."[17] The problem, then, is to determine whether the alternative to the full Egyptian name is an Egyptian nickname or a foreign name—no easy task, especially since the two may be spelled in exactly the same way.

Despite the inconsistencies, the more of the foregoing five criteria can be applied to any given example, the more certain we can be of its non-Egyptian origin. Unfortunately, in many cases even minimal precision is impossible, and the decision must be left to our own subjective devices. Short names are particularly troublesome. John Chadwick observes that in choosing Greek cognates for personal names found in Mycenaean Greek Linear B texts, "the degree of probability [that a given choice is correct] increases with the length of the word [and] shorter words often admit of several identifications."[18] This cautionary statement applies equally to foreign names in Egyptian texts. One can easily see in Egyptian *ʿIrmrk* the *ʿIlumilki* of the Amarna Letters, the correspondence between foreign rulers and the Egyptian court in the later fourteenth century B.C.[19] But many names in the Deir el Medina archives contain only one or two strong consonants, so that even when one suspects that a name is foreign, there may be possible cognates in two or three west Asiatic languages. In such cases, it is not possible to be certain that the name *is* foreign—and if it is, there remain problems in determining its origin. These difficulties revolve around two areas of evidence: the source material in foreign languages, and the often tricky issue of phonetic transmission and change.

First, the source material. It is clear from Egyptian textual and pictorial evidence that foreigners came to Egypt from all regions around the Nile Valley and that personal names from all these areas are preserved in Egyptian documents. But it is not always possible to suggest precise cognates in foreign languages: that is, exactly the same name actually *written* in a foreign language. For the major languages of western Asia—Akkadian, Hittite, Hurrian, Amorite, and a number of more local dialects such as Ugaritic, Hebrew, and Phoenician—we possess an enormous store of personal names; their collection and study has been a major research effort for generations, so that our ability to compare foreign names in Egyptian texts with those in the whole of western Asia is almost unlimited. By contrast, because we have no contemporary texts in other African languages, comparable African names simply do not exist. We know that Libyans and Nubians lived in Egypt and that some Libyan and Nubian personal names are preserved in Egyptian texts, but the names as originally written down in those languages are lost to us. The Sudanese Meroitic texts preserve a large number of personal names, but they date to Hellenistic and Christian times. The earliest Libyan names written in a local language appear in Punic texts from such places as Carthage, again from Hellenistic and Roman times.[20] One cannot use these later languages as comparative material for African names found a thousand years earlier during Egypt's New Kingdom. In other words, though we can be reasonably sure that Libyans and Nubians lived at Deir el Medina and that some Libyan and Nubian names appear in the village archives (indirect evidence warrants the assumption in a few cases: see Appendix A, nos. 31, 32, and 34), it is only rarely that we can define a specific personal name as African—and even then, we are unable to produce a cognate in an African language. This means, of course, that we are unable to assess accurately the extent of African penetration into the native population of Egypt. Unless contemporary inscriptions in the African languages are discovered, the African elements in Egyptian society —other than individuals specifically stated to be Libyan or Nubian— will remain largely anonymous.

In selecting foreign cognates from the sources—mainly West Asiatic, —that we do have, we confront the complicated matter of phonetics. Because Egyptian scribes in recording a foreign word or name tended to write down what they *heard,* we are dealing with oral, not written, transmission and all its intricate phonetic problems. This simple fact opens a veritable Pandora's box of difficulties. Let me illustrate this with a modern example. In a small Arabic restaurant in Beirut our waiter, who spoke neither English nor French, asked if we would like some "obble bye." Of course, he meant "apple pie," but there is no *p* phoneme in Lebanese Arabic, so he heard this sound as a *b.* Likewise, he said "obble" rather than "abble" because his ear could not distinguish the English *a* sound in "apple."

We face exactly this kind of phonetic problem in trying to isolate the original of a foreign name, recorded in Egyptian, which we suspect came from one of the languages of western Asia. When the Asiatic foreigners who came to live at Deir el Medina pronounced their names, the transmission of those names into Egyptian depended on how they sounded to Egyptian hearers. The village scribes therefore had to make do with what *they* heard and then spell foreign names and words as best they could. Since the languages of western Asia contained phonemes not present in Egyptian (and vice versa), such phonemes were reproduced in writing by Egyptian phonemes that only approximated the correct pronunciation.

Some years ago, I lived in a small town in Massachusetts where, because of the local strong New England accent, I was known as "Mr. Wad." I tried vainly to correct the error but finally gave up in the face of a whole community that did not hear the *r.* Had written records depended on a local scribe, the archives of a Massachusetts village would forever have preserved the temporary presence of one "Wad." Much the same happened at Deir el Medina, so that even though we have an enormous amount of comparative material in the West Asiatic languages, we are often hampered by having to deal with what an Egyptian scribe heard and wrote down as he heard it, not as it was really pronounced. Every language has phonemes that are simply not heard by those who do not speak it, as any English speaker knows who has wrestled with the sounds of Arabic, Russian, or Chinese.

Social Status of Foreigners at Deir el Medina

I have so far identified in the Deir el Medina texts twenty-two masculine and ten feminine names of West Asiatic origin: for example, Semitic *Bariya* and *Delilah,* Hurrian *Tulpiya* and *Zilli.* Of these thirty-two names, nineteen are of Semitic origin, five are Hurrian, six are either Semitic or Hurrian/Hittite, and two are the ethnic appellative "the Cypriote," which may indicate these two women's origin, though it could as easily be defined as Canaanite. With one or two exceptions, these are all names of people who lived in the village. I think it safe to assume that all these people or their recent ancestors came from Canaan; the linguistic mix of West Asiatics at Deir el Medina certainly reflects that of Canaan. The contemporary archives of Ugarit on the Syrian cost prove that the population of Canaan was made up chiefly of Semitic and Hurrian speakers, with Hittites and other groups constituting minorities.[21] Archaeological evidence indicates also the presence of Aegeans at Ugarit, though to the best of my knowledge no attempt has been made to identify Aegean names in the considerable archives of the city. The other main textual sources of the period—the Amarna Letters, the archives of Alalakh (again on the Syrian coast), and the Old Testament—also reflect the population mix at Ugarit.[22] It is therefore logical that the Canaanites who came to Deir el Medina would represent the various linguistic groups that made up the population of their homeland.

What was the personal situation of those of foreign extraction who lived at Deir el Medina? Within the community, the Canaanites all belonged to the lower functional levels of village society.[23] Nine of the women were housewives and, where their husbands can be determined, were married to ordinary workmen. The tenth woman was attached to a work gang as a servant.[24] Of the twenty-two men, one was a necropolis guard, two were gardeners, and the others were all ordinary workmen. So far, no Canaanites have shown up in the ranks of Foremen, Scribes, or other professionals who formed the upper levels of the Deir el Medina social structure with the single exception of the Chapel Scribe Zabû (see Appendix A, no. 35), whose office places him in the lower temple bureaucracy. If I am correct in assuming that this individual was attached to the small local chapels just outside the village, then we can consider him resident there, though he may well have come from elsewhere; in any event, his function derived from outside the village, no matter what his origins may have been. A second possible exception, the Ship Captian *bl* (Appendix A, no. 25) was probably not a resident of Deir el Medina; in any case, his position too would have been granted him by a larger temple in the area. Whether it represents the true picture or not, the evidence so far collected indicates that within the confines of the village, Canaanites did not have the same opportunities as the native population. This seems to apply to descendants of Canaanites as well as the original immigrants.

In the wider population of the whole Theban region, however, both in the government and in the administration of the great funerary temples, one finds Canaanites in very responsible positions, such as the Semite *Zabû*, a Scribe of the Vizier, (also in no. 35) who penned one of the Deir el Medina papyri.[25] This leads to a suggestive but very preliminary conclusion: Canaanites could advance to high positions in the wider Theban population, but local prejudice—perhaps "custom" is a better word—in the village denied them the upward mobility enjoyed by their counterparts in the temples and across the river. If so, the reason may have been no more complicated than that the more important and better-paying jobs were kept within a few native village families.[26]

At this stage I hesitate to comment on the Libyan component at Deir el Medina since I can point to only three personal names that are Libyan. But one of these, *Knr/Kl*, was common throughout Egypt and was borne by no less than thirteen inhabitants of the village (see Appendix A, no. 31, and Appendix B, nos. 1–11). There were also at least three individuals named *Kr* (Appendix A, no. 32), and one *Dydy* (no. 34). This gives us seventeen Libyans, which is far too little evidence on which to base more than tentative suggestions. Among them we find not only individuals in the lower ranks of village society but also a Chief Craftsman, a Guardian of the Tomb, a scribe, and a priest. Perhaps the Libyans who moved to Deir el Medina had a somewhat better chance for upward mobility than the Canaanites. But with only thirty-two Canaanite and seventeen Libyan names so far identified, such a conclusion is premature.

Chronologically, it is not possible to fix precise dates for all the Canaanites, so we must be content for the present with very general observations. Three date to the Eighteenth Dynasty (though the evidence is not completely certain), seven to the Nineteenth Dynasty, nine to the Twentieth, one to the Twenty-first, and nine to the general Ramesside age. The remaining three are of uncertain date. This does not really tell us much except that in Ramesside times there was a small but fairly constant minority of western Asiatic origin living in the village. The Libyan element at Deir el Medina can be somewhat better dated. One lived around the time of Ramses II, five are of the late Nineteenth Dynasty, eight of the Twentieth Dynasty, three in the general Ramesside period. This apparent concentration in the late Nineteenth and Twentieth Dynasties may be only because Libyan names are so difficult to identify. Or, since at this time Libyan groups were moving in and out of the Nile Valley, it is just possible that a few individuals decided to stay on and seek their fortunes in Egypt. We just do not know enough to draw conclusions.

The population mix at Deir el Medina was in any case a microcosm of all Egypt. We find, for example, this same mixture of Canaanites and other foreigners in the Tomb Robbery Papyri, which are concerned with the whole Theban region, and the Wilbour Papyrus, which records the population of a region in Middle Egypt.[27] The village was thus very much like other parts of the country with respect to the diverse origins of its inhabitants.

There remains an intriguing question for which I have no answer. In the hills and mountains above the village the rocks are covered with well over three thousand graffiti naming people who passed that way; they include a sum total of almost five thousand names.[28] Much of the village is represented here, as well as officials from across the river and the major funerary temples in the region, but there are just five examples of foreign personal names. Does this mean that foreigners—or even residents of foreign extraction—were not allowed to roam freely in the sacred hills of the royal tombs? West Asiatics in particular had a totally different view of life after death from that of the Egyptians; with their belief in a grim underworld and gloomy view of life beyond the grave, might they have been considered bad luck among the tombs of Egyptian royalty? If something like this was so, then these people, even if buried as Egyptians, must truly have remained all their lives strangers in a foreign land.

Appendix A: Foreign Names at Deir el Medina

Names 1–22 are discussed in Ward, *Essays . . . Kantor*, pp. 295–299, and are therefore only briefly commented on here.

1. *'Ibnt(t)n:* the non-Egyptian consonantal structure suggests a Semitic name of the Akkadian type *Ibne-X*, "(the god) X has created," or perhaps Hurrian *Abenatal, Abinadal.*

2. *'Inṯ:* the consonantal structure suggests a derivation from Semitic *nsʿ*, "to leave, depart."

3. *'Irʿ:* the writing of the element *'ir-* was commonly used for Semitic *'ilu, 'el*, "god." The full spelling seems to represent a partial translation of the Ugaritic name *ilrb*, "El is the great one."

4. *ʿbd:* a west Semitic hypocoristicon (shortened name or nickname) from *ʿbd*, "to serve," e.g., Ugaritic *ʿbdu*, Hebrew *ʿŌbēd.*

5. *ʿmṯ* and *Tʿmṯ:* masculine and feminine names from Semitic *ʿms*, "to carry," as Hebrew *ʿAmôs*, Akkadian *Yaḫmus, Taḫmus*, Ugaritic *ʿms.*

6. *ʿdr:* from west Demitic *ʿzr*, "to help," e.g., Hebrew *ʿĒzer*, Amarna *Aziru.*

7. *ḫr Bsy*, "The Syrian *Bsy*": Akkadian *Basi, Basiya;* Amorite *Yabasi-Dagan.*

8. *P³-il:* the Semitic element *-il*, "god," is written as no. 3, with the Egyptian definite article. This and the following name have been "Egyptianized" by the addition of the definite article; see n. 47, below.

9. *P³-Ym:* the element *-Ym* is west Semitic *ym(m)*, "sea; (the deity) Yamm," not generally used as a personal name except in Ugaritic, e.g., *ʿbd-Ym, Ym-il. P³-Ym* as a deity appears in the Legend of Astarte, an Egyptian version of a Canaanite myth.

10. *Prs:* from West Semitic *pls*, "to view, observe," e.g., Amorite *Pilsu*, Ugaritic *Pls.*

11. *T³- irs* "the Cypriote." Egyptian *irs* is *Alašiya*, now generally recognized as the Akkadian name for Cyprus. Again, this is an "Egyptianized" form with the definite article.

12. *Tnḥm.t:* a feminine name from west Semitic *nḥm*, "to comfort, to console." No Semitic feminine form is preserved, though there are many masculine names, e.g., Akkadian *Yanḫamu.* Hebrew *Tanḥumet, Tnḥm.*

13. *Trby:* Hurrian *Tulpiya*, one of the rare Hurrian names at Deir el Medina.

14. *Dmr:* from west Semitic *zmr*, "to protect."[29]

15. *'Inrn* (*'Iln*) from Semitic *'ln*, e.g., Hebrew *Ēlōn*, Akkadian *Iluni, Ilâni.*

16. *Ybḫy:* cognate to Amarna *Yapaḫi,* Babylonian *Yapaḫum,* with the shift *b* > *p* in Egyptian. This could also represent an Amorite hypocoristicon such as *Yabḫiya.*

17. *Bry:* though spelled with the masculine determinative, it is the name of a female servant. The name is derived from Semitic *bry,* e.g., Akkadian *Bariya, Biria,* Hebrew/Phoenician *Bry.*

18. *Mntḥ.t:* a female name, obviously not Egyptian. No certain cognates are forthcoming, though there are possible Akkadian and Hurrian parallels.

19. *Ktwn:* possibly an attempt to transcribe a name like Amarna *Kuzuna* or Hittite *Kizzuwa.*

20. *Tkrny:* either a hypocoristic *Takilayu,* or perhaps Hurrian *Takkaraya.*

21. (not used).

22. *Ṯr:* Hurrian *Zilli.*

Following are new foreign names from the Deir el Medina texts.

23. ⟨hieroglyphs⟩, *ꜣti,* mother-in-law of Sennedjem, owner of Theban Tomb 1. She and her husband *Ṯr* (= Hurrian *Zilli*) were the parents of Sennedjem's wife Iyneferty.[30] There is an excellent contemporary parallel for this couple. Another woman named *ꜣti,* also married to a Hurrian, appears on a family stela from Thebes which is replete with foreign names, those of the owner, his wife, a daughter and her husband, several children, and the owner's brother, who dedicated the stela.[31] The brother is the chief charioteer ⟨hieroglyphs⟩, *ʾItnm,* which is the Semitic name *ʾAda-num(mu),* or the like.[32] The owner of the stela is ⟨hieroglyphs⟩ *Bt,* Hurrian *Batta/Patta,* and his wife is ⟨hieroglyphs⟩, to be read *ꜣti* (rather than *Ti*), which can be compared with Hurrian *Ataya.* The son-in-law *Ḥty* has the common Hurrian name *Ḥutiya,* though his wife and her siblings have Egyptian nicknames.[33]

The genealogy of the *Patta* family can be traced for only two generations, but that of *Zilli* at Deir el Medina is better known.[34] His daughter Iyneferty has an Egyptian name, but foreign names reappear in the next generation: a son of Sennedjem and Iyneferty named Bunakhtef was also known as "the Canaanite," and a niece was named *Ataya* after her maternal grandmother. Analogous situations, where children have Egyptian names but foreign names emerge among the grandchildren, are seen in other Deir el Medina families: *Knr*, grandson of *Dydy* (Appendix B, no. 3), and *Knr*, grandson of *Kr* (Appendix C, no. 1).

24. [hieroglyphs] , *ᶠIrsy*, "the Alashian (Cypriote)," reign of Ramses XI. Not to be confused with *Tȝ-irs*, another woman at Deir el Medina. Cognate personal names seem to be rare, but compare Alalakh ᵐ*Alašia*, Ugaritic ᵐ*alṯn*, ᶜ*altt*.[35]

25. [hieroglyphs] , *ᶜbl*, a ship's captain, noted once on a jar label. Ugaritic *ᶜbl*, and the Hebrew gentilic names *ᶜôbâl* and *ᶜêbâl*, referring to Arabia and Edom. The name is rare in West Semitic, but fairly frequent in Old South Arabic.[36]

26. [hieroglyphs] , *Pȝ-mhrn*, mentioned once in a broken context in a letter from the Painter Hor-Min.[37] Reign of Ramses IV. The passage in question reads: "I have sent the letter . . . with *Pȝ-mhrn*. . . ." so that at first sight this could be taken as a title with the actual name of the messenger lost in the lacuna; however, the seated man determinative indicates a personal name, and through *mhr* was used as a title (see below), it never appears elsewhere with the definite article. Furthermore, the final *-n* speaks in favor of a name rather than a title.

The root *mhr*, borrowed from Canaanite in New Kingdom times, has been discussed by several scholars.[38] As a noun, it means "champion," "warrior," and the like, and is distinct from its homograph *mhr*, "marriage price."[39] The sense "warrior" is certainly indicated in the rare Semitic personal names that contain the root. A perfect analogy to the Egyptian spelling is *Mahranu(m)*, an Amorite name in a text of the Third Dynasty of Ur; the word is included in the name *Mahriel* in a slightly later text and, with the elements reversed, in Ugaritic *ilmhr*.[40] It is most frequent in the Punic name *Mhrbᶜl*.[41]

The element *mhr* appears in several Semitic personal names in

Egyptian texts: *B'l-mḥr*, "Baal is a warrior" or "Baal is [my] champion";[42] *P³-mḥry-ḥ³.t-f*, "The warrior is before him";[43] *Mḥr*, "the warrior";[44] *Mḥry*, with the hyocoristic ending -*y*, "My champion is . . . ";[45] *Mḥry-B'l* and *Mḥr-B'l*, "A warrior is Baal" or "[My] champion is Baal."[46] The names *P³-mḥrn* and *P³-mḥry-ḥ³.t-f* have been "Egyptianized" by the addition of the deifnite article.[47]

27.   ⟨hieroglyphs⟩ , *Ptr*, occurs alone on O. Turin 57257; because of the throwstick determinative, it should be considered foreign. Compare Hittite *Pisiri*, or Semitic *Pazzalu, Pazzulu*. Probably also related is ⟨hieroglyphs⟩ , *Ptr*, the name of a Chief Gardener, with the West Asiatic hypocoristic ending -*ya*.[48]

This name must be distinguished from ⟨hieroglyphs⟩ , *P³-ṯr*, the nickname of one Inherkhawy, apparently a great-grandson of the well known Chief Workman Hay. Among the many other family members named in his tomb and on the related monuments, there are no other foreign names, as is also true of the genealogy of Hay himself. This and the lack of the throwstick determinative indicate an Egyptian name *P³-ṯr*. Other individuals at Deir el Medina with similar names are *Ṯr*, a workman who lived under Ramses III and IV, a Wood Carrier with the same name, and the well-known Scribe of the Necropolis Thutmosis, also called *Ṯr(y)*, writer or recipient of several letters of the late Twentieth Dynasty.[49]

28.   ⟨hieroglyphs⟩ *Mgyr*, occurs once in a list of names.[50] This is not an Egyptian name and illustrates the difficulties of finding a suitable cognate out of many possibilities. One can compare Hittite *Magallu, Mugallu*; Hurrian *Mukaru, Mugaru*; Semitic *magir*, "obedient," in many Akkadian names such as *Magir-addu*;[51] and Hebrew *Mâkîr*. But none of these can account for the -*y*- in the Egyptian spelling, which normally represents a consonant in transcriptions of foreign words and should reflect, e.g., a Semitic form—**Mugayyalu*, or the like. Names of the same structure appear in an Egyptian list of foreign names dating to the Seventeenth Dynasty: *Mtyb, Mnyni*.[52]

29. ⟨hieroglyphs⟩ , *Ḥsy,* a Gardener.[53] Cf. the very common Hurrian *Ḫašiya, Ḫasiya,* and Hebrew *Ḥûsay,* according to J. J. Stamm an abbreviated form of *Hᵃšabyâhû.*[54]

30. ⟨hieroglyphs⟩ , *Šmy,* a Chief Gardener. Akkadian *Šumaya,* Amorite *Sumaya,* a hypocoristicon.[55]

31. ⟨hieroglyphs⟩ , *Knr (Kl).* No less than thirteen individuals at Deir el Medina bore this name. Since the indications are that it is a nickname given to Libyans, all the evidence, including that from elsewhere than Deir el Medina, is presented in Appendix B. The personal name *Knr* is quite common in Egyptian texts from the New Kingdom and slightly later, mostly as a masculine name but also as a feminine (Appendix B, nos. 13, 16, 29). Černý suggests

that the name was also spelled ⟨hieroglyphs⟩ , *Kr,* though he

offers no proof, and Ranke gives ⟨hieroglyphs⟩ , *Kr,* as a variant spelling based only on a statue group in Leningrand (Appendix B, no. 16).[56] Here, the lady Kel is shown with her son Amenemhab and his wife. On Kel's figure her name is spelled out in full (*Knr*), but on that of her son it is spelled in the shorter form—not really a variant spelling but an abbreviation: the end of this text gives the formula "Amenemhab, born of Kel," and there was room for only part of Kel's name. I know of no other instance where *Kr* was used in place of *Knr.* The latter was very common in the New Kingdom; the former less so but still frequent (see no. 32). There appears to be no case, save for the Leningrad stela, where the two names are applied to the same person in spite of the large number of individuals involved.

The name *Knr* appears to be Libyan, though that supposition can be supported only indirectly. We have no individual specifically identified as "the Libyan Kel" (as we have "the Nubian stonemason *Trki*" who worked at Deir el Bahri or "the Canaanite *Bsy*," a workman at Deir el Medina.[57] Nor is there contemporary evidence from the Libyan language, since no texts in that language exist. But the indirect case seems satisfactory enough to warrant the conclusion that we are dealing with a Libyan name, or at least a hypocoristicon of one. That *Knr* is not Egyptian is certain in that well over half its occurrences use the throwstick determinative (see note 9). Another indicator is that where the double-name formula occurs—Neferrenpet, Minmose, and Thutmosis, all of whom are "called Kel" (Appendix B, nos. 19, 20, 24)—*Knr* is most often spelled with the throwstick; hence, it is a foreign name rather than an Egyptian nickname.

Two details, both from Deir el Medina, point to a Libyan origin: Kel, son of Amennakht, is shown with two plumes in his hair after the Libyan fashion; and Kel, son of Penduau, was the grandson of *Dydy* (Appendix B, no. 3), a demonstrably Libyan name (see no. 34 below)—apparently another case of a foreign name cropping up again in the third generation (as happened in the family of the well-known Sennedjem; see no. 23 above). One should also consider here the *ꜥ n ḫꜣs.t Knr*, "Chief of the Desert, Kel," who led expeditions into the desert to obtain gold and galena for the Amon temple at Karnak (Appendix B, no. 28). His name, which appears many times in the papyrus dealing with these expeditions, is uniformly spelled with the throwstick; and he is obviously an official familiar with the desert and, as such, likely to have been a Libyan—though one could argue that Nubians would also be experts in desert travel.

The name *Knr* seemingly belongs to a group of rather common names with the same construction: *Wrnr, Ḥnr, Snr, Tnr,* and a unique *Ḥnr*, names collectively considered foreign, specifically Libyan.[58] This is not the case, however. *Knr* is treated differently in that only *Knr* uses the throwstick determinative and, with rare exceptions (noted below), does not enter into compound names such as *Bꜣk-n-Wrnr, Pꜣ-Snr, Pꜣ-Tnr*. Those compounds, like their simplexes, do not use the throwstick determinative because, unlike *Knr*, they are Egyptian names. *Tnr* is derived from the common verb *tnr*, "be strong."[59] *Wrnr* and *Ḥnr* are feminine hypocoristica for *Tꜣ-wr.t* and *Ḥw.t-Ḥr*, respectively; *Snr* and *Ḥnr* are probably the same for names compounded with *Stḫ* and *Ḥnmw*.

One may reasonably wonder why more than thirty individuals bearing the same foreign name can be identified in Egyptian texts.

We might expect many native Egyptians to have the same name over four hundred years, the time represented by the examples of *Knr* given in Appendix B, but hardly so high a frequency of a single Libyan name during the same period. It is possible, and I suggest this *only* as a possibility, that *Knr* was a nickname applied to Libyans much as other peoples today may refer to the English as "Brits" or Americans as "Yanks." Libyan personal names must often have been difficult for Egyptians to pronounce.[60] Hence, it seems plausible that Libyans or their descendants living in Egypt would be called by a nickname on the pattern of such common Egyptian nicknames as *Wrnr* and *Snr*. A possible origin for such a nickname might be *Knm.t,* the ancient name for the Khargeh Oasis in the western (Libyan) desert.[61] *Knr,* Kel, would thus be a hypocoristicon, following an Egyptian name pattern, for *Knm.ty,* "Khargian."

This does not mean that all the individuals named Kel were Libyan immigrants; most of them probably were not. Where the patronymics are known, several fathers have Egyptian names (Appendix B, nos. 1–4, 9); in only one instance does the father have a Libyan name (nos. 24–25). In a few cases an ancestor has a foreign name, indicating that the name Kel was given in honor of the foreign origins of either the father or mother. And we must also consider that the name Kel, like "the Canaanite" or "the Nubian," may have come to have little or no foreign connections at all.[62] There are thus several rasons why an individual might be given a name that was non-Egyptian in origin, though our inability to trace family trees prevents our determining the reason in specific cases.

It remains to note those rare cases of names that *seem* to include the name *Knr*. The only occurrences of *Knry* are found in the Wilbour Papyrus, as a personal name ⟨hieroglyphs⟩ and in place name ⟨hieroglyphs⟩, *P₃-n-knry*, an unknown location in Middle Egypt.[63] A single instance of an apparent ending *-ri* is found on an early Nineteenth Dynasty funerary figurine.[64] A second example with this ending is quoted in the literature but does not exist.[65]

32. [hieroglyphs], *Kr*. Three, or possibly only two, individuals with this name are known from Deir el Medina (Appendix C, nos. 1–3), and several others appear from outside the village (nos. 4–10). The rare spellings [hieroglyphs], *Kri*, and [hieroglyphs], *Kry*, are variants of the much more common *Kr*. The name of the Guardian of the Tomb *Kr* is spelled all three ways and there is even a unique *Kriy* for the same person. These variants indicate that the name is a hypocoristicon. That this name is foreign is shown by the use of the throwstick determinative and its appearance in two lists of foreign names (nos. 4–5). The question arises, of course whether all the instances I list are actually the same name, given its brevity and the widespread appearance of names with this consonantal structure in other languages.[66] I am inclined to consider all these occurrences as representing the same foreign name, though I cannot prove it.

Whatever its origin(s), this name with the initial [hieroglyphs] should be carefully distinguished from its homophone, [hieroglyphs], [hieroglyphs], (and the variants *Kri*, *Kry*), which is characterized by an initial k^3 sign and, as far as I can tell, never uses the throwstick determinative. There are four persons with this name at Deir el Medina, and it is fairly common elsewhere.[67] This is undoubtedly an Egyptian nickname. It should be emphasized that though both foreign *Kr* and Egyptian *Kr* are quite frequent, there is no case in which both spellings apply to the same person.

Nor are the foreign *Kr* and the Libyan name *Knr* (see no. 31 above) ever used for the same individual—though both do occur in the family of Qaha (Appendix C, no. 1). Qaha's brother-in-law was named *Kr*, and both men were grandfathers to a *Knr* (Appendix B, no. 1), son of *Kr*'s daughter and Qaha's son. The parents of this *Kr*, owner of Theban Tomb 330, both have Egyptian names, so—on the analogy of *Knr*, grandson of *Dydy* (Appendix B, no. 3)—one of *Kr*'s grandparents should be foreign. *Kr* thus comes in the third generation and *Knr* in the fifth, both names recalling the now unknown ancestor. If this is the case, *Kr*, like *Knr*, is possibly a Libyan name, since it is unlikely that Libyan and West Asiatic names would occur in the same family.

There is evidence to support such a suggestion in the person of "the Great Chief of the Libu, Great Chief of the Ma, *Kr*," written as foreign *Kr*, who may or may not be the same as "the Great Chief of the Meshwesh, *Kr*."[68] These occurrences establish at least that *Kr* is a Libyan name but not that all individuals with this name were of Libyan origin or descent. As already noted, names based on the consonants *k* + *r*/*l* can be found in all linguistic groups. As a tentative conclusion, I would count the Workman *Kr*, grandson of *Knr*, as Libyan (Appendix C, no. 1) and perhaps also the "Guardian of the Tomb, *Kr*," because of his rank (Appendix C, no. 3), since western Asiatics do not appear to have achieved any status above the lower ranks at Deir el Medina.

33. , *Trr*, a woman mentioned once on a piece of mummy linen found in the tomb of Huy. Reign of Ramses II. The foreign cognate that comes immediately to mind is Hebrew *D^elîlâh*, meaning "flowing locks of hair" or, possibly, "little one."[69] An Akkadian name of the same structure is ᵐ*Dalilu*, ᶠ*Daliluša*, the latter meaning "her (a goddess's) fame, glory." It is possible that the Hebrew and Akkadian names ultimately derive from the same root *dadâlu*, "be submissive; praise."[70] *Dalilu*, the masculine form of this name, is probably represented by

, *Trr*, the name of a Canaanite mercenary portrayed on a stela of the Amarna period.[71]

34. , *Dydy*, a Chief Craftsman (*ḥmww wr*) mentioned many times in his tomb and on funerary objects.[72] This is one of the few personal names which can with certainty be called Libyan. A Libyan chieftain *Mwry*, son of *Dydy*, the latter spelled exactly as at Deir el Medina, is mentioned in the account of Merneptah's Libyan campaign.[73] The Chief Craftsman *Dydy*'s parentage is unknown, though two of his sons, Amennakht and Penduau, appear frequently; and a son of Penduau was named *Knr*, carrying on the Libyan tradition of the family (Appendix B, no 3). The only other

instance of the name *Dydy* spelled with the throwstick of which I
am aware is a Sherden in Papyrus Wilbour (A 44, 17). This Libyan
name should be kept separate from Middle Kingdom *Dd*, a gemi-
nated form of the verb *rdi*, and from New Kingdom *Dydw*, which
is never written from the throwstick.[74]

35. 𓀀𓃀𓅱𓏲 , *Db*, a Scribe of Chapels (*sš n r-prw*) mentioned in
a letter from the Vizier Nefer-renpet penned by his namesake

𓀀𓃀𓅱𓏲 , *Db*, Scribe of the Vizier.[75] The letter is addressed
to certain "Administratiors of the Tomb" and concerns business
having to do with the work force of Deir el Medina. This Scribe of
Chapels was probably attached to the small chapels just outside the
village. Aside from these examples, the name does not occur elsewhere.[76] It is cognate to Semitic *Zabû/Sabû*, "warrior" as a personal name.[77] The plural noun "warriors = army" occurs a few
times in New Kingdom texts.[78]

Appendix B: Occurrences of the Name *Knr/Kl*

Each individual known to me with the name *Knr/Kl*, primarily in New
Kingdom texts, has been isolated from the others on the basis of patronymics, double names, or dating. Though it is possible that in one or
two instances the same person may be listed under two entries, I have
made every effort to avoid such suplication. The several funerary figures,
for example (nos. 15, 17, 22, 26, 29), are of different materials, work-
manship, or date; no two can be considered as belonging to the same
person. The dating of the Deir el Medina sources for the Twentieth
Dynasty generally follows that of Gutgesell, *Datierung*, vol. 1 (for this
and other sources cited, see the Abbreviations preceding the Notes in this
volume).

At Deir el Medina

1. Workman, Deir el Medina, son of Inherkhau; later Nineteenth Dynasty. Mentioned with patronymic on O. Geneva 12550 and in
   Spiegelberg, *Graffiti*, no. 589. He is said to have been dead for some
   time on the Geneva ostracon, dated to year 11 of Ramses III, and his

father was a Chief Workman under Ramses II and Merneptah (Černý, *Workmen,* pp. 297–298). This Kel should thus date to the later Nineteenth Dynasty and is probably the one mentioned on O. Cairo 25507, I, 10; 25510, 13; 25522, II, 7; 25796, II, 24. His maternal grandfather was the *Kr* (also a foreign name) of TT 330.

2. Workman, Deir el-Medina, son of Amennakht; second half Nineteenth Dynasty. Shown with two Libyan plumes in his hair which were effaced in favor of the label "Workman Kel": FIFAO 5/2, 74, fig. 51; MIFAO 71, pl. 1, sc. 8. In neither case are the plumes visible in the photographs, but Bruyère was quite definite about their presence.

3. Workman, Deir el Medina, son of Penduau; second half Nineteenth Dynasty. Grandson of the Libyan *Dydy.* This Kel is shown with his parents in a statue group in Turin and on a Louvre stela, and is mentioned elsewhere. The generation sequence *Dydy*—Penduau—Kel is certain: FIFAO 8/2, 14; FIFAO 14, 89; MIFAO 71, pl. 4, sc. 25; *RecTrav* 2 (1880): 169; Turin stelae 240, 296; Louvre stela A 63.

4. *Wab* priests, Deir el-Medina. At least three *wab* priests with the name *Knr* are mentioned in the Deir el Medina texts.

   a. *Wab* priest: O. Cairo 25555 v. 6; late Nineteenth Dynasty.

   b. *Wab* priest of the Lord of the Two Lands; on a stela seen in a dealer's shop; late Nineteenth Dynasty; Jaroslav Černý, "Le culte d'Amenophis 1er chez les ouvriers de la nécropole thébaine," *BIFAO* 27 (1927): 202 (69); and Jean J. Clère, "Monuments inédits des serviteurs dans la place de vérité," *BIFAO* 28 (1929): 191.

   c. *Wab* priest of (the goddess) Maat; reign of Ramses III; O. Gardiner 130, 6 (KRI 7:304, 10–11).

In light of the practice of village workmen serving as lay priests in the cult of Amenhotep I (Černý, *BIFAO* 27 [1927]: 193–197), the first two priests noted here probably refer to workmen of the same name; they would thus correspond to any of nos. 1–3 above. The third, a priest of Maat, can be understood as it stands, since such priests are well documented in the Theban area; see Borghouts, *Divine Inter-*

vention, pp. 85–87. Borghouts suggests that such priests served a shrine at Karnak under the Vizier, also a priest of this goddess. O. Gardiner 130 is simply a list of officials serving at various places, though the place is not specified for this priest. It would appear that he was not a resident of the village.

5. Workman, Deir el-Medina, son of Userhat; reign of Ramses III. Mentioned on an offering table fragment: FIFAO 20/2, 52; probably the same person named without the patronymic on ostraca dating to years 14–22 of Ramses III: O. DeM 222, 364; O. Cairo 25555, 1, 4. Two other ostraca naming Kel also date to this period on the basis of other names: O. DeM 582; Černý-Gardiner, *HO* pl. 31, 2, II, 1. This may be the same person as the *Knỉ* (son of) Userhat of O. Turin 57039 and 57056, dated to Year 24 of Ramses III.

6. Water Carrier, Deir el-Medina; early in reign of Ramses III. Mentioned on ostraca dating to years 13–16 of Ramses III: O. Turin 57151, 5; O. DeM 432; 433; O. Michaelides 2, 4; perhaps also in the Turin Strike Papyrus: *RAD*, 46, 11.

7. Potter(?), Deir el-Medina; reign of Ramses III. No title given but noted as a supplier of pottery vessels: O. DeM 55. This could, however, be one of the workmen of that time who delivered but did not make the pottery.

8. Policeman, Deir el-Medina; reign of Ramses IV. O. DeM 433, 3.

9. Workman, Deir el-Medina, son of Amenkhau; reign of Ramses III or IV. O. Michaelides 7, Vs. 2.

10. Scribe, Deir el-Medina; Ramesside. O. Cairo 25504, I, 8.

11. Stablemaster, Deir el-Medina; Ramesside. O. Turin 57151, 6.

Elsewhere than Deir el Medina

12. Workman, Deir el Bahri; mid-Eighteenth Dynasty. Hayes, *Ostraca and Name Stones*, no. 89, 3.

13. Female relative of Thutmosis called Paroy, owner of TT 295; reigns of Thutmosis IV and Amenhotep III. El Sayed A. Hegazy and M. Tosi, *A Theban Private Tomb: Tomb No. 295* (Mainz, 1983), p. 18, pl. 2. It is not possible to define the relationship, if any, between this Kel and Paroy. In the tomb scene Osiris is being praised by Paroy, behind whom is an unidentified man. The latter is followed by a

woman, identified as "his mother," whose name is lost in a lacuna. She, in turn, is followed by her three daughters, one of whom is the Kel in question. Kel is thus either a sister of Paroy or of the unidentified man behind him.

14. Relative of the owner of a stela; Eighteenth Dynasty. Otto Koeford-Petersen, *Les stèles égyptiennes* (Copenhagen, 1948), no. 29; Ny Carlsberg Glyptotek AEIN 1552. The editor gives the name as *Pskl*, though there are actually two names labeling the first two figure in a line of worshipers before a tree goddess. The first name is $P^3 \ldots s^3$ with the determinative below the arm of this individual because of lack of space above the head. I know of no other name similar to this. Signs following P^3 may be $y + r$, but the surface is damaged at this point. The second figure is *Knr,* who is shaved as a priest but bears no title. (I thank Mogens Jorgensen of the Ny Carlsberg Glyptotek for sending a photograph of this stela and verifying the reading on the original.)

15. Funerary figurine; Deputy of P^3-*mnw.* W. F. Petrie, *Shabtis* (London, 1935), no. 83.

16. Songstress of Amon, mother of the Steward in the Temple of Amenhotep I west of Thebes, Amenemhab; time of Horemhab. LD Text III, 238–239, from Amenemhab's tomb at Thebes. Shown in statue group in Leningrad, Hermitage 740: B. Piotrovsky, *Egyptian Antiquities in the Hermitage* (Leningrad, 1974), p. 10, pl. 51. Mentioned on a funerary cone of Amenemhab: N. DeG. Davies, *A Corpus of Inscribed Funerary Cones* (Oxford, 1957), no. 532.

17. Funerary figurine; Beginning of Nineteenth Dynasty. J.-L. Chappaz, *Les figurines funéraires égyptiens du Musée d'Art et d'Histoire et de quelques collections privées* (Geneva, 1984), no. 006, private collection.

18. *Wab* priest, Head of the Magazine of Khonsu; early Nineteenth Dynasty. Usurper of TT 54 of Huy; PM² I, i, 104–105.

19. Scribe of the Treasury of the Estate of Amon, Neferrenpet called Kel; TT 178; time of Ramses II. André Lhote, *La peinture égyptienne* (Paris, 1954, pls. 35, 108; Ludwign Borchardt "Friesziegel in Grabbauten," *ZÄS* 70 (1934): 26 n. 5; Mahmud Abdel-Raziq, "Bemerkungen zu Grab 178 in Theben-West und zu dem *Pr-ḥd* des *Pr-Jmn,*" *MDAIK* 37 (1981): 409–416.

20. Royal Scribe and palace official, Minmose called Kel; time of Ramses

II. Louvre stela C 218. It has often been assumed (e.g., Černý, *Workmen*, p. 210) that he is the same person as the Deir el Medina Scribe Minmose (mentioned, e.g., in TT 335), son of the Royal Scribe Amenemopet, though this can hardly be the case. The Minmose of the Louvre stela was indeed a scribe, but his many titles show him to have been a palace official and a priest of Neith. He was also a "True Scribe of the Place of Truth," which places him in the ranks of necropolis officials, but his career was obviously as a Royal Scribe in the central government. Statements that the Scribe Minmose of Deir el Medina was also named Kel, and identical to the Minmose of Louvre C 218, are, as far as I can see, based on no evidence other than that stela: FIFAO 20/2, 51, 99 (no. 208); FIFAO 26, 34; etc.

21. Chief Vintner; Nineteenth Dynasty. Wilhelm Spiegelberg, *ZÄS* 58 (1923): 34.

22. Funerary figurine; Nineteenth Dynasty. Petrie, *Shabtis*, no. 126.

23. Chief Weaver; Nineteenth Dynasty. Owner of a headrest, Heidelberg 290: Siegfried Schott, *ZÄS* 83 (1958): 141–144.

24. Thutmosis called Kel; Year 6 of Ramses III. Marek Marciniak, *Les inscriptions hiératiques du temple de Thoutmosis III* (Warsaw, 1974), no. 9.

25. Scribe Kel the Younger; son of no. 24, above; Year 6 of Ramses III. Marciniak, *Inscriptions*, no. 9.

26. Funerary figurine, *Wab* priest of Khonsu; Twentieth Dynasty. Cairo 47234; Percy E. Newberry, *Funerary Statuetts and Model Sarcophagi* (Cairo, 1930–1937), no. 47234.

27. Without title; Ramesside. Marciniak, *Inscriptions*, no. 112. This must be a third *Knr* in these texts, since the handwriting is different from that of nos. 24–25, above.

28. Chief of the Desert; reign of Ramses VII. Mentioned many times in an IFAO papyrus as the leader of expeditions to obtain gold and galena: Yvan Koenig, "Livraisons d'or et de galène du trésor du temple d'Amon sous la XXᵉ dynastie," in *Hommages Sauneron I*, IFAO BdE 81 (Cairo, 1979), pp. 185–220; Additional fragments in Yvan Koenig, *BIFAO* 83 (1983): 249–255; full text in KRI 7:364–368. Since these raw materials were brought to the temple of Amon at Karnak, we can assume that this official worked for that institution. The title is rare (Koenig is able to quote only one parallel), but it is evident that such officials were familiar with the desert.

Third Intermediate Period

29. Two funerary figurines of a woman; Twentieth Dynasty or later. Newberry, *Funerary Statuettes,* Cairo 48311, 48312.
30. Chief of the Hall of the Double Brazier of Khonsu; post–New Kingdom. Owner of Cairo statue 571.

Appendix C: Occurrences of the Name Kr(i, y)

1. Workman, Deir el Medina, son of *Sꜣ-mwt*; reign of Ramses II. Owner of TT 330: BM 144; BM 328; Turin 169=1636=50012; Turin 44; Dominique Valbelle, *Ouchebtis de Deir el-Médineh,* IFAO, Doc. et Fouilles, 15 (Cairo, 1977), no. 25; FIFAO 2/2, 94–97. His genealogy (simplified after Bierbrier, *Late New Kingdom,* p. 36, and Černý, *Workmen,* p. 314) is as follows:

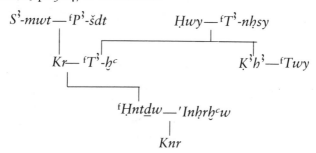

2. Workman (?), Deir el Medina; late Twentieth Dynasty. Mentioned on O. Turin 57297, 2–3, in a list of three names. One of these is *Pꜣ-šdw,* a workman who lived during the second half of the Twentieth Dynasty. It is possible that this *Kr* is the same as no. 3 below.
3. Guardian of the Tomb, Deir el Medina; late Twentieth to Twenty-First Dynasties. Appears eleven times in letters: Černý, *LRL,* p. 79. He is also mentioned once as Gatekeeper (*iry ꜥꜣ*) in P. Turin 2071/244 + 1960: Allam, *HOP,* p. 329, pl. 125. This papyrus also lists the Chief Workman Hormes, active in the reign of Ramses IX: Černý, *Workmen,* pp. 308–309. He can thus be added to the list of gatekeepers promoted to the rank of Guardian of the Tomb: Černý, *Workmen,* pp. 168–169.
4. In list of foreign names; Seventeenth Dynasty. Erman, *Hymnen,* Anhang, no. k1.

5. In list of Canaanites; Eighteenth Dynasty. Steindorff, *ZÄS* 38 (1900): 17.

6. Female relative of Amenmose on stela from Abydos; New Kingdom. Cairo Cat. 34067.

7. In list of householders on Theban West Bank (not Deir el Medina); reign of Ramses IX and later. P. BM 10058, v. 2, 14.

8. In list of names probably related to the tomb robbery trials; reign of Ramses IX. P. Abbot 8, 2, 13: see Peet, *Tomb Robberies*, p. 29.

9. Porter ($k^{3}w.ty$) mentioned three times in the tomb robbery trials; reign of Ramses IX. P. Mayer A 4, 8; 5, 1; 3c, 10.

10. Priest of Amon; end Twenty-First Dynasty. Cairo coffin J 29644, now in Florence: Georges Daressy, "Les cercueils des prêtres d'Ammon (deuxième trouvaille de Deir el-Bahri," *ASAE* 8 (1907): 8, 19.

Tomb of Queen Nefertari, Valley of the Queens, Nineteenth Dynasty. Photo by L. H. Lesko.

Workers at the funeral of their father from the tomb of Sennedjem (TT #1), Deir el Medina, Ramesside Period. Photo by B. S. Lesko.

Depiction of the deceased tomb owners in the Field of Hetep, tomb of Sennedjem, Deir el Medina, Nineteenth Dynasty. Photo by L. H. Lesko.

Workman praying under a dom palm tree. Tomb of Pashed (TT # 3), Ramesside Period, Deir el Medina. Photo by L. H. Lesko.

Burial chamber of the tomb of Ramses VI, Valley of the Kings, Twentieth Dynasty. Photo by L. H. Lesko.

Workmen decorating a shrine to the deified Amenhotep I. Tomb of Ipuy (TT # 217), Deir el Medina, Nineteenth Dynasty. Photo by L. H. Lesko.

The deceased tomb owners' family, tomb of Sennedjem, Deir el Medina, Twentieth Dynasty. Photo by L. H. Lesko.

The foreman Inherkhau and his wife from their tomb in Deir el Medina, Twentieth Dynasty. Photo by L. H. Lesko.

PART II

Spiritual and Intellectual Matters

Do not raise your voice in the house of god.
He abhors shouting;
Pray by yourself with a loving heart,
Whose every word is hidden.
He will grant your needs,
He will accept your offerings.
Libate for your father and mother,
Who are resting in the valley;
When the gods witness your action,
They will say: "Accepted."

—Maxims of Ani

It is always difficult to understand the psychology of people who lived so long ago and about whom we have only random knowledge. At Deir el Medina, where the workmen's whole lives were devoted to excavating and decorating royal tombs intended for life after death, there had to be a special aura of magic and mystery that would have particularly touched the most religious among them. Since the decoration of the burial chambers of their own tombs contains mythological vignettes from Books of the Dead, if not from the royal tombs, combined with the more customary ritual and daily life scenes that they could have studied in the tomb chapels of the elite, it would seem that the villagers were generally quite religious, optimistic about a blessed hereafter, and willing to devote much of their time and resources to that end. Their expectation for the afterlife would probably not have been equivalent to that of their kings and queens, which they like few others would have understood, but they presumably believed that they were capable of attaining a state not less blessed than that of the bulk of the nobility or at least of the local Theban officialdom buried in other nearby cemetery hills.

Private votive stelae provide perhaps the best evidence of the personal piety and religion of the common people of Deir el Medina. These were individual expressions of faith or confidence in one or another deity, gratitude for divine favors, and petitions in adversity. Physical ailments required a deity's attention as much as a physician's; the carved and painted ears on many stelae were intended to get a god's attention rather than to call attention to earaches. The votive stelae show insistent public action, which the members of the community as a whole would have understood and sympathized with, and a closeness to the gods that borders on familiarity rather than awe or dread. Among the household deities favored at Deir el Medina, women looked to Hathor, Taweret, and Bes for protection in childbirth, and all looked to Renenutet and Meretseger for food and safety. The workmen themselves seem to have particularly honored Ptah and Reshep in connection with their patronage of craftsmanship and strength, and shrines to Thoth and Seshat reflect the scribal activity of some.

The number of chapels dedicated to various deities is indicative of the workmen's devotion, tolerance, and need for public religious expression. The villagers had a total of sixteen to eighteen small temples or chapels; the larger ones among them were those dedicated to Hathor and Ramses II at the north end of the village and another to Ptah on the southwestern path leading to the Valley of the Queens. Any individual chapel would have provided a local residence for the god or goddess to whom it was dedicated and a locus for offerings to that deity. Finds from some of the chapels suggest that a few were devoted to ancestor cults, and this perhaps should not be too surprising, since shrines to the greatest gods mingle with those of local (Meretseger), distant (Khnum, Satis, and Anukis), and foreign (Reshep, Anath, and Kadesh) gods and of royal ancestor cults. The chapels symbolize the community's recognition of both national and local gods, and in the important matter of their mortuary beliefs—which are perhaps the best documented—it would seem that the local Meretseger, "Lady of the Western Mountain" was at least as important as the great god of the dead, Osiris.

Although the small temples or chapels may have been places for some ritual observances and oracular pronouncements, textual references to religious activities involve the gods' images in procession rather than in their shrines. The gods' images, even that of the great Amon-Reʿ, had to come out among the people. The workmen themselves engaged in the simple priestly activities documented; the villagers probably had no professional clergy, though some chapels had attached chambers or guardhouses. Serving as priests for the processions they conducted on numerous feast days, the majority were acting as ordinary *wab* priests (pure ones), though the titles of "lector," "fan bearer," and "*bak*" (servant) are

Religious scenes from the tomb of Inherkhau at Deir el Medina (TT # 359). Photo by L. H. Lesko.

Chapel area in the north end of Deir el Medina. Photo by L. H. Lesko.

A chapel at Deir el Medina. Photo by B. S. Lesko.

The workmen's cemetery on the western foothills of Deir el Medina. Photo by L. H. Lesko.

also known. Whether those priests did more in the way of instruction, preaching, blessing, or assisting the workmen is not known and therefore perhaps not likely.

The cult of the long-deceased Amenhotep I, known as "Lord of the Village" and regarded as its founder, was among the most important for these particular villagers. This deified king had many feasts during the year at which his statue was carried in procession by the *wab* priests, and he was called upon to resolve disputes, particularly those involving real estate. The god's oracular pronouncements—however they were made and with the help of whatever priests—had great weight, and his processions were a high point in community life. There were cult chapels to at least eight other pharaohs of the New Kingdom as well, since they were the patrons for whom the workmen toiled. But even though Amenhotep I could replace Amon-Re' in a ritual performed by Ramses II, and could also replace Osiris in a tomb painting of the judgment of the deceased, the annual parade of Amon-Re' from Karnak to the West Bank was part of the beautiful Feast of the Valley, the greatest festival in which the villagers participated, and Osiris was one of the deities most frequently represented.

In addition to cult statues (probably of wood), votive stelae, and libation basins, several chapels had benches for twelve persons, seven on one side and five on the other. These benches and seating arrangements have no parallel elsewhere and no satisfactory explanation as yet. Persons may sometimes have slept in the forecourts of the chapels to effect cures or to secure a communication from a god, as Ashraf Sadek has suggested (*Popular Religion in Egypt during the New Kingdom;* Hildesheim, 1988). In any case, these chapels—with hidden oracles, animal pens, resident guardians, libation basins, ash from cooking, benches, and cult objects for gods of all kinds, including ancestors—must have been very special gathering places, where so-called reversion offerings were consumed by like-minded people or family groups who perhaps belonged to or attended one or more of these confraternities or assemblies.

The settlement on the path from Deir el Medina to the Valley of the Kings, where the workmen spent their nights during the ten-day work week, also contained more than 50 small shrines, indicating the widespread personal devotion of the workmen even when away from home and family. They also suggest that social deviants—such as a woman known to have stolen temple property and to have sworn a false oath;

and the notorious Paneb, who was accused of stealing, misappropriation of equipment and workmen, sexual assault, drunkenness, and even murder—were exceptional in the community.

Gods were frequently called upon to intercede in the villagers' personal problems, and an instruction from the Maxims of Ani, which was found in the village (see the epigraph above), tells how one should pray meaningfully.

Two aspects of personal piety and the religion of commoners in the village of Deir el Medina, relevant to our understanding of ancient Egyptian culture in general, are the veneration (worship?) of or at least close involvement with household deities and ancestors, and the invocation and use of magic with its roots in mythology. Florence Friedman's contribution deals with the former, and Joris Borghout's with the latter. My own concluding chapter discussed some literary and educational matters that link the Deir el Medina workmen with Egyptians who lived hundreds of years earlier.

FOUR

Aspects of Domestic Life and Religion

Florence D. Friedman

Religious concerns and obligations were a part of everyday life for the people of Deir el Medina. It is well documented that workers frequently took days off to perform a variety of cultic duties in the village: brewing beer for local festivals, making libations to the dead, or preparing and assisting at funerals.[1] There were festival celebrations in honor of deified kings, most notably Amenhotep I, the traditional founder of the village and oracle par excellence.[2] There were also devotions to Thutmose III of the Eighteenth Dynasty, and celebrations of the jubilee festivals of Ramses II and III.[3] Furthermore, the villagers participated, at least in some cases, in such major Theban celebrations as the Festival of the Valley and the festival of Opet, possibly even developing a local variant of the Opet festival within their own community.[4]

The inhabitants of Deir el Medina seem to have enjoyed a shared religious culture with Thebes, and probably Egypt as a whole, but religious practices within their village life were often focused on personal concerns that could be addressed to favorite deities, and deified kings or forebears. Individuals made pleas to the gods through votive offerings in their local temples and private chapels, and through funerary offerings at the tombsites of deceased relatives whom they honored and whose aid they implored. In seeking the help of the gods or the dead, the settlers adapted formal religious experience to personal and family needs, liberally employing magic, divination, oracles, and seers peculiar to their settlement.[5]

The movement from the broader, formal structure of worship of the standard deities to the more specific and personal veneration of gods and divinized beings who could help in private life was undoubtedly the norm in settlements everywhere, but it is clearer in Deir el Medina, thanks to the material remains that have survived there. At such a uniquely preserved site one can see evidence of beliefs that are less the result of theological engineering than the product of naturally evolving popular tradition. One personal aspect of this tradition concerned domestic religion, practices carried on in the household, some of which mirrored cult practices conducted in the votive chapels and at tombsites.

Housing in Deir el Medina, which was provided by the state, was fairly standard in plan.[6] Though there were certainly variations in size and the number of rooms, the typical village house in Ramesside times consisted of an antechamber, or first room, followed by a main room characterized by the presence of a mudbrick divan. From this second room stairs led to a cellar that was possibly used as a storeroom, though burials of children were discovered there in a few instances. Two smaller rooms—a bedroom, possibly, and a kitchen—and finally another underground cellar issuing off the kitchen concluded the layout (fig. 1). The walls, though poorly or unevenly preserved, appear generally to have been whitewashed with simple bands of gray and black above the floor. The paintings that we assume decorated many walls have unfortunately not survived, with the exception of a lower band of figures from a mural that seems to depict a naked mother, seated and attended by three figures, with tendrils of convolvulus leaves (which often suggest a female-related context) appearing between the legs.[7]

Depending upon the number of men employed by the pharaoh at any given time, the houses, of which we count the roofless remains of seventy today, might all have been occupied or some left vacant.[8] The size of the average family residing in a house is not entirely clear and could fluctuate with such variables as how often the father returned home for the night (as opposed to sleeping close to the site of the royal tombs or being away on a special mission); the number of children still living at home; the number of servants within the family; and the addition of widowed, unmarried, or other relatives to a multigenerational household.[9] Domestic animals, their presence attested by numerous droppings, must have added to already cramped quarters.

A given for any Egyptian settlement was that fertility, birth, disease, suffering, and death were critical and long-term concerns—as they are today—and that complaints and grievances, ranging from property disputes to adultery, were inevitable.[10] It was the home where, at least in part, such concerns were undoubtedly aired. At Deir el Medina we find, in the midst of what was probably a malodorous dwelling crowded with children, servants, and the activities of cooking and weaving, evidence of domestic arrangements that addressed or alluded to ways these concerns were handled, at least in part.

Bedlike Constructions

Found in a corner of the first room of many dwellings is a rectangular bedlike construction of mud brick, originally plastered and painted or whitewashed (figs. 2 and 3). Some bear decoration that appears to identify them with birth-related and other female activities. Bruyère found remains of such structures in twenty-eight of the sixty-eight houses known to him at the site and dated their appearance to the second half of the Eighteenth Dynasty. They have seven different forms (fig. 4). The two sides, which are free from the corner of the room, may take the form of low walls, or they may reach nearly or all the way to the ceiling and be crowned with a molding that creates, in some instances, a sort of canopy. The structure is thus partially or fully enclosed except for an opening on the long side, which is approached by three to five steps set either perpendicular or parallel to the platform.[11]

Bruyère described the brick structures as generally rectangular blocks with average dimensions of 1.70 meters long, 0.80 meters wide, and 0.75 meters high (for the platform) (that is, about 5½ by 2½ by 2½ feet), a size capable of accommodating one but probably not two adults. Their appearance, much like modern box beds, prompted Bruyère to compare these constructions with "des lits clos bretons."[12] The structure does not appear to have been permanently affixed to any of the walls or consistently located in any one corner of the room. Its frequent appearance in the first room of the house, however, suggests that it held some prominence in domestic life, and its painted decoration (discussed below) may have reflected traditions of popular belief regarding aspects of female sexuality in its most comprehensive sense.

It is tempting to interpret such blocklike, legless, canopied constructions as beds, yet they do not accord with representations of ordinary Egyptian beds (mainly known from examples from the elite class), which are typically lighter, open pieces of furniture equipped with a mattress of sorts and often having a headrest, footboard,[13] and legs carved in the shape of bulls' or lions' legs. Mattresses and headrest could certainly have been added as needed, and headrests were, in fact, found on two of the platforms of these structures. Bruyère suggested that the bedlike construction may have been not an ordinary bed but a bed-altar, possibly a conjugal bed or a birthing bed, and possibly an altar to an ancestor cult as well.[14]

The painted imagery that has survived on the exterior panels of some of these "box beds" is instructive. Several fragments reveal figures—or parts of figures—of Bes, the household dwarf god associated with fertility and the protection of women in labor and childbirth.[15] He is typically shown in a celebratory mood, dancing and making music. One painting fragment shows most of a dancing female flute player who has a Bes tattoo on her thigh and is surrounded by leafy convolvulus vines; another shows part of a marsh scene that Bruyère believed referred to the life of the young god Horus in the Delta; a third reveals the lower portion of a scene of a naked woman kneeling in the course of her toilette, with convolvulus vines behind her and a servant girl opposite.[16] The subject matter in all these paintings specifically involves themes in female life: labor, childbirth, and daily grooming.

Bruyère's birthing-bed notions would certainly be in keeping with the appearance of Bes and the other female-related evidence. Yet one could counter that the images of Bes on these structures may merely have served a protective role, just as they typically do in furniture decoration and on toilet articles. James Romano has suggested that the representation of Bes on the box bed was in fact intended as nothing more than a means of protecting the sleepers within it, and indeed, the purpose of placing the platform several feet off the ground may have been to protect potential sitters or sleepers from such common night intruders as scorpions and snakes. Romano also suggests that the structure probably served as just an ordinary bed; though it could *also* have been used for the delivery of a child, he thinks it unlikely that the villagers would have sacrificed a good 10 percent of the room's floor space to a ritual birthing bed that would likely be needed no more than once a year.[17]

More recent discussions of the beds, therefore, revolve around whether they were used just for sleeping, for giving birth, or, as one scholar has suggested, simply as a place to sit down and get one's feet off the animal droppings on the floor.[18] In fact, it is probable that the inhabitants used the structure for both sleeping and sitting, though one would guess only in cooler temperatures, since such a partially or almost fully enclosed structure would have been uncomfortable in warmer weather (when it was hot, the villagers probably slept and lounged on the roof, just as Egyptians do today). At the same time, however, the box bed very likely had associations with the procreative and child-related life of the woman, a key element in domestic life, which could be invoked as needed.

Convincing evidence marshaled by previous scholars makes a birth-related function seem, if only in part, unavoidable. The appearance of Bes immediately suggests a birthing theme, as witnessed, for example, in the Deir el Bahri scenes of Hatshepsut's birth.[19] Even more noteworthy evidence, giving prominence to Bes, is found in a variety of scenes on the Deir el Medina figured ostraca, most of which were found in the excavations of the village of the Nineteenth and Twentieth Dynasties. They depict mothers and what are probably meant to be infants (an otherwise uncommon theme in Egyptian art), though the babies are proportionately larger than actual newborns. These mothers and children, often shown on or beside beds with Bes-decorated legs, appear with reddish skin, the color traditionally used for men. The images, collected by J. Vandier d'Abbadie, are quite varied and do not seem to be stock scenes. A few examples include a mother attending to her child on a bed, with a servant nearby to help; a mother holding her baby on her lap; and a mother nursing her child while attendants extend offerings to her.[20] On one ostracon without Bes imagery, the new mother sits naked but for a large, fancy wig (typical in images of nursing mothers) and broad collar, and she nurses her child while a naked servant to her left offers a mirror and what is possibly a kohl container or menat necklace (a broad necklace with a counterpoise at back). Here the flesh of the figures is yellow, the normal coloring for women, and the figures appear to be situated within a columned bower hung with convolvulus leaves (fig. 5).[21]

These scenes of mothers and children and attendants recall subjects from Eighteenth Dynasty wall paintings found in the front rooms of two houses in the Amarna workmen's village, a site with numerous parallels to Deir el Medina.[22] The first painting depicts a scene with dancing figures of Bes before what appears, on reconstruction, to be Taweret the hippo goddess, who is also a protectress of pregnant women and appears frequently in scenes with Bes. The second scene reveals fragments of the lower portions of four women and two girls who appear to be dancing and possibly making music. Barry Kemp interprets this painting as a scene of joyful festivities in honor of childbirth. It extends around the interior corner of the first room of the house; in that corner and below the painting of dancing figures is what appears to have been a square bin, possibly meant as an offering table, with an original height of 0.75 meter—also the average height of the box beds at Deir el Medina.[23] Given the similarity of placement and height, might the Amarna bin and the Deir el Medina box bed have served similar or related functions, despite clear differences in surface structures, perhaps as altars? Kemp concludes that the paintings at both sites—in the front rooms of the Amarna workmen's village houses and in the first rooms of the Deir el Medina houses—point to the "celebration of childbirth."

The Deir el Medina ostraca and box bed paintings should be understood in conjunction with not only the Amarna paintings but also a body of works known as fertility figurines (not to be called concubines), which appear at several sites throughout the New Kingdom, beginning in the Eighteenth Dynasty. Geraldine Pinch discusses examples from both Amarna and Deir el Medina. In most, the figures are naked and attached to a bed or slab; some are accompanied by a figure of a child as well as toilet articles such as a mirror. Though Pinch found some of the figurines painted yellow ("sometimes with the pubic triangle outlined in black"), she and Bruyère observed that red was generally used for the skin, as it was for many of the painted figures on the ostraca. But unlike the ostraca, which depict beds with Bes-shaped legs, the fertility figurines generally present beds that Pinch describes as "much simpler, with plain legs, a high footboard and criss-cross patterns to indicate the string webbing."[24] The difference in the beds, however, may simply be a result of the different media and the modes of representation on two- and three-dimensional surfaces.

It seems evident that the figurines were meant largely for domestic use, since they were found predominantly in houses and sanctuaries, less often in tombs. Most probably these figurines were used for and by women and, at least in part, reflect the sort of domestic fertility cult that has been determined for comparable material from Medinet Habu.[25] Enough examples come from Hathor shrines, however, to indicate a connection with this goddess of sexuality and fertility. Gay Robins suggests the figurines may have been offerings to Hathor in hopes of bearing a child.[26] In keeping with the fertility theme, many of the modeled female figures wear the elaborate wigs that characterized the figures of nursing mothers on the ostraca. The wig, however, may have multiple connotations; as Philippe Derchain has noted, it could be an erotic symbol indicating the wearer's receptivity to sexual activity.[27] Such a signal, one must assume, would have been used only in a separate but obviously related sexual erotic context that might ultimately have resulted in the conception of the child who is so often shown nursing.

As Bes is found at Deir el Medina in bed paintings and on ostraca, he is associated with a portion of the fertility figurines as well.[28] He figures appropriately on such a range of items, not only because he is generally connected with female activities but because he is specifically "the protector of anything to do with the private life of a woman."[29] This could mean protecting not only mothers but also women in more erotically charged roles, such as musicians, acrobats, or prostitutes.[30] A sexual interpretation in its most comprehensive sense, encompassing the procreative and erotic, the maternal and nurturing sides of female life, seems to apply to the box bed paintings, the ostraca, and the fertility figurines. This interpretation is underlined by the appearance on all these objects of the convolvulus, whose leafy vine marks a specifically sexual or at least fertility-related context.[31]

Emma Brunner-Traut some years ago pointed to the images on Deir el Medina ostraca and painting fragments as illustrations of the critical events of childbirth, convalescence, and nursing, which she posited as having taken place in a temporary outdoor structure that she termed a *Wochenlaube* (birth arbor). She viewed the images as representations expressing or alluding to the birth arbor theme and probably repeating subjects that once decorated the interior walls of Deir el Medina houses. On the basis of ostraca bearing suckling and offering scenes, she convincingly reconstructed the fragmentary wall mural from a Deir el Medina house, noted earlier, showing the lower portion of a scene with the legs of a seated woman and three standing figures surrounded by convolvulus leaves. Her reconstruction of this mural (fig. 6), somewhat different from an earlier attempt by Bruyère, depicts a mother—naked except for a broad collar, anklets, and a fancy wig—seated and nursing her child, with the servant to her right offering a mirror and some other object.[32] Brunner-Traut's reconstruction, in conjunction with images from painted fragments on Deir el Medina bed structures and in the Amarna wall paintings, verifies that themes related to childbirth occur in both villages, settlements of possibly comparable status and purpose. The forms of mural decoration are "largely female-oriented," as Kemp notes, and reflect the "status accorded to this aspect of life by the community as a whole."[33] This emphasis on female life clearly involved not solely the birth of the child but also postdelivery activities concerned with nurturing the new member of the village community.

The birth and the subsequent care of the infant may have occurred in two different locations. We can assume that as elsewhere in Egypt, the event of birth was understood as rendering the woman unclean; if so, the child would likely have been delivered outside the house in a court or garden area or on the roof, where a temporary arbor could be constructed and hung with foliage such as the convolvulus vines that appear in the painting fragments and on the ostraca and fertility figurines.[34] In the arbor the mother-to-be might squat or kneel on bricks or stones during labor.[35] Then, as suggested on the ostraca, she would spend a period of seclusion from the rest of the family (fourteen days, if Papyrus Westcar can be relied on as evidence), which would constitute her time of purification following delivery.[36] Care of the infant, however, was an obviously ongoing process, and nursing the child may have continued for up to three years.[37]

Perhaps after the purification period in the outdoor birth arbor, the subsequent nursing and other mother-child bonding activities took place in one of the bedlike structures at Deir el Medina; this would have provided an intimate, secluded area for mother and child within the turmoil of the everyday occurrences in the home. Or, because the ideally separate outdoor arbor would not always have been possible, the indoor bed area could itself have served as the birth arbor: that is, the place where delivery of the newborn and the following period of purification could occur.[38] In keeping with these functions are the enclosed nature of the Deir el Medina structure, its size (which would more easily have accommodated a mother and child than a husband and wife), and the Bes and other female-related imagery sometimes used in its decoration.

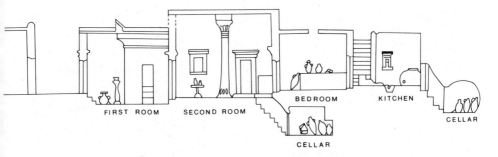

Figure 1. Plan of a typical Deir el Medina house. Drawn by Mary Winkes, after a drawing of Mrs. C. Barratt, in Morris Bierbrier, *The Tomb-builders of the Pharaohs* (London, 1982), p. 69.

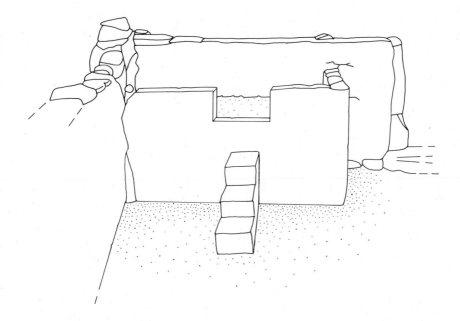

Figure 2. A so-called box bed. Drawn by Mary Winkes, after a photograph in R. E. Freed, *Ramesses the Great* (Memphis, 1987), p. 89.

Figure 3. A so-called box bed in situ from a Deir el Medina house. Photo by B. S. Lesko.

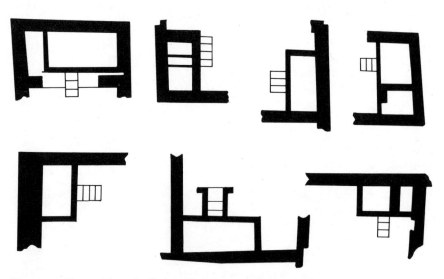

Figure 4. Plans of box beds found at Deir el Medina. Drawn by Mary Winkes, after an illustration in Bernard Bruyère, *Rapports sur les fouilles de Deir el Médinah*, FIFAO 16 (Cairo, 1934–35), p. 56.

Figure 5. Ostracon of mother and child. Drawn by Mary Winkes, after an illustration by Emma Brunner-Traut in *Mitteilungen des Instituts für Orientforschung* 3 (1955), p. 14, fig. 4.

Figure 6. Restored wall painting of a birth arbor. Drawn by Mary Winkes, after an illustration by Emma Brunner-Traut in *Mitteilungen des Instituts für Orientforschung* 3 (1955), p. 15, fig. 5.

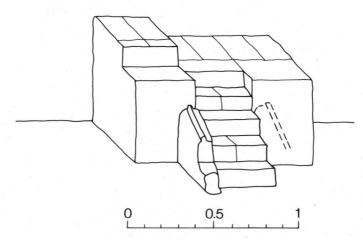

0   0.5   1

Figure 7. Indoor altar from Tell el Amarna. Drawn by Mary Winkes, after a drawing from Ludwig Borchardt and Herbert Ricke, *Die Wohnhäuser in Tell el-Amarna* (Berlin: Gebr. Mann Verlag, 1980), p. 255, fig. 38.

Figure 8. ꜣḫ iḳr n Rꜥ stela from Deir el Medina. Drawn by Mary Winkes, after a drawing from R. J. Demarée, *The* ꜣḫ iḳr n Rꜥ *Stelae* (Leiden, 1983), pl. VI, A17.

Figure 9. ꜣḫ iḳr n Rꜥ stela from Deir el Medina. Drawn by Mary Winkes, after a drawing from R. J. Demarée, *The* ꜣḫ iḳr n Rꜥ *Stelae* (Leiden, 1983), pl. XII, A49.

Figure 10. An ancestor bust from Deir el Medina. Courtesy of the Staatliche Museen zu Berlin—Preußischer Kulturbesitz Ägyptisches Museum und Papyrussammlung, no. 20914.

Figure 11. Stela of offering to an ancestor bust. Drawn by Mary Winkes, after an illustration from J. Vandier d'Abbadie, *Revue d'Egyptologie* 5 (1946): 135, fig. 1.

Given the motifs relating to female life in the bed paintings, ostraca, fertility figurines, and related Amarna wall paintings, it seems unlikely that the box beds in the front rooms of the house were solely sleeping quarters for the owner and his wife. Besides their general everyday reception and industrial purposes, these rooms appear to have been areas that focused broadly on female life in all its aspects, including the procreative, the maternal, and even the erotic. Because here Bes and other deities favored by women could be invoked, there remains the question of whether the bed enclosures were actual places of worship.[39] Bruyère suggested that they could have been used as altars, and, indeed, in Amarna there are Eighteenth Dynasty outdoor and indoor constructions of similar plan and shape which did serve as shrines. There the well-to-do homeowner might worship Akhenaton and Nefertiti, who would act as intermediaries between the worshiper and the Aton. The outdoor versions in Amarna are walled, with raised brick platforms approached by stairs; a brick or limestone altar is set within some, and the remains of columns and cornices suggest that most were partially or fully roofed. They vary in area from "tiny" to 25 meters square for simple shrines (the most common form), to 39 meters square for more complex, bipartite ones (the next largest category). In general, the dimensions of the outdoor shrines, studied by Salima Ikram, considerably surpass those of the box bed.[40] Stelae, fragments of statues, and other objects depicting the royal family have been found in many of the garden shrines, supporting the idea that they were places of worship.

The indoor house altar at Amarna is usually placed against a wall in the central room. On the platform of the altars is a space set aside for a stela or statue, undoubtedly dedicated to the royal couple.[41] The indoor Amarna altars, however, though consisting like the outdoor versions of walled brick platforms approached by steps, have just simple, low walls around their perimeters. Dimensions for one such altar are about 1 meter wide, 0.60 meter high and perhaps 0.50 meter deep (fig. 7), measurements much reduced from those of the usual garden shrine and also smaller than the standard dimensions of the Deir el Medina box beds but not much different from those of the Amarna bin altar noted above.[42] The form of these Amarna indoor altars, however, is similar to that of the Deir el Medina structures, though the latter had the higher walls and more enclosed design of the outdoor garden shrine type. Further, just as the small Amarna indoor altar was placed in the central room of the house, so the larger Deir el Medina structure was placed in the first room. Similarity of form and similarity in prominence of placement suggest the possibility of similarity in function, despite the fact that no birth or female-related imagery was found on the Amarna structures, and no space for a stela or statue for worship inside the Deir el Medina ones. It is possible that just as a wealthy Amarna householder prayed at such a household shrine to the Aton through Akhenaton and Nefertiti, so the Deir el Medina villager might have worshiped figures of deities or supplicated a recently deceased relative within the bed-altar.[43] If this was the case, then the enclosed beds may have served as house shrines in addition to their other functions. Surely using the same structure for multiple purposes in the limited space of the Deir el Medina house would have been practical and thus not unlikely.

Cultic Household Items

Just as concern for one's offspring is universal, so are individuals' expressions of need for help in daily living. Cultic items in the Deir el Medina household reveal that the villagers looked not only to standard deities of the royal and elite class—such as Hathor and Ptah—for succor but also to intermediaries in the form of divinized royal and private ancestors. Amenhotep I and his mother, Queen Ahmose Nefertari, of the early Eighteenth Dynasty were understood as divinized patrons of the village. The villagers' close relationship to and dependency on this pair is illustrated, among other ways, by false-door dedications to them found in the second room of most houses.[44] These patron saints functioned as objects of devotion and supplication in the home and even served as funerary gods. As Černý has outlined, Amenhotep, for example, appears on funerary stelae, lintels, offering tables, and even some wall paintings. The numerous sanctuaries in the village and other votive chapels throughout the Theban area testify to his profound popularity, surpassing even that of the major Theban god Amon.[45]

The villagers also displayed their belief in a more personal cult through particular forms of stelae and ancestral busts, by means of which they hoped to invoke the aid of the recent dead. Indeed, the stelae and busts were objects for offerings and worship not only in the home but in many other village locations as well.

The stelae (fig. 8) that were used for this purpose—a purpose well documented by R. J. Demarée as part of a private ancestor cult—are rectangular limestone slabs, originally painted, with round or pointed tops; they range in size from larger examples of 50 by 40 centimeters to fragments of 7 by 9 centimeters. Men of the village appear to have been the primary dedicatees; only a small number of selae are dedicated to women.[46] The dedicators, though not always mentioned or represented, do sometimes include women. Typically, the stelae depict a seated man (sometimes there are two) holding a lotus in one hand, with the other outstretched to a table of offerings, or grasping a cloth or an ankh sign.[47] Usually, this person is identified as the *ꜣḫ iḳr n Rꜥ*, the term by which these stelae are known today, which can be translated as "the able *ꜣḫ* [spirit] of Reꜥ," or "a *ꜣḫ* (one) who is (continually) *iḳr* [effective] to/for/on behalf of Reꜥ," and represents the divinized private ancestor to whom petitions could be made by the living.[48]

The inscriptions are generally rather laconic: for example, "The Osiris, the *ꜣḫ iḳr n Rꜥ*, Pashedu, justified." Some, however, are more expansive. In one example a relative of the deceased is shown offering the *ꜣḫ iḳr n Rꜥ* a libation, while censing him with a brazier. Termed *sn*, "brother" or "cousin," this relative figure is said to be "making a boon which the king gives, pure, pure, for your *ka*, *ꜣḫ iḳr*, by his *sn* who make his name live." The text below identifies the dedicator as "the workman in the Place of Truth, Huy, son of Sebay [or Duay]"[49] (fig. 9). A stela such as this provided a place where a villager could bring offerings to a recently deceased relative whom she or he had known personally. Demarée's work suggests that the figures being worshiped, implored, or offered to were not remote ancestors but more likely those known and remembered by the living. In many of the verifiable cases the persons dedicated to are fathers, husbands, brothers, and sons of the villagers. Through the powerful afterlife nature of the *ꜣḫ iḳr* relative, the villager could gain intervention and aid in this life or the next.[50]

Fifty-five examples of these stelae, discussed in detail by Demarée, are known primarily from the Nineteenth Dynasty, though their dates extend from the late Eighteenth to the Twentieth, essentially the same period in which the household structures already discussed appear. Demarée first believed that forty-seven of these were from Deir el Medina but has since added another three examples. The *ꜣḫ iḳr n Rꜥ* stelae are, however, neither a phenomenon unique to Deir el Medina nor exclusively objects of the home. Besides those from the cemeteries and Osiris

Temple at Abydos (already known to Demarée), Alan Schulman offers
eight other excavated examples, none of which, to his knowledge, had a
household or even a private chapel origin. Two come from the palace of
Merneptah in Memphis; one is from the mortuary temple of Ramses III
at Medinet Habu; four from a Memphite excavation; and one from
Aniba in Nubia. Others come from "various West Bank Theban temples,
the Valley of the Tombs of the Kings and, in one case, possibly from the
area of Gurna in the Theban necropolis."[51]

Despite the range of discovery places, it seems clear that some stelae, at
least, were used in Deir el Medina homes, as suggested by two examples
found near shallow rectangular and arched wall niches (which occur in
the first and second rooms of several houses) as though having fallen
from the niches.[52] Finding limestone offering tables in the same vicinity,
also dedicated to the ^{3}h *iḳr n R^{c}*, seems to indicate that the stelae, the
tables, and other dedicatory items were used together in a domestic
cult.[53] Another ^{3}h *iḳr n R^{c}* stela, however, was found with other votive
stelae on a bench in a votive chapel and another in a Temple of Hathor.
What is noteworthy, therefore, is that the use of the ^{3}h *iḳr n R^{c}* stelae and
associated items in Deir el Medina was apparently not confined to the
houses and that given the geographical range of those found, their use
seems to have been widespread throughout Egypt.[54]

The images on these stelae, generally of the seated man, may well be
modified depictions of statues of the deceased to whom offerings were
made.[55] The tradition of feeding the ^{3}h by means of offerings given to his
or her k^{3} goes back to the Old Kingdom, when Egyptian texts of the
period make clear the need to appease and supplicate the dead, who
could make mischief from the grave. Letters to the dead dating from the
Old and Middle Kingdoms illustrate this tradition, and a letter from the
Nineteenth Dynasty addressed to one ^{3}h *iḳr* who is clearly wreaking
havoc in the writer's life reveals that the belief in the power of the dead to
meddle in earthly affairs was still fully operative in the thinking of ordinary people in Ramesside times.[56] A villager could therefore set up a
stela to his father, for example, in a wall niche in his house and, using
offering tables and libation basins also dedicated to the ^{3}h *iḳr n R^{c}*, make
offerings to him and ask him either to effect some action or possibly to
stop causing trouble.

In the Book of the Dead the ^{3}h *iḳr* tows the bark of the sun-god Re^{c},
sails at his rising, and is free from all wrongdoing. He is also one who

knows and becomes at one with Re‛ and Osiris, with the transforming element often being knowledge, as a passage from the Book of the Dead Papyrus of Iouiya indicates: "O Atum, I have entered as an ignorant one; I have come forth as an ᵌḫ iḳr. . . . I shall be seen in my human form forever."[57] The ᵌḫ iḳr is thus knowledgeable and equipped with human form, characteristics that accord with the practice of worshiping and supplicating the deceased as a human figure who is understood, in general, to be a wise entity.[58] Equipped with such elevated credentials and powers, one's dead forebear was consequently iḳr—effective (or able, worthy, perfect, excellent) to intercede on one's behalf in time of need. This wish for intercession is found worldwide and continues today.[59]

Because the range of discovery locations for the stelae indicate that their cult activity could be carried on in houses, temples, chapels, or tombs, it appears that the domestic, votive, and funerary functions of these objects flowed easily into one another in village life without sharp distinctions. The smaller stelae could easily have been carried from one location to another, so that those found in temples, chapels, or tombs might well have originated in houses and vice versa.[60] The same principle applies today, in fact, when a devotee transfers a statue of the Virgin Mary from his home to his garden, place of business, car, or votive chapel. Intercessory prayers were, and are, sought in multiple settings, each one being perceived as effective in and of itself. Just as a modern-day believer would probably not rename a sacred statue of Mary depending on its placement, so the ancient Egyptian did not, in general, distinguish a funerary from a votive stela and, in fact, appears to have called each by the same name (wḏ).[61]

Another body of material from the Eighteenth to Twentieth Dynasties, made up of what are known today as anthropoid or ancestral busts (fig. 10), is also associated with private ancestor worship. Seventy-five of some 150 known examples originate from Deir el Medina, with the remainder coming from fourteen other sites.[62] Typically small, averaging from 10 to 25 centimeters high, and made usually of limestone or sandstone, they are readily portable objects. Though we can assume that most were originally painted, only a few now retain paint traces in red, with a possible example showing evidence of yellow.[63] The gender of the busts, therefore, is open to question; though the predominance of red paint traces favors their being generally male, we have seen that red was sometimes used for female figures on the ostraca and fertility figurines.

Of the busts that have survived with the head intact, most show a tripartite wig and a painted lotus blossom that hangs from the neck, the latter two elements being common features of Deir el Medina examples, as is a painted *wsḫ* collar (a "broad collar," a form of necklace).[64] A few anthropoid busts display what appears to be a caplike or shaven head, though they are rare.[65]

The busts rarely bear an inscription—a lack that frustrates our efforts to understand them. That the workmen's families actually used the busts in their homes, however, is evident from the fact that five were found in houses at Deir el Medina, where a few may have fallen from wall niches in the first and second rooms.[66] Given their simplified shape and generally small size, their placement in wall niches of comparable size seems probable. In several cases the house busts apparently functioned in conjunction with the *ꜣḫ iḳr n Rꜥ* stelae and offering tables; hence, it seems likely that such a bust, at least in the domestic context, represented the deceased relative who was the object of the *ꜣḫ iḳr n Rꜥ* worship. It appears then that the dead relative in the village can be represented both by an uninscribed bust and by the depicted and identified person being worshiped on the stelae. Like the *ꜣḫ iḳr* depicted on the stelae, the house busts seem to represent the *ꜣḫ iḳr* deceased member of the family to whom petitions could be made.[67] In the domestic Deir el Medina context, then, the largely uninscribed busts may be understood as three-dimensional, abbreviated statue versions of the figures found in relief on the stelae.

Geographic distribution, as for the stelae, is varied; as Keith-Bennett has shown, the busts have been found at numerous sites from the central Delta to the Third Cataract, discovered "at least as frequently in or near tombs and temples as in houses."[68] Thus their place of use, like that of the stelae, included but was not limited to the home. Whether their meaning was perceived somewhat differently by the Egyptians depending on where they were used we cannot be sure. We can posit, however, that whatever the context, for the worshiper the busts conjured up memories of a deceased relative. Some of the amulet-sized examples[69] found at numerous sites may have been carried or hung about the neck like lucky charms bearing the powers and protection of a deceased loved one.

Still, though it seems likely that the busts from Deir el Medina are identifiable with the *ꜣḫ iḳr* deceased, other possibilities have been raised. B. V. Bothmer, for example, has suggested that the tripartite wig typical of these small sculptures in the round is specifically Hathoric, a deliberate reference to the goddess. The wig, he believes, would establish such a bust as representing the "mistress of the house" in identification with Hathor, who was the traditional protectress of the home. Bothmer takes one bust that has an inscription to Hathor as evidence that all busts with tripartite wigs are to be understood in this manner and thus concludes that "it is the female ancestor who was remembered in the house more than the male," an enticing suggestion considering the emphasis on female life in the village. As to busts identified as males, Bothmer singles out those with a shaven head or skull cap, which he associates with the traditional treatment of the head of the Memphite god Ptah, noting that both Hathor and Ptah had extensive cults at Deir el Medina and that numerous monuments to both have been found in the houses as well as in votive chapels at the site.[70]

Arguments against these suggestions include the fact that neither the wig nor the scant evidence of one Hathoric inscription can conclusively verify the sex of the busts. According to Keith-Bennett, who has examined virtually all the known examples in detail, the wig is by no means indicative of gender; the sex of the majority of busts, she feels, remains uncertain. Supporting her position, she cites the fact that the tripartite wig is found on both male and female deities since the Old Kingdom and on male and female mummy masks since the Middle Kingdom.[71] And the one Hathor inscription is most likely a later addition and thus an anomaly that cannot be used as a point of reference for determining either gender or divine association.[72] Moreover, according to both Werner Kaiser and Keith-Bennett, busts with the shaven head or skull cap rarely appear at Deir el Medina and thus may not be an appropriate model for distinguishing male busts at the site.[73] Whatever or whoever the busts represented, it seems clear that residents of Deir el Medina carried them about the village and set them up in a variety of places, including their homes, apparently without feeling the necessity of identifying the small-scale works by either name or sex.[74] Given the absence of inscriptions and general lack of portrait features, they may well have been reused, over time, for different though related purposes and in a variety of contexts.

That the villagers worshiped and made offerings to the busts—in the same manner as they worshiped and offered to the $^{3}ḫ$ ikr n R^{c} figures on the stelae—is suggested by images found on two New Kingdom works.

A (non–$^{3}\underline{h}$ *i$\underline{k}$r n R^{c}*) stela from Abydos depicts a worshiper offering incense and a libation to a bust sculpture(fig. 11); and a British Museum stela similarly depicts a worshiper, sketchily painted, offering to a large painted bust shown in profile, while two other busts are modeled in relief above.[75] Neither of these examples, however, indicates the location where the offerings were made. That the house was one such locale is clear in a line from Papyrus Sallier IV which enjoins one to make invocation (that is, funerary) offerings to the $^{3}\underline{h}w$ in the home.[76] Nevertheless, one can reasonably posit that just as a villager might worship Ptah either at home or in nearby votive chapels, he or she might similarly make an offering to a bust in any and all such locations. Whether praying to gods (Hathor or Ptah), kings (Amenhotep I), or personal ancestors who had become $^{3}\underline{h}w$ in the afterlife, the ordinary person wanted to connect with and gain the protection of those outside the bounds of ordinary moral existence. That connection, believed to be effected through offerings and supplications, could apparently be made equally effectively in multiple settings.

Summary

The box bed structures, the $^{3}\underline{h}$ *i$\underline{k}$r n R^{c}* stelae, and the anthropoid busts all reflect the villagers' desires to obtain personal protection and aid in areas ranging from mother and infant care to a myriad of other daily life concerns. The bed structure apparently alludes to the fertility of the family through its future offspring; the stelae and the busts, to the family's relations with and dependence on the recent dead, these objects thus illustrating, as others have noted, the settlers' desire to preserve ties among present, past, and future generations.[77] The bed area within the home could provide seclusion for a mother and babe under the protection of household deities and may also have been a place of worship, while cult objects in the home and elsewhere allowed one to appeal to recently deceased relatives. Both the stelae and busts appear to have been means by which the householders of Deir el Medina—and possibly of Egypt as a whole—hoped to attain some measure of security in an otherwise uncertain world.

FIVE

Magical Practices
among the Villagers

Joris F. Borghouts

It is a curious paradox that the New Kingdom village of Deir el Medina is the best-documented community in the whole history of Pharaonic Egypt and, at the same time, a most exceptional one. It was not an agricultural settlement, which could have had a natural growth, but an artificial one. Its inhabitants were stonemasons and painters and their families, people who probably had a higher degree of literacy than those elsewhere.[1] Also, as workers in the service of the state they were relatively well paid, and when their salaries, which they received in the form of rations, were in arrears, they could complain directly to such high officials as the vizier and, later, the high-priest of Amon in Karnak or even go on strike, as surviving administrative records show.[2] The workmen were well aware of their own importance, for theirs was the duty of building and decorating tombs for kings and nobles, and stoppage of the work would be a reason for concern in high places. They were privileged people, even though their employment was sometimes subject to the arbitrary decisions of the mighty pharaonic bureaucracy.[3] The village—its inhabitants never referred to it otherwise than as "pa demey" (*p³ dmi*), "the Village"—ended its existence in a disturbing way. When continual raiding by Bedouin from the neighboring Libyan deserts made it an insecure place to live, the community was moved in its entirety to the safe precincts of the funerary temple of a former king, Ramses III, at nearby Medinet Habu. Thereafter, its members' history is characterized by reports of many years of thieving in the tombs where their forefathers had been working.[4] It may have been that hard times so impoverished the villagers that they somehow had to make a living by pilfering objects from the burial equipment.[5]

In the four hundred years or so of its occupational existence, however, the Village developed certain religious customs of it own, such as the high esteem for their chief saint, the deified king Amenhotep I. So far, no overall study of the religious life of this community has been undertaken, although there are studies on festivals, individual gods, and some of the cultic aspects.[6] Yet we are still waiting for the integrated research that would be based on both archaeological and textual sources and would put all these things together in a coherent pattern. It would be a unique opportunity to study popular religion in its relationship to all kinds of aspects of the daily life.[7]

I will not attempt to do anything of the kind here. I will merely touch on certain aspects of magical practice, as far as reported by the written sources, and this magic is of the everyday type. Yet in what has so far been written on the religious life of this community of artisans, the subject of magic has been almost completely neglected. One reason for this disregard is perhaps that magical practice has mostly a private character, whereas present-day Egyptology focuses rather on the abundantly documented funerary and temple religion: that is, on official theology. Further, there is a tendency to dissociate what is generally regarded as religion from what is considered magic, although from the viewpoint of anthropology, separating the two often makes little sense.

Indeed, in ancient Egypt magic was firmly rooted in theology. According to a statement made some seven hundred years before this village began its history, in the famous "Teaching for King Merikareʿ" of the early Middle Kingdom (c. 2000 B.C.), magic was sent to mankind as a gift from the creator god himself and served "to ward off the stroke of an unexpected event."[8] A recent discovery has identified a part of this teaching among the many literary pieces coming from the remains of Deir el Medina, so some of the more enlightened inhabitants may have known this statement, too.[9] The term used in this source is "heka" (*ḥk3*), and though there are more terms (as we shall see), it is also the most frequent one in the documentation from the Village. In agreement with this ancient statement, everyday Egyptian magic normally served defensive purposes, setting itself modest aims. Magical texts from the Village, always easily recognized by their slightly overheated tone, have none of the theological depth and involvement of magical texts dealing with the netherworld, such as those in the Book of the Dead. On the other hand, if there is anything to mark magic off against, I would think of the cult, although sometimes here, too, magical ritual may be involved. For example, the most widespread and characteristic of all Pharaonic cults was, no doubt, that of the sun. There are many sun hymns, in tombs, on stelae and statues, and in papyri. A brief introduction to such a hymn appears on an ostracon from Deir el Medina: "An adoration of Re' when he sets in life, by the decorator Hori. Whereby he lets the Bark of Re' sail forth in peace, while the crew is in joy."[10] By reciting this hymn, the pious Hori helps the sun boat accomplish its daily course, which is not without danger, as mythical texts tell us. But in a magical spell the course of the sun boat may be mentioned in quite a different spirit. Here is a characteristic quotation from a charm against poison: "If the poison goes up on high, then the Bark of Re' will founder on that spine of Apap."[11] Apap (Apopis) is the monster of chaos that forms a daily threat to the sun god when he journeys to visit what he has created.[12] The difference in style is obvious. In both cases the words uttered by the speaker attempt to achieve something (respectively, safeguarding the sun bark and stopping the course of the poison in the body of a patient), so both texts are "performative," to borrow a term from fairly recent linguistics.[13] But the one takes a descriptive attitude in a (cultic) spirit of veneration;[14] the other has a manipulative (magical) intention.

Defensive magic is the sort best represented in the Deir el Medina texts. Defense against what? In order of frequency, dangerous animals, demons, and dead persons. The tendency to personify those ailments whose causes were difficult to identify (giving such an elusive ailment a name was the first effort to cope with it) led to their demonization. Spells against headaches, for example, developed a mythology of their own.

Dangerous animals are certainly a clearer objective, and references to snakes and scorpions are especially frequent. A bite or sting by one of these could be a legitimate reason for absence from the job, as a work journal on a large ostracon tells us several times.[15] Although such incidents could be quite nasty, however, the prominence of these particular spells was perhaps motivated also by religious considerations. In many texts the victims are the gods Horus and Re', and various allusions point to such sinister beings as Seth and Apopis as the real perpetrators of the attack. As a magical papyrus from Deir el Medina puts it quite blandly, a snake is "a sister of Apap."[16] On the symbolic level, then, being bitten by one of these animals also implies being temporarily delivered to the powers of chaos. From the New Kingdom on, one may find a parallel but positive view regarding those who drown in the Nile: they are thought to become "saints" by coming into immediate contact with the primeval waters (Nun), represented on the earth by the River Nile.[17]

What makes magical texts such fascinating material is more often the verbal element than the relatively simple ritual complement. The Egyptian search for a mythical antecedent that would connect the case at hand with the world of the gods was a search for divine salvation, and it gives us a unique insight into living and productive mythology, different from the more learned and principal temple mythology. The charter myths of a temple must include a number of cultic "facts," and because these have grown haphazardly in the course of the sacred history of the temple complex, such narratives often lead one into very thorny problems of reading and interpretation.[18] But scorpion- and snake-spell myths have a much more straightforward purpose—which does not mean that they lack sophistication—and in them, if anywhere, the plasticity of myth is most transparent.

One example is a well-known myth on a papyrus from Deir el Medina which is the core of a spell against snake poison. It is well known because the manuscript has for many years been in the Museo Egizio in Turin, and its facsimile was published in the second half of the last century. Moreover, there are several variants, down to the Late Period (until ca. 350 B.C.).[19] The myth tells how the goddess Isis, daughter of the sun god Reʿ (at that time an old man), went about securing the kingship of her father for her own son Horus. She fashioned a snake—the first snake that ever was—which bit the sun god when he walked over the earth. Unable to help himself, Reʿ turned to Isis for rescue. His daughter prepared to conjure the poison, but for a charm to be effective it is an absolute requirement that the victim's real name be known and worked into it. In this way Isis sought to obtain possession of Reʿ's most secret name—the name that probably subsumed the whole of the sun god's creative power and thus was the key not only to the divine kingship but to control of the world. The sun god cited a number of his majestic names—such as those one may find in hymns—but none of these appeared to satisfy Isis, and in the end Reʿ could stall no longer and had to give in. Thereupon, he was cured indeed, but this particular name (we are not told which one) passed on to Horus—so there was also a change of reign.

This has all the appearance of a trickster story. Another one, much less familiar, is in another part of the same magical handbook, now in Turin, and proceeds in much the same way. Its antagonists are the god Horus and a minor falcon god, Nemti.[20] The two find themselves in a boat, the golden boat of Horus, the text tells us. Nemti is bitten; the animal is not specified, but we may suppose that Horus had a hand in the incident. Nemti too must tell his most secret name if Horus is to heal him. Again, we hear many names, but the remarkable difference from the former story is that Nemti's litany of titles includes some that seem far above his station. He is known as a local god in, among others, the eighteenth Upper Egyptian nome,[21] and the names he attributes to himself sound either boastful or downright weird: "I am a Quiver, Full of Arrows; a Pot, Full of Unrest." Nemti was provoked by his companion to proceed in this way. The name that finally satisfies Horus is far from flattering; it is "Evil Day."

Several ostraca and papyri provide us with another five texts whose individual wording varies between these two myths.[22] The very variety in the way they exploit the theme is quite interesting. Though they all appear to be abbreviations of the Re῾ and Isis myth, several of the names mentioned by Re῾ are far from majestic. Rather, they are of a speculative nature, and some are the same as those in the Horus and Nemti version. We do not know who was responsible for the composition of these individual magical spells, but obviously popular imagination ran away with the original theme, and it seems to me that we have a satirical tendency here: if we compare the Horus and Nemti myth (where Horus is overdoing it a bit) to the Isis and Re῾ story, the minor variants make it obvious that the sun god is often the object of downright ridicule. In fact, the spirit of these minor myths is not much different from that of a literary composition—which comes from Deir el Medina in a single papyrus version—known as the Contendings of Horus and Seth.[23] In this story, in which the pantheon divides into two parties that take sides with the two antagonists, the community of the gods is represented as a group of quarrelsome dignitaries whose chief care is their personal prestige.

The ritual element that comes at the end of a magical spell is itself, surprisingly simple—sometimes even omitted altogether. The long Reʿ and Isis spell is to be recited over a drawing of its three main persons—Reʿ, Isis, and Horus[24]—which must be copied on the hand of the sufferer of a bite or sting and then licked off. In this way the magic efficacy of the three divinities, vested in the drawing, will enter the body and combat the poison. As a double precaution, the three figures should also be drawn on a piece of linen and hung about the victim's neck. And although they are not expressly prescribed here, we may be almost certain that knots were made in the linen, for on the symbolic level knots are blocking points; most ancient Egyptian spells specify seven. Finally, the spell prescribes the eating of a certain herb, to be ground and gulped down with beer or wine. All this has little meaning of its own and merely endorses the spell itself, which, the text concludes, is "a true killer of the poison, proven a million of times." If you know how a problem started, you are well on your way to solving it, by posing the problem in terms of myth, the magician finds his solution.[25]

A third class of beings was much feared: dead persons, who should have been in their graves but were often believed to be roaming about to plague the living.[26] For the people of Deir el Medina, the dead were always within sight. Not only did the workmen ply their trades in royal tombs, but their own tombs were built into the slopes on both sides of the village. Yet at all times there was an ambiguous attitude with regard to the dead ancestors. They were entitled to a cult, chiefly in the cult chambers of their tombs but also in the homes of their relatives, where they were present in small shrines or in portrait busts.[27] They were indicated by the word "akh" ($\jmath\underline{h}$) or spirit, mostly as "akh iqer" ($\jmath\underline{h}$ *i*$\underline{k}$*r*), honourable spirit.[28] But these spirits, ancestors or not and honorable or not, were at the same time first-rate troublemakers. A story preserved on potsherds from this village recounts the dealings of a high priest, Khon-suemhab, with the spirit of a former Theban citizen who had completely lost his bearings and, at the time of their meeting, was in miserable circumstances because his place of burial had been disturbed long before.[29] Apart from this ghost story, Deir el Medina also has its examples of the so-called Letters to the Dead, where hope and fear intermingle in what the living say to or expect from their dead relatives.[30]

What is probably the most revealing testimony on the attitude toward the dead comes from a famous instruction text, the Maxims of Ani. This scribe's work may have been well known to the educated villagers, for

Workmen in a religious procession, Tomb of Nakht-Amun, Sheikh Abd el Gurna, Nineteenth Dynasty. Photo by L. H. Lesko.

several copies of portions of it have survived on ostraca and even on a papyrus from the debris of Deir el Medina.[31] Such instructional texts are usually concerned with social behavior, norms, and the like, and not with weird subjects such as ghosts. However, a particular passage of this literary text blamed all misfortunes in everyday life on the dead: "Any loss is due to him: the game, seized in the field: it is he who does a thing like that. As for a loss on the threshing-floor: 'that is the spirit [akh]!' so says one likewise."[32] Similar accusations concerning the disturbance of nature have turned up in an as yet unedited magical text from Deir el Medina which addresses a malignant "akh" as follows: "You enter heaven and then you eat the stars that are in it. You sit down on the soil and then you dislodge the seed which people have sown in it. You stretch your hand toward the desert and you kill all the game that is in it. You are put on the border of the sea and you make all the fishes die that are in it."[33]

Another quite interesting piece in connection with the influence exercised by evil forces is a catalog of dangers that may lead to death, all caused by spirits of the dead. Since the spirits are under the orders of the god Osiris, king of the netherworld, the decree used to protect someone against these instigators of evil is issued by Osiris himself. The inventory includes such curious entries as "death of the eyes," "death of a bird's bone" (stuck in the throat, probably), "death of falling," and so on. There is even "death of a man who acts as a woman, and vice versa," which looks like a reference to homosexual behavior.[34] A few centuries later, many of the same incidents and accidents are mentioned in texts written on long, narrow strips of papyrus which were rolled up and worn as amulets. These are the so-called Oracular Amuletic Decrees of the Twenty-Second and Twenty-Third Dynasties in Thebes (about 800 B.C.), when the rulership over this region had officially been laid in the hands of the Theban gods—or, in more realistic terms, was largely exercised by high Theban priesthoods—and it is these gods who declare, as did the Osiris decree, that they shall protect the bearers of the amulets against an encyclopedia of everyday dangers.[35]

If so much could be attributed to the occult influence of the dead ones, it is surprising that so few instances have come down to us of magic exercised by the Deir el Medina inhabitants among themselves. There seem to have been other ways to deal with internal conflicts in this tightly packed village, where greed, enmity, quarrels, and the like are attested in a number of documents as normal aspects of daily events.[36] For example, the "qenbet" (literally, corner-group) was a kind of village council of elders where people could seek redress for injustice.[37] Or they could invoke the help of their patron, the deified Amenhotep I, when his image was carried around the village during a weekly procession. The judgments of these two authorities (in both cases, decisions made on the basis of what must have been popular consent)[38] are abundantly documented and throw much light on all kinds of conflicts. One well-known case of juridical investigation is the written indictment collected from many testimonies to the outrageous behavior of a chief workman, Paneb. This person had terrorized the village for some years and had "really been behaving like the *udjat*-eye!" as one indignant official concluded at the end of the document, which amounts to saying "who played Providence."[39] These accusations, which we have only in the form of a draft, must somehow have led to the demise of this notorious individual.

But although Deir el Medina need not have been a sorcery-ridden community, there are recorded cases of magic being turned to purposes other than self-defense. A love spell found on an ostracon—a very rare specimen—bearing the unmistakable tone of magic addresses the god in order to win the favor of a certain female: "Make so-and-so, born of so-and-so, run after me like a cow after grass, like a servant after her children, like a drover after his herd!"[40] We have to wait several centuries before this type of charm turns up with greater frequency, in demotic magical papyri. But there the wording appears to be almost the same, so that we may perhaps reconstruct a similar background and telescope it back in time from these fuller sources to the Ramesside period. The intention of the demotic charms is usually to break up an existing relationship or a marriage in favor of the user of the spell. Such spells, then, reflect a spirit of envy, and perhaps this Ramesside predecessor should also be seen in this light.

Another magical text, written by a scribe named Amenemhat, is a spell directed against someone he calls "the one hot of mouth" ("shemu-ra"). In other texts one may find a simpler term, "the hot one" ("pa shemu," p^3 *šmw*), probably referring to the same type of person. The "hot one" always appears as a contradictory figure, one who does not really fit the accepted standards of social behavior. Instruction texts, always eager to exploit the theme of such norms, contrast him with "the silent one" ("pa geru," p^3 *gr.w*), who is a polite and modest person with an exemplary way of bearing himself.[41] But our Amenemhat, though he has not given the name of his opponent, must have had a particular person in mind, whom he curses as follows: "Begone, be on your way to the East, you hot mouth! You will not be brought [back], you will be [exposed] to a cold shadow in wintertime, you will be [relegated] to a hot spot in summertime."[42]

In still another revealing document from Deir el Medina the "shemu" occurs as someone's antagonist. In the French Institute in Cairo there is a carefully reconstructed pot of which a number of pieces are, probably irretrievably, lost. This jar, whose ritual use (if any) is unknown, is inscribed with a partly preserved hieratic text giving a kind of preview of the future.[43] The title it bears is "seeing the good things in the months of the year," and for each month some happy event is predicted for the "I" of the text, who is also indicated by the name Nakhi. At the same time this brief ritual calendar foresees all kinds of mishaps for Nakhi's opponent, who is none other than the "shemu," also referred to here in a personal way as "your hot one."[44] For example, on New Year's day the whole community is chasing after the "hot one" with sticks, while Nakhi is sitting on the stairs of the local temple, quietly sipping his wine. Now this invites one to stretch the meaning of the "hot one" a bit further than the instruction texts allow us to do: it is perhaps not far-fetched to think of an Egyptian prototype of the village witch. We should not immediately compare him with the European witch, who was usually a woman acting in concert with the devil (as was believed of the Salem witches). Rather, what I have in mind is the witch as documented in many reports of African rural life.[45] Although there is great local variation, certain recurring characteristics are unconventional behavior and an asocial attitude that distinguish the typical witch from other members of the community. Also, many of these testimonies mention certain occult abilities as characteristic for the witch, and we may infer something of the kind from the final words of the fascinating document on this particular pot: "come now, throw the hot one out, and save Nakhi! Set him at his ease. The one who blinks with his eyes, he has fallen down!" This may be taken as a reference to the "shemu's" giving his fellows the evil eye.

One additional variety of Egyptian magic as it functioned in applied forms among the population of this small Ramesside settlement was that exercised by the gods against humans. People of the Village relate a number of instances of the appearance of a supernatural power, an event of which they say that "the 'bau' [$b^3.w$] of a god has taken place."[46] The word "bau" is a usual term for the "manifestation" of a god in all periods and places of ancient Egypt. The texts of Deir el Medina do not specify either its nature or the identity of the god or goddess who is behind it; hence, we can only guess what kind of incident would cause an individual to report such an appearance. Circumstantial evidence makes it likely that people who experienced it felt distressed by it. In fact, the "bau," another form of and term for "magic," was thought to appear as a vexation sent by the gods to ventilate their discontent over something.[47] What kind of discontent this was we learn only through backward analysis from statements about the reconciliation of some individual with one or more of the supernatural powers concerned. For instance, one man who had sworn a false oath to his wife reported the "manifestation [bau] of a god" and afterward pleaded with a number of gods to be forgiven.[48] Perhaps they had been mentioned by him in his oath and thus were implicated in the falsity of it—though we must keep in mind that we are reconstructing the course of events through the guilty conscience of the villager. Another individual, reported to have taken away an offering cake on the festival of the goddess Thoeris, made a similar confession.[49] We have also a brief ostracon letter from this village, asking urgently for a statue to be made of Thoeris; the writer's own, he says, had been stolen, and this prevented him from fulfilling his ritual duties toward the goddess. Perhaps he feared her scorn (she had a sanctuary nearby), for he added: "It may work a manifestation [bau] of Seth against me."[50] In other words, one god might act in league with another against a human being.

A "bau" was quite a serious disturbance; at least one text tells us that it amounted to a state of death.[51] The expression points to the individual's degree of uncertainty as to what was actually happening to her or him, giving rise to questions such as "Who is behind this?" and "What have I done?" For solving problems like these and tracing the origin of the vexation, people seem to have sought the advice of a woman expert who, according to the few texts that throw light on her activity, apparently acted as a kind of prophetess. Though so far attested with certainty only in this village, such a person may have been a common phenomenon elsewhere in ancient Egyptian society as well; similar intermediaries have been found in many other environments outside Egypt—in rural

Europe down to this century and in the Middle East up to the present day. The Egyptian documents describe the diviner's attempts to identify the origin of the "bau." Her response to consultation, brief enough to speak for itself and as enigmatic as all statements on this subject, appears in a fragmentary letter from a woman client: "She told me: 'the bau of Ptah is with you, because of the Light, on account of an oath by his wife. And the bau of Seth.'"[52] At that point—unfortunately, but not uncommonly—the text stops short. We do not know how the "wise woman" (as we may render the Egyptian term "ta rekhet") came by her insight. Perhaps it was less a matter of profound theological wisdom than of practical knowledge combined with current mythology and aided by a measure of inspiration.

Texts from the village of Deir el Medina offer a unique opportunity to study the practice of magic (*hekau*) in everyday life. Unexpected dangers like attacks by scorpions and snakes are documented in many spells. To counter ailments inflicted by such animals and demonic diseases the magician often set up a mythical narrative in which the origin of the illness is investigated with the sufferer finally emerging as the victor. Thus knowledge of the origin of snake poison, the theme of a long mythical spell with the gods Re' and Isis as the chief personages, averted the danger of dying of a bite or sting.

Roaming dead persons are another class of troublemakers; but surprisingly little testimony has come to light of villagers practicing magic against each other. Apparently for social conflicts the local oracle or the court of justice offered sufficient opportunity to straighten things out. On the other hand, spells and rituals make mention of a kind of stereotyped inimical person called "the hot one" (*shemu*), perhaps the equivalent of a village witch.

Magical influences caused by gods were another threat to be reckoned with. In order to restore peace between the victim and an offended god from whom these "appearances" (*bau*) were supposed to come, an expert had to be consulted, a woman; and such a female diviner reminds one much of similar customs in preindustrial Europe and the modern Middle East.

SIX

Literature, Literacy, and Literati

Leonard H. Lesko

"Do not turn your back on literary writings, or you shall be beaten thoroughly." Now we might prefer to translate *mdw-nṯr* in this student miscellany from the Deir el Medina papyri as "hieroglyphs" rather than as "literary writings" (as Alan Gardiner did).[1] But it probably would not have mattered very much to the ancients, considering what we know about their education. The many texts used in their scribal schools often served more than one purpose: that is, to teach writing as well as the subject of whatever was being copied. Of the papyri that Bruyère excavated at Deir el Medina the seventeen documents published by Jaroslav Černý and Georges Posener include a few literary but mainly nonliterary texts.[2] The former are useful for assessing both reading interests and pedagogy in the community (assuming that trade books and textbooks can generally be distinguished). The latter are important primarily because they furnish information about life in the community but also, from our present point of view, because they help tie together the considerably larger body of texts that came from this village. Many of the papyri acquired by the Egyptian Museum in Turin through Bernardino Drovetti's and Ernesto Schiaperelli's efforts obviously had come from Deir el Medina; a summary of parallels and direct links was provided by Alessandro Roccati in 1975.[3] Posener made the direct connection between the Deir el Medina papyri and the Chester Beatty papyri in 1978, and an exciting short article by P. W. Pestman in 1982 traced the history of a library of forty papyri through the generations for more than a hundred years.[4] The papyrus from which the line above is cited was part of this library collected by the scribe Ken-ḥer-khepshef, about whom I shall have more to say.

The tons of ostraca excavated from the great pit and picked up all around the village, the cemetery, the royal necropolis, and the nearby temples are mainly nonliterary, but a high proportion from Deir el Medina itself are literary, and over 1,500 pieces with literary excerpts are now known.[5] A huge piece such as the Ashmolean ostracon with the story of Sinuhe may contain essentially the complete text of a longish story, but most of these sherds have only excerpts, which are, however, generally easy enough to identify. Some, but far from a majority, may have been student copies, a few perhaps with teachers' corrections.[6] Some may have been practice pieces or even demonstrations of scribal skills; others may have been passages of special interest to the scribe, "file card notes" made while reading texts and copied for the writer's own use or enjoyment or for sharing with others. Some such ostraca were apparently placed carefully in tombs for further enjoyment in the afterlife.[7] What surprises is their quantity and the fact that certain texts are represented by more than three hundred examples.[8]

Among the literary works attested at Deir el Medina are the Instructions of Ptahhotep, Hardedef, Amenemhet I, Amen-nakhte, Ani, and Father to Son; the Satire on the Trades, the Book of Kemit, the Satirical Letter, and other wisdom, moral, and student texts; the Prophecy of Neferti, the Royal Panegyric, and the Ritual of Amenhotep I; the stories of Sinuhe, Khonsemheb, the Contendings of Horus and Seth, the Blinding of Truth by Falsehood; hymns to the Nile, the sun, Amon-Reʿ, and other gods, as well as monotheistic hymns; and love songs.[9] William K. Simpson has pointed out allusions to stories known as "The Shipwrecked Sailor" and "The Eloquent Peasant" in an ostracon at the Oriental Institute of the University of Chicago (originally from Deir el Medina) and noted that although the original vocabulary of the seven-hundred-year-old narratives had been retained, the grammatical forms had been changed from Middle Egyptian to Late Egyptian.[10] Clearly, many of the texts copied at Deir el Medina were hundreds of years old and written in a stage of Egyptian that can be labeled "synthetic" to distinguish it from the "analytic" (periphrastic) Late Egyptian used in the Ramesside period. The differences are roughly comparable to the differences between Latin and Italian, but at least some of our ancient scribes could either maintain the original language or translate the old texts to their colloquial when they wanted to do so. The Deir el Medina texts generally do not provide a great deal of help in editing the Middle Egyptian stores, but they are not nearly as bad as the attempts found at the nearby mortuary temple of Ramses III at Medinet Habu to write historical texts in the old classical language; there inconsistencies abound even in the same sentence.[11]

Clearly, the literary texts documented at Deir el Medina represent most of the literature surviving from ancient Egypt with the exception of a few texts still known from only a single copy. In addition, the archive includes a few historical works, a large number of medical and magical texts (spells against scorpions, fever, headaches), a book of dreams interpretion, a book of aphrodisiacs, and illustrated satyric and erotic pieces.[12]

As Deir el Medina was not a very large community, averaging perhaps few more than one hundred adult residents, there should have been no more than one or two official scribes at a time. Yet some texts point to as many as five or six in a very brief time span with the tenure of some clearly overlapping. Černý listed the data he collected on sixty-six names of men associated with the title "scribe of the tomb" (*sš n pꜣ ḥr*), trying to screen out claimants to the title who may really have been draftsmen (*sš ḳd*) or persons who were merely literate.[13] Some adjustment to his findings may be posited now, but through his work something of most of the ranking scribes at Deir el Medina during the Ramesside period is known, as well as something about individual draftsmen, workmen, and even a carpenter who could evidently read and write. We cannot say that any of the most famous or best texts were composed by Deir el Medina scribes, but we do have semiliterary texts, literary allusions on ostraca, and an elaborate hymn that may have originated at the village, though these were not always the work of the chief scribes.

The two versions of the Battle of Kadesh copied by the scribe Ken-her-khepshef have phrases now lost in lacunae on the monumental versions; it remains to be determined whether he took his versions from the temple walls themselves or from a draftsman's copy or from a circulating book roll.[14] Since he and at least one other scribe entered the community from the outside world (rather than inheriting their positions), and since at least one of the books in his collection had been copied by a Theban scribe and the names of other nonlocal scribes are also represented in the archive, there was clearly potential for interaction between the village and the intellectual center of the big city across the river, and from the evidence at hand it seems highly likely that such existed.[15] One text that was copied and possibly authored by a Deir el Medina draftsman named Merysekhmet (1) is a long reverential hymn to Amon-Reʿ-Atum-Harakhte in Papyrus Chester Beatty IV. A later Merysekhmet (3), well documented as being from Deir el Medina and considered by Jac. J. Janssen to have been a nasty fellow, appears in a text describing his wanderings and calling him a "wild one" (nb^3-hr); this is the same Oriental Institute ostracon with literary allusions referred to above.[16] This particular text appears to be a semiliterary composition (even verse points are provided) though purporting to be a letter from his father, Menna, who was a draftsman in the village. If he actually wrote this, Menna was clearly capable of some creative writing. Of course, this suggestion opens the door to consideration of the indictment against Paneb as literature;[17] we must draw the line somewhere. Perhaps the ancient Egyptians too enjoyed their soap operas.

Recently, several scholars have argued that perhaps four-tenths of 1 percent of the ancient Egyptian population was literate. They based this estimate largely on the number of tombs of bureaucrats in one Old Kingdom cemetery and went on to suggest that the rate of literacy might actually have declined in the later periods. Because the evidence from Deir el Medina seems so counter to such an argument, they deemed the village exceptional and therefore excluded it from consideration.[18] As I see it, these scholars should not have so quickly dismissed the evidence from this village, since it is perhaps the only site in Egypt with adequate data upon which to make any assessment of literacy—especially for the New Kingdom.

We are indeed fortunate to have so many papyri, ostraca, and graffiti that can be associated with individual owners of stelae and tombs found at Deir el Medina, but surely, finds from other sites—the Kahun and Abu Sir papyri; the Sinai, Hatnub, Wadi Hammamat, and Deir el Bahri graffiti; and the Tell el Amarna letters—are all exceptional and remarkable. What is missing is 99 percent of the documentation from the most important of Egypt's cities, towns, temples, and other worksites—yet the fact that little more than jar labels survives from vast excavated palace sites indicates not that no libraries or archives ever existed there but rather that literacy extended at least to the household servants who had to fetch the required provisions in sealed but labeled containers. The workmen who labeled the jars knew what information to include and also knew enough to erase old labels when jars were reused.[19] Egypt could hardly be considered a preliterate or nonliterate society, unless, of course, we use very different definitions of literacy. If at Deir el Medina foremen, scribes, draftsmen, some common workers, and some wives could read and write, as we know to be the case, this indicates a much higher percentage of literacy than John Baines and others are prepared to accept.[20] Numerous scribal titles and actual or even representational scribal equipment can be taken as good indications of literacy.

This is not to say that all the people who have been identified at Deir el Medina could read and write; professional scribes may have handled some of the correspondence between individuals and the preparation of religious guidebooks, execration texts, and even some so-called autobiographical texts. But such scribes could not have written all the known correspondence—including letters to the dead—and the notes on thousands of ostraca and graffiti found in so many out-of-the-way places.[21] Surely, many members of the Deir el Medina community would have recognized the scribe Ramose's graffiti and stelae, which were written to record the date of his arrival and were illustrated to show his piety as well; and Ken-her-khepshef's name on his seat at the settlement in the mountain pass and at his work station in the shade beside Merneptah's tomb would certainly not have been intended for his own use in identifying these places; rather, they would keep others *who could read* from using his reserved seats.[22] The scribes' notes sent from the settlement above Deir el Bahri to their womenfolk in the village below would have gone unanswered when the scribes were all at work unless some of these women too could read.[23] Many of the workmen at Deir el Medina could write their names at least, and as it is easier to read than to write, a good number must have been able to read the messages that were being exchanged.[24] Would threats against trespassers, written on blocks and left at the entrances of tombs, have been thought effective if less than one in two hundred people could read them? What response could one have hoped for from a graffito asking passers-by to say "a thousand bread, beer, oxen, and fowl" if, of the few who would pass by, such a small percentage could read?[25] Obviously, there was a magical element in some of these writings, but surely not to the extent that the writers would have written their texts knowing that almost no one could read them.

Of course, none of this means that any great percentage of the ancient Egyptians were well read or even bothered to try to read most of the texts available to them on the outsides of buildings. Nor does it prove that the Egyptians generally were able to understand the subtleties of the propagandistic texts surrounding them. On the basis of the comparatively few literary texts that survive, it is probably impossible and unwise to estimate how many creative writers there were in ancient Egypt. Clearly, however, there were some to record the past and instruct for the future, and there were also storytellers, prophets, poets, philosophers, and theologians.

And even though no great author is known to have been from Deir el Medina, the village did have at least one important bibliophile, the man whom Pestman identified as Ken-her-khepshef, scribe of the tomb in the latter half of the Nineteenth Dynasty. The internal clues that link his collection of papyri and help us trace their history are adequate to make the case, but as is true of most old puzzles, there are still a few missing pieces. Linking Ken-her-khepshef to the library was easy, since at the end of an early Nineteenth Dynasty dream book he added copies of Ramses II's poem of victory in his own unmistakable hand, and also a copy of a letter that he had written to the vizier of Pharaoh Merneptah—about seventy years later than the original text on the papyrus. This scroll eventually came into the hands of a workman named Amen-Nakhte, who inserted a colophon in the middle of the dream book falsely claiming that he had written it (and incidentally providing information about the identities of his mother and his three brothers).[26]

This Amen-nakhte also added probably the finest roll of all to the collection: Papyrus Chester Beatty I, which contains a cycle of love songs and the mythological story of the Contendings of Horus and Seth. The text had originally been copied by a scribe from across the river in Thebes, who added his name in a colophon, but a friend of Amennakhte's from the village erased the original scribe's name and put his own name, Nakht-Sobek, in its place. Since the archive also contains letters from this Nakht-Sobek to Amen-nakhte, it is assumed that Amennakhte acquired the roll from him. It has long been known that some of the Chester Beatty papyri were deliberately mutilated in antiquity. Sheets were torn off and reused with or without erasure; some were used for notes and copies of letters sent by a workman named Maanakhtef, who happens to have been the brother of Amen-nakhte.[27]

The link between the scribe Ken-her-khepshef and the workman Amen-nakhte became evident in the will of Naunakhte, who was Ken-her-khepshef's wife and the mother of Amen-nakhte. These facts seem clear enough but do not make Amen-nakhte the son of Ken-her-khepshef. He was in his fifties when he married Naunakhte, a young girl of perhaps only twelve years. They lived together for thirty years or so but had no children. After he died, Naunakhte married again and had eight children, four of whom, because they did not treat her well, she disinherited. Gardiner commented years ago that the items she bequeathed to her other heirs were probably not as valuable as the papyrus on which her will was written. For example, her favorite son, named after her first husband, received just one bronze washing bowl more than the others. But since it is now known that Ken-her-khepshef's library passed through his widow to her son Amen-nakhte, and her will with it, Naunakhte seems to have maintained the library herself for twenty or thirty years and thus had an estate worth more than Gardiner estimated. One roll that had broken, perhaps from use (Papyrus Chester Beatty IX), had been carefully mended, but it is not known who made this repair.[28] The same roll, moreover, had been unrolled once when it was wet and in the process had picked up a considerable amount of dirt and sand. Interestingly, a letter survives referring to such an occurrence, written by the scribe of the tomb Thutmose at the very end of the Twentieth Dynasty (c. 1070 B.C.) about two hundred years after the beginnings of this whole collection. Thutmose said: "Now as for the documents on which the sky rained in the house of the scribe Horsheri (my grandfather), you brought them out, and we found that they had not become erased. I said to you: 'I will unbind them again.' You brought them down below, and we deposited them in the tomb of Amen-nakhte (my great-great grandfather)."[29]

Now the problem here is that there were two men named Amen-nakhte; though roughly contemporary, they are evidently not the same person.[30] The scribe of the great tomb who was a successor in that office to Ken-her-khepshef was the son of Ipuy—not the son of Kaiemnun, Naunakhte's second husband; the two also had different sons as successors. It would appear, then, that either Naunakhte, her son Amen-nakhte the common workman, or his brother Maanakhte the carpenter sold or traded some portion of this inheritance to Ken-ḥer-khepshef's successor, Amen-nakhte the scribe, whose own family treasured it for five more generations. Thus far, for the history of the archive, the scribe Ken-ḥer-khepshef must still be seen as the principal bibliophile, though several others helped preserve the collection and even added to it, and at least one heir, Maanakhtef, destroyed some—and who knows how many—of the books.

On the basis of the surviving records of the village, many nasty things can be said about Ken-ḥer-khepshef, and they have been.[31] He was not a very likable person. I only wish that even a part of the archive could be traced to the widely loved scribe of the tomb Ramose, Ken-ḥer-khepshef's adoptive father, so that we could point to *him* as the real bibliophile.

Among the texts in the Deir el Medina archive that were intended to keep students at their books is the famous passage from Papyrus Chester Beatty IV—one of the texts from Ken-ḥer-khepshef's library—which speaks of the learned scribes of the past who foretold the future and whose writings cause them to be remembered: "Is there any here like Hordedef? Is there another like Iyemhotep? There have been none among our kindred like Neferti and Khety, that foremost among them. I recall to you the names of Ptahemdjedhuty and Khakheperrê-soneb. Is there another like Ptahhotep or Kaires?"[32]

Since authorship was rarely attributed in preclassical antiquity, and abiding fame should be a hallmark of greatness, it is significant that a school text survived at Deir el Medina with a list of eight authors who were referred to as "great." Three of the four Old Kingdom sages (the first two and last two named in the passage) are well known from other sources. Ptahhotep was a Sixth Dynasty vizier and Hordedef a Fourth Dynasty prince; both were known as the authors of instructions, many of which would have been irrelevant to the sons to whom they were ostensibly addressed (some obviously were intended for children in different levels of society).[33] If not merely compendia of useful information that these "sages" compiled, their works may have been literary pieces attributed to famous men to give the instructions more authority. Imhotep was known as a sage, as well as the architect of the very first pyramid and the patron of medicine, identified later with the Greek god Asclepius. The fourth famous Old Kingdom scribe, Kaires, may have been author of the Instruction for Kagemni, only a small portion of which survives.[34]

Imhotep, Ptahhotep, and Kagemni each had an important tomb at Sak-kara, and Hordedef at Giza.

The few surviving literary texts from the Old Kingdom together with this list of famous authors seem to point toward a single genre of litera-ture for that period: that is, wisdom literature, specifically instructions. But is this all that existed or even the best that was written at that time? I think not, and I find the text's list of Middle Kingdom scribes much more revealing. These four sages, whose names are grouped between the two pairs of Old Kingdom scribes, were apparently not prominent men in the Egyptian bureaucracy, nor did they have famous tombs that were prac-tically pilgrimage sites. We know that their complaints, prophecies, and instructions (again, all in the genre conveniently labeled wisdom litera-ture) did not represent the totality of literary output for the period, and most would agree that the surviving works attributed to them, which are representative if not comprehensive, are not as good as some of the contemporaneous works of other, unnamed authors.[35] Since this is the case, what is the justification for the Chester Beatty IV list? Perhaps the explanation lies in some surviving works by and about the four.

The Heliopolitan priest and scribe Khakheperreʿ-seneb wrote a lamen-tation (part of which survives) in which he tried to unload all his misery and sought to formulate his complaints with "unknown words, unusual phrases in new speech which has not yet been used, free from repetition, not the phrases of familiar utterance which the ancestors spoke." This statement is significant because it indicates that much had already been written in this vein and also suggests that Khakheperreʿ-seneb may have been more interested in the form than the substance of his complaints. Khakheperreʿ-seneb wanted to avoid plagiarism in his own work; specifi-cally, he did not want to be accused of presenting "a tale of telling after the fact: they did it long ago. Nor a tale whose telling they anticipate. This is seeking misfortune. It is falsehood. There is no one who shall remember such a one's name to others."[36] In this passage Khakheperreʿ-seneb was here describing the major works of two of his predecessors of the Twelfth Dynasty. In spite of the fact that their tales were patently false, the names of Neferti and Khety were remembered by others for hundreds of years—partly because they were included in the list in P. Chester Beatty IV—and their fame and their works survive even to the present. Because Khakheperreʿ-seneb's name derived from the prenomen of Senusret II, he can safely be placed later in the dynasty than Senusret I's propagandists, and he may actually have been lamenting a contemporaneous turn of events rather than merely writing the formulaic type of text made popular by the disruptions of the First Intermediate Period. That event could indeed have been the suppression of the nomarchs' power by Senusret III.[37] The situation would have had more urgency then, and the complaint could also reflect some criticism of this royal move by someone outside the royal court: that is, a priest. Khakheperreʿ-seneb's criticism of the earlier court scribes Neferti and Khety could have had political as well as literary motives.

Neferti obviously had been used by either Amenemhet I or his son Senusret I to write a piece justifying the new Twelfth Dynasty.[38] Amenemhet appears in Neferti's work as Ameny, the savior from the south, but since Amenemhet's assassination was the spur to so many other propaganda pieces ordered by Senusret I, Neferti's prophecy could also have been forged as one more link in the chain of texts written to justify and glorify the usurpers. At any rate, the work is an ex post facto prophecy set in the Old Kingdom reign of Seneferu which purports to foretell the horrors of the First Intermediate Period and the coming of Ameny. It omits any mention of Mentuhotep II, who actually succeeded in reuniting the country and whom Amenemhet had served as vizier before he took the throne for himself. Clearly, Neferti's work was flawed by falsehood, and Khakheperreʿ-seneb was incensed by it. His anger could have been a priestly response to a political fiction, but he obviously thought that such fictions were serious, perhaps because he saw that they were believed. It is not the same as if he had criticized the author of the Shipwrecked Sailor for telling lies.[39] He saw the harm in misrepresenting history, and this in itself is a significant first, or at least the earliest documented case. It is unfortunate that he could not have expressed himself more clearly, but under the circumstances we are fortunate that he was able to write anything and that what he wrote has survived.

Papyrus Chester Beatty IV refers to Khety as the "foremost" of the writers listed and also mentions that he was the real author of the Instruction of Amenemhet I.[40] Since that text clearly alludes to the assassination of that king, it is another misrepresention on several counts and was recognized as such in antiquity. Senusret I, who promoted the ghost-written work, was the beneficiary of the text as well as the beneficiary of the death of his father. The piece alleges (as does the separate but contemporaneous story of Sinuhe) that he was far away at the time of the assassination, asserts that he was to have had the throne "handed over" to him anyway, and prophesies for him a very successful reign.

Assuming that this "famous" Khety is the same scribe Dua-Khety who wrote the Satire on the Trades, we have a second work of a very different kind that can be used in assessing his merit.[41] The satire—apparently the most popular work at Deir el Medina[42]—is not very subtle but does show a teacher's concern for his students and the entertaining tricks he would use to keep them at their studies. The scribe's lot is depicted as far better than that of persons in any other occupation that Khety considers, and he wants his students to emulate him. The idea is quite clever, so if he had invented it or even perfected it, he would deserve credit. But the work itself refers to the Book of Kemit, which probably did much the same kind of thing and was obviously an earlier work known to Khety.

Khety's Instruction of Amenemhet I also had a precursor with which he was probably familiar, the Instruction for King Merikare῾.[43] This posthumous work from the end of the Tenth Dynasty, if authentic, explains a negative turn of events in moral terms and is a very pietistic document. Khety wrote in much more practical terms and provided a variety of excuses for the king's assassination, none of which have anything to do with divine retribution. Even without this difference of attitude, Khety's king and the royal office come across as very weak and very human—not the picture his patron would ideally have wanted—so aside from the few pointed references employed for the exculpation of Senusret, this successor was not really well served by the work. The question still remains whether the texts that have survived are really Khety's best. Lacking any other evidence, it is impossible to say, but these two alone should hardly have merited him such high acclaim.

Hans Goedicke suggested that Khety could himself have written Merikare῾'s Instruction, and the scribe's name could indeed reflect a Heracleopolitan connection.[44] If he did write both instructions, we could readily accept his greatness, the more so since he would have succeeded in placing the Heracleopolitans in a better light than the Thebans he ostensibly continued to serve. Aside from the style, tone, and date arguments that I raised against Goedicke's suggestion earlier,[45] the Merikare῾ text could have been written well after the fact by a not unbiased historian, but I still find it hard to believe that the person who wrote it could also have produced, even for hire, such an inferior imitation. Interestingly, though, the Instruction of Amenemhet I was the second most popular literary work found among the ostraca at Deir el Medina, and there was also a copy in the papyrus archive of Ken-ḥer-khepshef.[46]

Finally, Ptahemdjedhuty, although his name is not directly connected with any known Middle Kingdom work, has been suggested as the likely author of the Loyalist Instruction known from a late Middle Kingdom stela and later copies, many from Deir el Medina.[47] This work is a hymn of praise for the king and an exhortation to share in the adoration of him which seems excessive on both counts: "Adore the King . . . in the innermost part of your bodies. Be friendly with His Majesty in your hearts. He is Perception, which is in hearts, and his eyes search out every body. He is Reᶜ (the sun god) by whose rays one sees; he is one who illumines the Two Lands more than the sun disk."[48]

Three of these four renowned Middle Kingdom authors, then, were apparently blatant propagandists for Twelfth Dynasty kings. They may have written other works, but the fact that these "books of instruction" survived in numerous copies at Deir el Medina, where the authors were also found listed on the Chester Beatty papyrus, would seem to demonstrate that these are the works for which they were remembered. All three may have been employed in the court schools, perhaps at different times during the Twelfth Dynasty—schools such as Dua-Khety described when he took his son "to the Residence to place him in the school of writings among the children of the magistrates, the most eminent men of the Residence."[49] The fourth author, Khakheperreᶜ-seneb, who condemned the lack of originality, the plagiarism, and the false prophecies the other three authors were guilty of, can at least be credited as one of the world's first literary critics. Since he has been identified as a priest, and his brief work does not show the same clear inclination to propagandize for the crown, he could have come from a different background, perhaps from a temple school. After saying how difficult it was to find anything new to say and pointing out what sorts of things were to be avoided, however, he unfortunately did not have very much of his own to offer.

Since all four of these scribes were textbook authors whose works were used in the scribal schools, their reputations would probably have been enhanced considerably by having their names sandwiched between those of four of the most famous writers of the Old Kingdom. I suggested earlier that this may have been done intentionally by a later teacher in the scribal school system.[50] It would certainly be interesting to know more about the scribe who authored the text on the verso of Papyrus Chester Beatty IV. He was obviously familiar with the works used in the schools. He also advocated writing above all else, sounding very much like a teacher himself. Gardiner said that he "was obviously a scribe of great experience," and Pestman has suggested that Amen-nakhte, the son of Naunakhte, may have been the scribe who wrote these exercises.[51] Whoever he was, he does not seem to display either a religious or political bias of his own, and he may not even have been aware of the flaws that we see in the works of his predecessors.

The four Middle Kingdom scribes who taught in the schools probably possessed no elaborately decorated tombs of their own at least none has survived. Their fame, however, did survive for hundreds of years—even among the Egyptians living in a comparatively new village such as Deir el Medina—most probably because their texts had been repeatedly copied by succeeding generations of teachers and students. Even though their original purposes might have been forgotten, the works magnified the fame of the Twelfth Dynasty kings to such an extent that the name Senusret (Sesostris) was ranked among the greatest pharaohs of Egypt even to the time of Herodotus and Diodorus Siculus.[52]

The list in Papyrus Chester Beatty IV obviously omits some good Middle Kingdom fiction writing and a few psychological and inspirational works that have also survived.[53] It makes no mention of any New Kingdom works written in Late Egyptian, passing over even the two exceptionally good instructions of Amenemopet and Ani.[54] Since the text with the list is itself essentially a Middle Egyptian piece with many Late Egyptian corruptions, it may have been an earlier composition badly preserved in the Ramesside copy.[55] The original could well have been closer in time to the Middle Kingdom authors mentioned; this would at least explain its omissions, its own flawed nature, and the exaggerated assessment of authors who clearly were not among the best of ancient Egypt. The much more sensitive Instruction (or Maxims) of Ani, found at Deir el Medina among the rolls that had belonged to Ken-her-khepshef's library, praises mothers, defends the independence of wives, extols the virtues of marital fidelity, advocates the planting of flower gardens, and recommends praying with loving heart in words that are hidden.

Perhaps the most distinguished and exciting texts of the Chester Beatty papyri are those in an anthology of romantic lyric poems which, together with poetic texts from elsewhere in Egypt, have been shown to possess many themes in common with the lyric poetry of later Mediterranean and Near Eastern cultures and include examples of courtly love poetry as well as the more down-to-earth songs of women.[56] Seventy percent of these songs are presented as coming from the mouths of women, but unfortunately, we have not yet identified any of the original authors.

As the copyist of Chester Beatty IV was probably himself a scribe, teacher, or advanced student, it is clear that though his colloquial language was Late Egyptian, he understood enough Middle Egyptian to make his substitutions, however careless, in the right places without being terribly bothered by them. Obviously, the schools were urging continued use of the classics written in the very different older language. Keeping Middle Egyptian alive would have been useful for anyone involved, as these workmen were, with copying monumental inscriptions and archaizing religious texts.[57] The old literary texts being copied for writing practice would logically have been used also to help scribes learn the old language in preparation for these practical tasks. But perhaps they were also kept alive for their own sake, as historical anachronisms, even if they were not as good as some of the then current literature.

Abbreviations

AEL	Miriam Lichtheim. *Ancient Egyptian Literature*. 3 vols. Berkeley, 1973–80.
AEMT	Joris F. Borghouts. *Ancient Egyptian Magical Texts*. Leiden, 1978.
AJA	*American Journal of Archaeology*.
Allam, *HOP*	S. Allam, *Hieratische Ostraka und Papyri aus der Ramessidenzeit*. Tübingen, 1972.
Anast. V	Papyrus Anastasi V.
ASAE	*Annales du Service des Antiquités de l'Egypte* (Cairo).
BAe	Bibliotheca Aegyptiaca, Brussels.
Bakir, *Slavery*	Abd el-Mohson Bakir. *Slavery in Pharaonic Egypt*. Cairo, 1952.
Bauer, *Ostkanaanaer*	Theo Bauer. *Die Ostkanaanaer*. Eine philologisch-historische Untersuchungen uber die Wanderschicht der sogenannten "Amoriter" in Babylonien. Leipzig, 1926.
BdE	Bibliothèque d'Etude, Institut Français d'Archéologie Orientale, Cairo.
BES	*Bulletin of the Egyptological Seminar* (New York).

Abbreviations

Bierbrier, *Tomb-builders*

Morris Bierbrier. *Tomb-builders of the Pharaohs*. London, 1982.

BIFAO

Bulletin d'Institut Français d'Archéologie Orientale (Cairo).

BiOr

Bibliotheca Orientalis (Leiden).

BM

British Museum.

Borghouts, Divine Intervention

Joris F. Borghouts. "Divine Intervention in Ancient Egypt and Its Manifestation." In *Gleanings from Deir el Medineh*, ed. R. J. Demarée and Jac. J. Janssen, pp. 1–70. Leiden, 1982.

Breasted, *Ancient Records*

James H. Breasted. *Ancient Records of Egypt*. Vol. 3. Rpt. New York, 1962.

Brunner-Traut, *Sketches*

Emma Brunner-Traut. *Egyptian Artists' Sketches: Figured Ostraka from the Gayer-Anderson Collection in the Fitzwilliam Museum*. Cambridge and Istanbul, 1979.

Bruyère, *Rapports*

Bernard Bruyère, *Rapports sur les fouilles de Deir el Médinah*, FIFAO 1–8, 10, 14–16, 20–21, 26. Cairo, 1924–1953.

Cat. Mus. Eg. Tor.

Catalogo del Museo Egizio di Torino.

CdE

Chronique d'Egypte (Brussels).

Černý, *LRL*

Jaroslav Černý. *Late Ramesside Letters*. BAe 9. Brussels, 1939.

Černý, Note . . . Family

Jaroslav Černý. "Note on the Ancient Egyptian Family." In *Studi in onore di A. Calderini e R. Paribeni*, 2:51–55. Milan, 1957.

Černý, *Valley of the Kings*

Jaroslav Černý, *The Valley of the Kings: Fragments d'un manuscrit inachevé*. BdE 61. Cairo, 1973.

Černý, *Workmen*

Jaroslav Černý. *A Community of Workmen at Thebes in the Ramesside Period*. BdE 50. Cairo, 1973.

Černý-Gardiner, *HO*

Jaroslav Černý and Alan H. Gardiner. *Hieratic Ostraca*. Oxford, 1957.

DeM

Deir el Medina.

DFIFAO

Documents de fouilles de l'Institut

	Français d'Archéologie Orientale du Caire.
DLE	*Dictionary of Late Egyptian.* 5 vols. ed. Leonard H. Lesko. Berkeley and Providence, 1982–90.
Essays . . . Kantor	*Essays in Ancient Civilization Presented to Helene J. Kantor.* SAOC 47. Chicago, 1989.
Eyre, Employment	Christopher J. Eyre. "Employment and Labor Relations in the Theban Necropolis in the Ramesside Period." Diss., Oxford, 1980.
FIFAO	Fouilles de l'Institut Français d'Archéologie Orientale du Caire.
Giornale	Giuseppe Botti and T. E. Peet. *Giornale della Necropoli di Tebe.* Turin, 1928.
GM	*Göttinger Miszellen* (Göttingen).
Gröndahl, *Personennamen*	F. Gröndahl. *Die Personennamen der Texte aus Ugarit.* Studia Pohl, vol. 1. Rome, 1967.
Gutgesell, *Datierung*	Manfred Gutgesell. *Die Datierung der Ostraka und Papyri aus Deir el-Medineh.* Hildesheim, 1983.
Helck, *Beziehungen*	Wolfgang Helck. *Die Beziehungen Aegypten zu Vorderasien in 3. & 2. Jahrtausund v. C.,* 2d ed. Wiesbaden, 1971.
HPBM	Hieratic Papyri in the British Museum.
HTBM	*The British Museum. Hieroglyphic Texts from Egyptian Stela, etc.* 10 vols. London, 1911–1982.
Huffmon, *APN*	H. B. Huffmon. *Amorite Personal Names in the Mari Texts: A Structural and Lexical Study.* Baltimore, 1965.
IFAO	Institut Français d'Archéologie Orientale du Caire.
JA	*Journal Asiatique* (Paris).
Janssen, Absence from Work	Jac. J. Janssen. "Absence from Work by the Necropolis Workmen of Thebes." *SAK* 8 (1980): 127–152.

Janssen, *Commodity Prices*	Jac. J. Janssen. *Commodity Prices from the Ramesside Period: An Economic Study of the Village of Necropolis Workmen at Thebes.* Leiden, 1975.
Janssen, Khaemtore	Jac. J. Janssen. "Khaemtore, a Well-to-Do Workman." OMRO 58 (1977): 221–232.
Janssen, Legal Proceedings	Jac. J. Janssen. "The Rules of Legal Proceedings in the Community of Workmen at Deir el-Medina." *BiOr* 31 (1975): 291–296.
Janssen, Two Personalities	Jac. J. Janssen, "Two Personalities." In *Gleanings from Deir el Medineh,* ed. R. J. Demarée and Jac. J. Janssen, pp. 109–131. Leiden, 1982.
JAOS	*Journal of the American Oriental Society* (New Haven).
JARCE	*Journal of the American Research Center in Egypt* (New York).
JCS	*Journal of Cuneiform Studies* (Philadelphia).
JEA	*Journal of Egyptian Archaeology* (London).
Jean, Noms	Charles F. Jean. "Les noms propres de personnes dans les lettres de Mari." In *Studia Mariana,* ed. A. Parrot et al., pp. 63–98. Leiden, 1950.
JESHO	*Journal of Economic and Social History of the Orient* (Leiden).
JNES	*Journal of Near Eastern Studies* (Chicago).
JSS	*Journal of Semitic Studies* (Manchester).
Kemp, *Anatomy*	Barry J. Kemp. *Ancient Egypt: Anatomy of a Civilization.* London, 1989.
Koenig, *Catalogue*	Yvan Koenig. *Catalogue des etiquettes de jarres hieratiques de Deir el-Medineh.* Cairo, 1979–80.
KRI	Kenneth A. Kitchen. *Ramesside Inscriptions, Historical and Biographical.* Vols. 1–7. Oxford, 1975–89.

Abbreviations

LA	*Lexikon der Aegyptologie* (Wiesbaden). Vols. 1–7, 1975–92.
LAE	William K. Simpson, ed. *The Literature of Ancient Egypt.* Rev. ed. New Haven, 1973.
Laroche, *Noms*	Emmanuel Laroche. *Les noms des hittites: Etudes linguistiques.* Vol. 4. Paris, 1966.
LD	Carl Richard Lepsius, *Denkmäler aus Ägypten und Äthiopien.* 18 vols. Berlin and Leipzig, 1849–1913.
Lefebvre, *Grandes prêtres*	Gustave Lefebvre. *Histoire des grands prêtres d'Amon de Karnak jusqu'à la XXe dynastie.* Paris, 1929.
LRL	Late Ramesside Letters. (*See also* Černý, *LRL;* Wente, *LRL.*)
McDowell, *Jurisdiction*	Andrea G. McDowell. *Jurisdiction in the Workmen's Community of Deir el-Medîneh.* Egyptologische Uitgaven 5. Leiden, 1990.
MÄS	Münchener Ägyptologische Studien.
MDAIK	*Mitteilungen des Deutschen Archaeologischen Institut, Abteilung Kairo* (Cairo).
Mélanges Maspero I	*Mélanges Maspero* I. Orient ancien. MIFAO 66. Cairo, 1934–1961.
MIFAO	Mémoires publiés par les membres de l'Institut Français d'Archéologie Orientale du Caire.
MIO	*Mitteilungen des Instituts für Orientforschung* (Berlin).
NPN	I. J. Gelb, P. M. Purvis, and A. A. MacRae. *Nuzi Personal Names.* OIP 57. Chicago, 1943.
O.	Ostracon (followed by present repository or ancient site).
OIP	Oriental Institute Publication, University of Chicago.
OMRO	Oudheidkundige Medelelingen Leyden Rijksmuseum van Oudheden, Leiden.

Abbreviations

OrSuec	*Orientalia Suecana* (Uppsala).
P.	Papyrus (followed by identifying name, repository, or site).
Peck, *Egyptian Drawings*	William H. Peck. *Egyptian Drawings.* New York, 1978.
Peet, *Tomb Robberies*	T. E. Peet. *Tomb Robberies of the Twentieth Egyptian Dynasty.* Oxford, 1930.
PM	Bertha Porter and Rosalind L. B. Moss. *Topographical Bibliography of Ancient Egyptian Hieroglyphic Texts, Reliefs, and Paintings.* 6 vols. Oxford, 1927 (2d ed. in progress).
RAD	Alan H. Gardiner. *Ramesside Administrative Documents.* London, 1948.
Ranke, *Personennamen*	Hermann Ranke. *Die Aegyptischen Personennamen.* 2 vols. Glückstadt, 1935.
RdE	*Revue d'Egyptologie* (Paris).
RecTrav	*Recueil de Travaux Relatifs à la Philologie et à l'Archéologie Egyptiennes et Assyriennes* (Paris).
Rep. Onomastique	Jaroslav Černý, Bernard Bruyère, and J. J. Clère. *Repertoire Onomastique del Deir el-Medineh.* DFIFAO 12. Cairo, 1949.
SAK	*Studien zur Altägyptischen Kultur* (Hamburg).
SAOC	Studies in Ancient Oriental Civilization, Chicago.
Schulman, *Military*	Alan R. Schulman. *Military Rank, Title, and Organization in the Egyptian New Kingdom.* MÄS. Berlin, 1964.
Spencer, *Death*	Jeffrey A. Spencer. *Death in Ancient Egypt.* New York, 1982.
Spiegelberg, *Graffiti*	Wilhelm Spiegelberg. *Aegyptische und andere Graffiti aus der thebanischen Nekropolis.* Heidelberg, 1921.
Stamm, *Beiträge*	J. J. Stamm. *Beiträge zur Hebraeische und altorientalischen Namenkunde.*

	Orbis Biblicus et Orientalis, vol. 30. Freiburg, 1980.
Stamm, *Namengebung*	J. J. Stamm. *Die Akkadische Namengebung.* Leipzig, 1939; rpt. Darmstadt, 1968.
Studies . . . Lichtheim	*Studies in Egyptology Presented to Miriam Lichtheim.* 2 vols. Ed. Sarah Israelit-Groll. Jerusalem, 1990.
Studies . . . Parker	*Egyptological Studies Presented to Richard A. Parker.* Ed. Leonard H. Lesko. Hanover, 1986.
Tallqvist, *APN*	K. L. Tallqvist. *Assyrian Personal Names.* Acta Societatis Scientarum Fennicae, vol. 48, no. 1.
TT	Theban Tomb (followed by identifying number)
Urk.	Urkunder des ägyptischen Altertums
VA	*Varia Aegyptiaca* (San Antonio).
Valbelle, *Ouvriers*	Dominique Valbelle. *Les ouvriers de la tombe: Deir el-Medineh à l'époque ramesside.* BdE 96. Cairo, 1985.
Ventura, *Living*	Raphael Ventura. *Living in a City of the Dead.* Freiburg, 1986.
Wb.	A. Erman and H. Grapow, *Wörterbuch der ägyptischen Sprache.* Leipzig, 1926–63.
Wente, *Letters*	Edward F. Wente. *Letters from Ancient Egypt.* Atlanta, 1990.
Wente, *LRL*	Edward F. Wente. *Late Ramesside Letters.* SAOC 33. Chicago, 1967.
WER	Barbara S. Lesko, ed. *Women's Earliest Records from Ancient Egypt and Western Asia.* Providence, 1989.
ZA	*Zeitschrift für Assyriologie* (Berlin and Leipzig).
ZÄS	*Zeitschrift für Ägyptische Sprache und Altertumskunde* (Leipzig and Berlin).

Notes

1. Rank, Roles, and Rights

1. Alan H. Gardiner, "Coronation of Haremhab," *JEA* 39 (1953): 13–31.
2. Ahmed Kadry, *Officers and Officials in the New Kingdom*, Studia Aegyptiaca 8 (Budapest, 1982), pp. 20–35, 213–217.
3. Breasted, *Ancient Records*, §§ 32A, 32B.
4. Peet, *Tomb Robberies*, pp. 92–98.
5. Lefebvre, *Grandes prêtres*, p. 245; and Kadry, *Officers*, p. 94.
6. Kadry, *Officers*, p. 23.
7. Schulman, *Military*, p. 15; Barbara S. Lesko, "True Art in Ancient Egypt," in *Studies . . . Parker*, pp. 95–96.
8. R. J. Williams, "Scribal Training in Ancient Egypt," *JAOS* 92 (1972):218; and P. Chester Beatty IV, v. 4/3–6.
9. Černý, *Workmen*, p. 131 (O. Berlin 12654, v. 6; cf. Allam, *HOP*).
10. Černý, *Workmen*, p. 132.
11. Ibid., pp. 191, 229.
12. Ibid., p. 227.
13. Kadry, *Officers*, pp. 148–149. The villagers supplemented their diet with meat by raising small animals such as pigs. See Janssen, *Commodity Prices*, pp. 177–178, 525; and R. L. Miller, "Hogs and Hygiene," *JEA* 76 (1990): 131–140.
14. Janssen, "Khaemtore," p. 226.
15. Janssen, *Commodity Prices*, pp. 460 ff.

16. Ibid., pp. 461, 534; Černý, *Workmen*, pp. 191, 229.

17. Janssen, "Khaemtore," p. 229.

18. Janssen, *Commodity Prices*, pp. 180–193.

19. Alan H. Gardiner, "A Lawsuit Arising from the Purchase of Two Slaves," *JEA* 21 (1935): 140; and Janssen, *Commodity Prices*, pp. 172–176.

20. William F. Edgerton, "the Government and the Governed in the Egyptian Empire," *JNES* 6 (1947): 159.

21. Janssen, "Khaemtore," pp. 231–232.

22. Janssen, *Commodity Prices*, p. 534; and "Khaemtore," p. 231.

23. Eyre, "Employment," p. 113 and n. 57.

24. Barry J. Kemp, "The Amarna Workman's Village in Retrospect," *JEA* 73 (1987): 46.

25. Janssen, "Absence from Work," pp. 139–140.

26. Janssen, "Legal Proceedings," p. 295.

27. Janssen, "Two Personalities," p. 120; and McDowell, *Jurisdiction*, pp. 271–277, 296.

28. Černý, *Workmen*, p. 330; and Janssen, *Commodity Prices*, p. 536.

29. Eyre, "Employment," p. 151 n. 99.

30. Bierbrier, *Tomb-builders*, p. 36; and Černý, *Workmen*, p. 354.

31. Janssen, "Two Personalities," pp. 119ff.

32. Černý, *Workmen*, pp. 370, 380.

33. J. Vandier d'Abbadie, *Catalogue des ostraca figurés de Deir el Medineh*, DFIFAO 2 (1937), pls 4–8, 9–12; Peck, *Egyptian Drawings*, p. 84, pl 9; Černý, *Workmen*, p. 352; Brunner-Traut, *Sketches*, p. 5.

34. Any, *AEL*, p. 136.

35. For instance, out of the eighteen tombs recorded in *Rep. Onomastique*, only seven (TT 2, 4, 6, 10, 211, 215, 216) contain feminine clerical titles, and of these all but one of the women are related to scribes, foremen, or draftsmen (i.e., literate men). Such titles are missing on the numerous Deir el Medina stelae published by Mario Tosi, so they were not general to all wives in the village.

36. That the scribes of the tomb habitually addressed their own wives by their religious titles surely suggests that these women were exceptionally prestigious by way of their place in a temple's hierarchy, and lends credence to the view that not all the wives by any means were so associated. The existence, noted in Valbelle, *Ouvrier*, p. 330, of a woman who was $ḥsy.t^{ʿ\tiny{3}}.t$ (chief singer) of Sobek in the village, where there was no shrine for that god, would also indicate connections with cult places outside the village, in greater Thebes. See LRL 9, 16, 17; and Černý, *Workmen*, p. 369.

37. The sculptor Ken, himself well documented and perhaps wealthier than most, was the only man of the crew among the tombs listed in *Rep. Onomostique* to have a wife who was $ḥsy.t$ (TT 4).

38. Borghouts, "Divine Intervention," pp. 34–35; cf. Wente, Letters, p. 141 (no. 184).

39. Černý, *Workmen*, pp. 177–179.

40. *WER*, pp. 117–121, 314–315.

41. Černý, *Workmen*, pp. 369–370; Wente, *Letters*, pp. 217–219 (no. 353).

42. Carol Meyers, *Discovering Eve: Ancient Israelite Women in Context* (New York, 1988), pp. 172–181.

43. Barry J. Kemp, "Wall Paintings from the Workmen's Village at El-Amarna," *JEA* 65 (1979): 52–53.

44. See Barbara S. Lesko, *The Remarkable Women of Ancient Egypt*, 2d ed. (Providence, 1987), p. 143.

45. Černý, *Workmen*, p. 199; Wente, *Letters*, pp. 162 (no. 255), 165 (no. 270), 156 (no. 230); Leonard H. Lesko in this volume.

46. LRL, 37; and Wente, *Letters*, p. 174 (no. 290).

47. P. Chester Beatty (Group A, 32C), *AEL*, p. 183.

48. William A. Ward, "Notes on Some Semitic Loan Words and Personal Names in Late Egyptian," *Orientalia* 32 (1963): 430–432; K. Baer, "Temporal *WNN* in Late Egyptian," *JEA* 51 (1965): 138, example c.; Janssen, "Khaemtore," p. 229.

49. Ventura, *Living*, pp. 105, 179.

50. Černý, "Note . . . Family," pp. 52–53.

51. Janssen, "Khaemtore," p. 230.

52. Janssen, "Two Personalities," pp. 119–120.

53. One marriage agreement from the Twentieth Dynasty has to do with the settlement of property on a new, second wife by a widower advanced in years. See Jaroslav Černý; T. E. Peet, "A Marriage Settlement of the Twentieth Dynasty," *JEA* 13 (1927): 30–39.

54. Jaroslav Černý, "The Will of Naunakhte and the Related Documents," *JEA* 31 (1945): 29–53.

55. Shafik Allam, "Some Remarks on the Trial of Mose," *JEA* 75 (1989): 104.

56. Dominique Valbelle, *Catalogue des poids à inscriptions hieratiques de Deir el-Médineh nos. 5001–5423* DFIFAO 16 (1977), p. 21; Černý, *Valley of the Kings*, p. 53.

57. Miller, "Hogs," 136–40; Janssen, *Commodity Prices*, p. 538.

58. Gardiner, *JEA* 21 (1935): 141 (P. Cairo 65739, r. 1).

59. Bierbrier, *Tomb-builders*, p. 71; Jaroslav Černý, *JEA* 15 (1929): 243–258 (P. Salt 124 r., pl. 44); Janssen, "Khaemtore," p. 230 (Černý-Gardiner, *HO* 56, 1); Gardiner, "Paprus Salt 124 British Museum 10055," *JEA* 21 (1935): 141 (P. Cairo 65739 r. 1).

60. Spencer, *Death*, p. 115.

61. S. Allam, "Women as Owners of Immovables," in *WER,* pp. 123–135.

62. William F. Edgerton, "The Strikes in Ramses III's Twenty-ninth Year," *JNES* 10 (1951): 137–140.

63. Černý, *Workmen,* p. 351; Černý, *JEA* 15 (1929): 243–258.

64. Edgerton,; also Jac. J. Janssen, "Background Information on the Strikes of Year 29 of Ramesses III," *Oriens Antiquus* 18 (1979): 301–308; and P. J. Frandsen, "Editing Reality: The Turin Strike Papyrus," in *Studies . . . Lichtheim,* pp. 173–192.

65. O. Berlin 12654, v.; Černý, *Workmen,* pp. 104–5, 185. A porter's low wage was but 1 *khar* of wheat and ¼ *khar* of barley per month, barely a subsistence wage. R. L. Miller, "Counting Calories in Egyptian Ration Texts," *JESHO* 34 (1991): 262, 269, errs when he bases upon a family of four his calculation of the individual caloric intake possible from such a wage; larger families were the norm.

2. *Contact with the Outside World*

I am grateful to Rob Demarée and Richard Parkinson for reading drafts of this paper and making helpful suggestions; and I would like to thank Jaromir Malek and the staff of the Griffith Institute in Oxford for allowing me to consult Jaroslav Černý's unpublished manuscripts.

1. See esp. Valbelle, *Ouvriers,* p. 116.

2. Ventura, *Living,* pp. 54, 175–79.

3. See, however, brief discussions of the problem by Christopher J. Eyre in "Work and the Organisation of Work in the New Kingdom," in M. A. Powell, ed., *Labor in the Ancient Near East,* American Oriental Series, vol. 68 (New Haven, 1987), pp. 170–171; Valbelle, *Ouvriers,* p. 116; P. J. Frandsen, *JEA* 75 (1989): 116.

4. Some of the examples I cite are also discussed by Ventura, who interprets them differently. It is my contention that when the material is viewed as a whole, the assumptions of Černý and the others are more coherent and plausible than Ventura's alternative.

5. Valbelle, *Ouvriers,* pp. 111–113.

6. *Rep. Onomastique,* pp. 38, 41, 43; Alain-Pierre Zivie, *La tombe de Pached à Deir el-Médineh [No. 3],* MIFAO 99 (Cairo, 1979), pp. 126–130 and pl. 29 (Zivie's reconstruction of Pashed's career seems to me rather speculative). Pashed's title *bʾk n šnꜤ n Imn in niwt rsit,* "servant of the *šnꜤ* of Amun in the Southern City," is discussed at length by E. C. Bogoslovsky in *CdE* 57 (1982): 275–276, who suggests that "in the early period of the XIXth dynasty quite a number of workers retained their relation to the economy of the temple of Amun

from which they were transferred after the reorganisation of the necropolis on the 7th year of the reign of Haremhab."

7. $\underline{T}^{\gamma}y$-$M\underline{d}^{\gamma}t$ n Imn m hnw, $\underline{T}^{\gamma}y$-nfr; see *Rep. Onomastique*, p. 45.

8. O. Cairo 25671; Černý, *Workmen*, pp. 317–318; Valbelle, *Ouvriers*, p. 168; Bruyère, *Rapport (1935–1940)*, FIFAO 20, fasc. 3, p. 19; KRI 3:630, 10 and 631, 5.

9. Berlin statue group 6910, published in Gunther Roeder, *Aegyptische Inschriften aus den Staatlichen Museen zu Berlin*, vol. 2 (Leipzig, 1924), pp. 63–71, esp. 66–67.

10. On Amen-em-opet, see Černý, *Workmen*, pp. 194–195; on Pashed, see Zivie, *Tombe de Pached*, p. 132; on Ken, see PM 1:1², p. 11 (Ramses II features in his tomb). Ken-her-khepshef was recruited to the gang at approximately the same time, but we do not know from where (Černý, *Workmen*, p. 329).

11. We know of many workmen whose fathers had served in the same capacity, and several texts record the appointment of younger members of the community to the gang (Černý, *Workmen*, pp. 114–116).

12. O. Berlin 12654 (Allam, *HOP*, pls. 12–15); on the date, see Janssen, "The Mission of the Scribe Pesiur," in *Gleanings from Deir el-Medîna*, ed. R. J. Demarée and Jac. J. Janssen (Leiden, 1982), p. 140.

13. Černý, *Workmen*, pp. 116–117; *Rep. Onomastique*, pp. 61, 63.

14. Raphael Ventura also notes that the workmen were employed on other projects and at other sites when there was no work for them in the Valley of the Kings (in Sarah Israelit-Groll, ed., *Pharaonic Egypt* [Jerusalem, 1985], pp. 373–374, discussion of a conference paper).

15. P. Turin 2044 (KRI 6:340–343), dated to a year 1 (Valbelle, *Ouvriers*, p. 36 n. 1, dates this papyrus to the reign of Ramses V).

16. R. J. Demarée, personal communication, based on unpublished fragments of P. Turin 2044.

17. Černý-Gardiner, *HO* 47, 2. Hormose says, "When I was working in the granary of the Temple of Maat, I happened to be lying ill, and the *ms-ḥr* Riaʿ who was a servant of the court took a *ḥnk*-cloth of 6 cubits." The fact that Hormose appears to have been under the authority of the village court suggests that he was an employee of the royal necropolis even at the time he was working in the temple. See also Valbelle, *Ouvriers*, p. 92.

18. RAD 66, 9–11. Cf. Černý, *Workmen*, p. 190. By this date (the reign of Ramses XI), however, the community had already moved to Medinet Habu. For *Pr-Ḥwt-Ḥr* see Eberhard Otto, *Topographie des thebanischen Gaues* (Berlin, 1952), p. 93.

19. Černý, *Workmen*, p. 94; Ventura, *Living*, p. 21 (it is not clear why Ventura speaks of one path to Deir el Medina, or why he feels this was rarely used). References to going to *Ḏsrt*: O. Cairo 25291 (KRI 6:143), the guardian Hay; O.

Cairo 25309 (KRI 6:148), the scribe Amen-nakhte and others; O. Cairo 25746, seven individuals. Coming from there: O. Turin 57006 r. 2.

20. O. Cairo 25518.

21. E.g., on an ostracon from the temple of Amenhotep, son of Hapu (O. Gard 130 plus frag. Černý, MS. 17, Notebook 45, 30 (unpublished manuscript in the Griffith Institute, Oxford); KRI 7:304 (recto only). The recto lists the two captains of the gang of the necropolis and perhaps several workmen in a list of officials and their subordinates from various institutions. The verso bears a letter from the vizier, in which he tells the *rwdw* (administrators) to be diligent in the work he has just launched for them, suggesting that the men named on the recto are involved in a building project.

22. O. Cairo 25295.

23. Černý, *Workmen*, pp. 253–255. Pashed calls himself "quarryman of Amun in *Ipt-Swt* (Karnak)" (Zivie, *Tombe de Pached*, pp. 129–130). Djehuty-her-maktef was a "quarryman of Thoth" (*Hieroglyphic Texts in the British Museum*, vol. 7 [London, 1925], p. 12 and pl. 37; Guillemette Andreu, "La tombe de Thothermaktouf à Deir el Medina (TT 357)," *BIFAO* 85 [1985]: 14). Mes was a "quarryman of Amon in the work of the southern Ipt (Luxor)" (wooden door, Moscow State Pushkin Mus. I. 1.a.4867: see PM 1:2² 745; cf. Bruyère, *Rapport [1929]*, FIFAO 7, pt. 2, 22).

24. Djehuty-her-maketef dates to early Ramses II (Andreu, *BIFAO* 85 [1985]: 14).

25. Černý, *Workmen*, pp. 65–67.

26. Černý, *Workmen*, p. 65.

27. Goyon, *Nouvelles inscriptions rupestres du Wadi Hammamat* (Paris, 1957), p. 122, no. 100; Černý, *Workmen*, pp. 211–212; McDowell, *Jurisdiction*, pp. 79–80.

28. P. Turin 1879 + 1899 + 1969. See Černý, *Workmen*, p. 66; Valbelle, *Ouvriers*, pp. 197–198 (verso texts published in KRI 6:335–339, 377). For quarrying activity under Ramses IV at the Wadi Hammamat, see Jaroslav Černý in *Cambridge Ancient History*, 3d ed., vol. 2, pt. 2, *History of the Middle East and the Aegean Region c. 1380–1000 B.C.*, ed. I. E. S. Edwards, C. J. Gadd, N. G. L. Hammond, E. Sollberger (Cambridge, 1975), pp. 608–609.

29. KRI 4:73–74. See Černý, *Workmen*, p. 21; Valbelle, *Ouvriers*, p. 176.

30. Wadi Hammamat: Jules Couyat and Pierre Montet, *Les inscriptions hiéroglyphiques et hiératiques du Ouâdi Hammâmât*, MIFAO 34 (Cairo, 1912); Goyons, *Nouvelles inscriptions*. Gebel el Silsila: PM, 5:208–221; Friedrich Preisigke and Wilhelm Spiegelberg, *Ägyptische und Griechische Inschriften und Graffiti aus den Steinbrüchen des Gebel Silsile (Oberägypten)* (Strassbourg, 1915).

31. P. Turin 2002 r.; Jaroslav Černý, MS. 3, 571, 723–731 (unpublished

manuscripts in the Griffith Institute, Oxford; the section discussed here is cols. 3, 10 to 4, 21, part of which occurs in KRI 6:244–245). See further references in Valbelle, *Ouvriers*, p. 36 n. 2.

32. Černý, *Workmen*, p. 173; O. Berlin 12654 v. 8 (Allam, *HOP*, pls. 12–15).

33. O. DeM 440.

34. E.g., P. Turin 1879 (cont. of Pleyte-Rossi, 33, 7ff.; KRI 6:338–339) v. 2, 7–22; P. Turin 1884 and frags. (KRI 6:644–650) r. 1, 17 (the whole gang is said to be in *niwt*, Thebes, in r. 2, 7 to 2, 9); *Giornale*, pl. 5, line 11.

35. See Jac. J. Janssen, *De markt op de oever* (Leiden, 1980). See also Černý, *Workmen*, pp. 94–97.

36. N. de G. Davies, *Two Ramesside Tombs at Thebes* (New York, 1927), pl. 30.

37. Ventura, *Living*, pp. 79–82, argues that *mryt* refers to the cultivated area in general rather than specifically the riverbank. I do not feel that he has proved his case, but either way, activity at the *mryt* would represent contact with the outside.

38. O. University College London 19614 (see Allam, *HOP*, pp. 253–254, pls. 74–75); see also, e.g., O. Brookyn, acc. no. 37.1880E, v. 4–6 (KRI 7:310–311); O. Gard 200 r. 4 (KRI 7:175); O. DeM 569, 1; Černý-Gardiner, *HO* 53, 2 v. 7.

39. Janssen, *De markt*, pp. 13–14; Černý, *Workmen*, p. 95; Valbelle, *Ouvriers*, p. 116.

40. O. BM 5637 (*JEA* 12 [1926]: pls. 37, 42). The administration of the tomb also had a storage facility at the riverbank for tools and supplies, the *ḫtm n mryt* (McDowell, *Jurisdiction*, pp. 104–105); it was presumably more secure.

41. E.g., O. DeM 112 r. 4, *ḫb mryt;* v. 9, *tꜣ ḫb n mryt.*

42. E. C. Bogoslovsky, *Vestnik Drevnej Istorii* 1, no. 147 (1979): 7.

43. McDowell, *Jurisdiction*, pp. 219–222; O. DeM 103 (doorkeepers at *mryt*); O. DeM 550, r. 3–4; O. Mich 13, r. 3–4 (Hans Goedicke and Edward F. Wente, *Ostraka Michaelides* [Wiesbaden, 1962], pls. 46–47); O. DeM 324, etc. (various activities).

44. Valbelle, *Ouvriers*, p. 255. I discuss this possibility in detail in *JEA* 78 (1992): 195–206.

45. See, e.g., LRL 5, 15 to 6, 1; 11, 1–5; 11, 11–12; Černý, *Workmen*, p. 382.

46. TT 212; Bruyère, *Rapport (1923–24)*, FIFAO 2, fasc. 2, p. 65 and pl. 19; *Tablets and Other Egyptian Monuments from the Collect of the Earl of Belmore, Now Deposited in the British Museum* (London, 1843), pl. 5, upper left. See also Černý, *Workmen*, pp. 324–325; Valbelle, *Ouvriers*, p. 255.

47. O. Gard 165 v. 12–18 (Allam *HOP*, pp. 183–184 and pls. 44–45; KRI 3:548–550). Černý, *Workmen*, p. 270, suggests a date in the reign of Ramses II.

48. O. Strassbourg H 106 (Černý, Notebook 35, 69).

49. O. Toronto A. 11 r. 27 (Alan H. Gardiner, Herbert Thompson, J. G.

Milne, *Theban Ostraca* [London, 1913], 16g–16h); and the question addressed to an oracle on O. IFAO [855] (Černý, Notebook 105, 85): "Shall one cultivate (*iri*) this field (of) the chief of police Neb-semen?" For *iri* meaning "cultivate", see Edward F. Wente, *Late Ramesside Letters*, SAOC no. 33 (Chicago, 1967), p. 70 n. b.

50. Janssen, *Commodity Prices*, pp. 167–177, 536–537.

51. O. DeM 624 v. 4–5; Černý-Gardiner, *HO* 29, 1; 42, 3; 71, 1; O. IFAO 1310 (Černý, Notebook 62, 18).

52. Wolfgang Helck, *Materialien zur Wirtschafts Geschichte des Neuen Reiches*, pts. 1–6. Akad. Wiss. Lit. [Mainz], Abh. Geistes Sozialwiss. Kl., 1960–1969 (Wiesbaden, 1961–1969), 485.

53. See, however, Černý-Gardiner, *HO* 26, 3 v. 4; LRL 63, 13–15.

54. O. IFAO 1425 (KRI 6:372). See also Janssen, "Year 8 of Ramsesses VI Attested," *GM* 29 (1978): 45–46.

55. Arrangements by Paneb: O. Cairo 25519 v. 21; O. Cairo 25521 v.; P. Salt 124 r. 2, 20; see Černý, "Papyrus Salt 124 (Brit. Mus. 10055)," *JEA* 15 (1929): 257. Others: O. Cairo 25589; O. DeM 428. In Černý-Gardiner, *HO* 33, 2 v. 2–4, the speaker seems to be unable to find the animal in question: "Indeed, I do not know the place where the cow is. It is in order to hear what you will say that I do not go to bring it." O. DeM 636 r. mentions going to the temple of Seti, perhaps in connection with feeding an ox (text broken).

56. For basketry, see Bruyère, *Rapport (1948–51), FIFAO* 26, p. 90; sickle teeth: Bruyère, *Rapport (1934–35),* pt. 3, FIFAO 16, pl. 42.

57. Hoe from burial chamber 1347: Bruyère, *Rapport (1933–34), FIFAO* 14, pp. 95 (no. 3) and 101, fig. 43. Bernadette Letellier, *La vie quotidienne chez les artisans de Pharaon.* Catalogue, Musées de Metz, du 12 novembre 1978 au 28 février 1979. (no date, no place), pp. 62–63.

58. Zivie, *Tombe de Pached,* pl. 23.

59. *Rep. Onomastique*, pp. 61, 63; Henri Wild, *La Tombe de Néfer.hotep (I) et Neb.néfer à Deir el Médîna [No. 6]*, vol. 2, MIFAO 103/2 (Cairo, 1979), pls. 6 and 20.

60. Sir J. Gardiner Wilkinson, *Manners and Customs of the Ancient Egyptians*, 2d series, supplement: Index and Plates (London, 1841), pl. 86 (detail); in this scene from TT 113, discussed in Černý, *Workmen*, pp. 27–28, Amenhotep is identified as "draughtsman of the noble " which Černý very reasonably suggested should be read *ḥr;* see also Cathleen Keller, "How many Draughtsman Named Amenhotep?" *JARCE* 21 (1984): 124.

61. TT 65: PM I:1², pp. 129–132; this could be the same Iy-em-seba as the scribe of that name who commissioned a bed from the workman Hay (P. DeM 3 r. 1–5), an identification suggested to me by Cathleen Keller.

62. *[ḫft]irt ḥr sn;* if the text has been read correctly.

63. Spielberg, *Graffiti*, pp. 92–93. See the remarks of Keller, *JARCE* 21 (1984): 124.

64. Keller, *JARCE* 21 (1984): 124–25 n. 68, 127.

65. O. DeM 324.

66. Černý-Gardiner, *HO* 70, 1.

67. Others include O. DeM 114–126, 128–129, 132, 326; letters listed in Černý-Gardiner, *HO*, vol. 1, pp. 34–35 (Index B). We will not discuss official correspondence between the necropolis and the office of the vizier.

68. Louvre parchment SN 174, III, 3A (Černý, Notebook 115, 2–8); cf. *RAD*, p. xx.

69. P. DeM 8–13.

70. See P. W. Pestman, in "Who Were the Owners in the 'Community of Workmen' of the Chester Beatty Papyri?" in *Gleanings from Deir el-Medîna*, ed. R. J. Demarée and Jac. J. Janssen (Leiden, 1982), pp. 162–163.

71. P. DeM 9.

72. John R. Baines and Jaromír Málek, *Atlas of Ancient Egypt* (Oxford: 1980), p. 114; Ricardo Caminos, "Papyrus Berlin 10463," *JEA* 49 (1963): 32, 34. The site is called *Ḥwt* in P. DeM 8 and 18, and *Ḥwt-shm* in P. DeM 10; both names were in use for Diospolis Parva.

73. O. DeM 418, 2–5. "The prophet," *pꜣ-ḥm-nṯr*, is perhaps a personal name rather than a title.

74. P. München 19 (818) (Černý, Notebook 35, 52) rt. 2; see also O. Mond 175 (KRI 7:381–382).

75. P. Chester Beatty 1 r. 16, 9; see Alan H. Gardiner's remarks in *The Library of A. Chester Beatty* (Oxford, 1931), p. 1

76. P. Geneva MAH 15274 v. 4, 2 (*MDAIK* 15 [1957], pl. 38).

77. P. DeM 6, if this is indeed he; Černý attributed P. DeM 6 to Nakht-Sobek, without stating his grounds, in *Papyrus Hiératiques de Deir el-Médineh, Tome I (Nos. I–XVII)*, DFIFAO 8 (Cairo, 1978), p. 19.

78. P. DeM 4 v. 2–5.

79. Černý-Gardiner, *HO* 18, 1. Much less clear is P. DeM 7, v. 6–7, where the writer seems to propose going to the recipient's house to take something. As neither the writer nor the recipient is identified, however, we cannot be certain this case is relevant.

80. Particularly as the entry of even a doorkeeper into the village was reprehensible in at least certain circumstances (O. DeM 339).

81. The very few possible exceptions, such as a fragmentary graffito mentioning a scribe of the army in Deir el Bahri (no. 1314; Jaroslav Černý, *Graffiti hiéroglyphiques et hiératiques de la necropole thébaine, Nos. 1060 à 1405*, DFIFAO 9 [Cairo, 1956], p. 20), could have been left before or after the New Kingdom.

82. Bruyère, *Raport (1934–35),* pt. 3, FIFAO 16, pp. 360 and 359, fig. 209.

83. Valbelle, *Ouvriers,* pp. 173, 318–323; see also A. I. Sadek, *Popular Religion in Egypt during the New Kingdom,* Hildesheimer Ägyptologische Beitrage 27 (Hildesheim, 1987), pp. 169–182.

84. Cairo Jd'E 43591; see *BIFAO* 24 (1924): 67 and pl. 11; KRI 1:403.

85. They include a relief with a depiction of the divine bark *Wsr-ḥ'̓t (BIFAO* 24 [1924]: pl. 15), purchased in Luxor but presume to be from Deir el Medina because the words "Place of Truth" appear twice in broken context; an ostracon which records that Amon-Reʿ crossed over to West Thebes, to pour water for the kings in a year 5 on IV *šmw* 1 (O. Cairo 25265; Černý, Notebook 101, 23); and a morsel of a stela dedicated to the *Wsr-ḥ'̓t* bark of Amon (Bruyère, *Rapport [1935–40], FIFAO* 20, fasc. 2, p. 123, fig. 206 [stela no. 288]).

86. G. A. Gaballa and K. A. Kitchen, *Orientalia* 38 (1969): 68–69. Depictions of the festival of Sokar are found in TT 211 (Bernard Bruyère, *Tombes Thébaines de Deir el Médineh à Décoration Monochrome,* MIFAO 86 [Cairo, 1952], pp. 76–77) and TT 7 (Bruyère, *Rapport [1935–40], FIFAO* 20, fasc. 3, p. 111); title *sš ḳd n Imn m ḥwt Skr* used by Pashed in TT 323 (Bruyére, *Rapport [1923–1924]), FIFAO* 2, fasc. 2, pp. 83–84; and Bruyère, *Tombes Thébaines,* p. 77). See also the references in Valbelle, *Ouvriers,* p. 322.

87. Černý-Gardiner, *HO* 107.

88. TT 2: Valbelle, *Ouvriers,* p. 173; PM I:1² 6(5); sketch in *Rep. Onomastique,*p. 25.

89. PM II²:445; M. E. Grebaut, *Le Musée Egyptien* (Cairo, 1890–1900), 1:5–6 and pl. 3; Arthur Edward Pearse Brome Weigall, *Ancient Egyptian Works of Art* (London, 1924), pl. on p. 260. The foreman Pashed is dated by Černý (*Workmen,* pp. 292–293) to the early Nineteenth Dynasty; his use of the title on this stela shows that he was a member of the workmen's community at the time.

90. Berlin 20377. The stela was bought from locals, who were persuaded to reveal where they had found it; see A. Erman, *Sitzungsberichte der Koniglich Preussischen Akademie der Wissenschaften Phil.—Hist. Classe* 49 (1911): 1087–1095; *MDAIK* 12 (1943): 22. PM 1:2², p. 683, says it was reused as a threshold. Another stela (Berlin 20143) found in the same area was dedicated by the chief carpenter in the Place of Truth, Hwy (Roeder, *Aegyptische Inschriften,* 2:213), but Rudolf Anthes in "Die Deutschen Grabungen auf der westseite von Theben in den Jahren 1911 und 1913," *MDAIK* 12 (1943): 22, suggests that both these monuments were brought here from elsewhere.

91. A number of doorjambs found in the Ramesseum and Medinet Habi belonged to workmen who lived before the community was moved to the latter temple (Ramesseum jamb of *Imn-nḫt*: James Edward Quibell and Wilhelm Spiegelberg, *The Ramesseum* [London, 1898], pl. 26; also in KRI 6:379; three Medinet Habu doorjambs and other objects belonging to members of the gang:

Bruyère, *Rapport* [1945–1947], FIFAO 21, pp. 79–80). It is not unlikely that these were brought down from the village at the time of the move, however.

92. Valbelle, *Ouvriers*, pp. 317–318; Sadek, *Popular Religion*, pp. 152–161.

93. O. Berlin 14214 (Allam, *HOP*, pls. 16–19).

94. O. DeM 636 r. 3.

95. Cf. Eyre in Powell, *Labor in the Ancient Near East*, pp. 170–171.

96. Valbelle, *Ouvriers*, p. 165. See also Wolfgang Helck, "Arbeitersiedlung," in *LA* 1 (1975): 374–375.

97. See Valbelle, *Ouvriers*, p. 226, on reburial of royal mummies; Kenneth A. Kitchen, *The Third Intermediate Period in Egypt (1100–650 B.C.)* (Warminster, 1973), p. 419, no. 32, on Graffito 2138 in Jaroslav Černý and A. A. Sadek, *Graffiti de la montagne thébaine*, vol. 4 (Cairo, 1970), of year 20 Pinudjem ("Coming by the *w'b*-priest of Amon-Re' King of Gods the chief of the gang Horem-hepet-Ese of the Place of Truth in order to make the manner of opening the Great Valley together with the members [*w'w*] of the gang who were with him"); Černý, *Workmen*, pp. 124, 202, 312–313, on the two foremen Pa-di-Amon and Amen-mose, and the scribe of the tomb Bak-en-Mut, who attended the burial of the High Priest Pinudjem II.

98. Ventura, *Living*, pp. 120–144.

99. William F. Edgerton, "The Strikes in Ramses III's Twenty-ninth Year," *JNES* 10 (1951): 139 n. 10; he is followed by Elizabeth Thomas "*P³ ḫr ḥnï ḥnw/n ḫnw ḫnï*, a designation of the Valley of the Kings" (*JEA* 49 [1963]: 61), and Klaus Baer, "Ein Grab verfluchen?" (*Orientalia* 34 [1965]: 431 n. 3).

100. See Georges Posener, *L'enseignement loyaliste* (Geneva: 1976), p. 40; Jésus López, *BiOr* 45 (1988): 550 (review of Ventura, *Living*). In Anast. V, 20, 2 (Alan H. Gardiner, *Late Egyptian Miscellanies*, BAe 7 [Brussels, 1937], p. 67, ll. 4–5), a group of fugitives is said to have passed the northern *inbt* of the fortress of Sety Merneptah.

101. Ventura, *Living*, p. 141.

102. P. J. Frandsen, "A Word for 'causeway' and the Location of 'the five walls,'" *JEA* 75 (1989): 113; Lopez, *BiOr* 45 (1988): 550–551.

103. McDowell, *Jurisdiction*, pp. 93–105.

3. Foreigners Living in the Village

For my initial foray into this subject, see my article "Some Foreign Personal Names and Loan-words from the Deir el-Medineh Ostraca," in *Essays . . . Kantor*, pp. 287–303, cited as Ward, *Essays . . . Kantor*. After the present study had been completed, an important book appeared that will surely become the basic reference on foreign names in Egyptian texts: Thomas Schneider, *Asiatische Personennamen in ägyptischen Quellen des Neuen Reiches*, Orbis

Biblicus et Orientalis 114 (Freiburg and Göttingen, 1992). Most of the names I have discussed here and in *Essays . . .Kantor* are included in Schneider's comprehensive work, though due to the numerous difficulties inherent in the subject, there are many points at which we disagree. Rather than enlarge the present text to critique Schneider's views on individual names, I have left the discussion of such matters to my review of Schneider's admirable volume to appear in *Chronique d'Égypte*.

1. Georges Posener, "Les asiatiques en Égypte sous les XIIᵉ et XIIIᵉ dynasties," *Syria* 34 (1957): 145–163, and Rosalie David, *The Pyramid Builders of Ancient Egypt* (London, 1986), chap. 7, survey the Middle Kingdom evidence, though the latter goes much too far in her analysis of Aegean connections. The most important list of resident foreigners is the long catalogue of household servants, including many Asiatics, published by William C. Hayes in *A Late Middle Kingdom Papyrus in the Brooklyn Museum* (Brooklyn, N.Y., 1955). The foreign names of this papyrus have been studied by William F. Albright, "Northwest-Semitic Names in a List of Egyptian Slaves from the Eighteenth Century B.C.," *JAOS* 74 (1954): 222–233, and Posener's article adds notes on individual names. The most recent analysis of these names is in Thomas Schneider, "Die semitischen und ägyptischen Namen des syrischer Sklaven des Papyrus Brooklyn 35. 1446 Verso," *Ugarit Forschungen* 19 (1987): 255–282. While these servants are generally classified as "slaves" in the literature, they are as a group called *ḥnmw*, which, as Hayes observes (pp. 83–84), refers to members of a household and in this case is best rendered as "household servants." On Tell ed-Dabʿa, see, e.g., Manfred Bietak, "Avaris and Piramesses. Archaeological Exploraiton in the Eastern Nile Delta," *Proceedings of the British Academy* 65 (1979): 226–283, and "Problems of Middle Bronze Age Chronology: New Evidence from Egypt," *AJA* 88 (1984): 471–485.

2. The most comprehensive study on slavery remains Bakir, *Slavery*. Wolfgang Helck offers an up-to-date survey in *LA* 5 (1984): 982–987, and O. D. Berlev has touched on the subject in his *Social Relations in Egypt in the Period of the Middle Kingdom* (in Russian) (Moscow, 1978). The problem of slavery in Egypt is complicated by a lack of pertinent documents and vagueness in Egyptian legal terminology; e.g., in the discussion of the term *bᵓk* in Bakir, *Slavery*, pp. 15–22, the Egyptian evidence does not warrant the conclusions given or the range of meanings assumed.

3. A general survey is in Helck, *Beziehungen*, chap. 26. His list however, was drawn up on the assumption that group-writing represents foreign names, which is not always the case.

4. E.g. Bernard Bruyère, "Rapport sur les fouilles de Deir el Médineh (1933–1934). Partie 1: La nécropole de l'ouest," *FIFAO* 14 (1937), p. 33, n. 1, and *Tombes thébaines de Deir el-Médineh à decoration monochrome*, MIFAO 86

(Cairo, 1952), p. 52; Charles Boreaux, "La stèle C.86 du Musée du Louvre et les stéles similaires," *Mélanges syriens offerts à M. René Dussaud* (Paris, 1939), 2:683.

5. Wilhelm Spiegelberg and Adolph Erman, "Grabstein eines syrischen Söldners aus Tell Amarana," *ZÄS* 36 (1898): 126–129; Berlin 14122. See also App. A., no. 33.

6. FIFAO 15, pp. 43–44.

7. For the former, see Wilhelm Spiegelberg, "Mitanni(?)-Eigennamen in hieroglyphischer Wiedergabe," *ZA* 32 (1918–19): 205–206; Arnold Gustavs, "Subaräische Namen in einer ägyptischen Liste syrischer Sklaven und ein sudarabäischer(?) Hyksos-Name," *ZÄS* 64 (1929): 55; Torgny Säve-Söderbergh, "The Stele of the Overseer of Works Benya, called Pahekmen," *Or Suec* 9 (1960): 54–61. For the latter, see Wilhelm Spiegelberg, "Zu den semitischen Eigennamen in ägyptischer Umschrift aus der Zeit des 'nuen Reiches' (um 1500–1000)," *ZA* 13 (1898): 51, and "Bemerkungen zu den hieratischen Amphoreninschriften des Ramesseums," *ZÄS* 58 (1923): 33. Cf. also Ugaritic *Mlky* and Amorite *Milkiya*. The latter names are probably from a root meaning "to counsel."

8. Ward, *Essays . . . Kantor*, p. 292.

9. The throwstick determinative is omitted in the two major collections of foreign personal names compiled in the Middle Kingdom—the Execration Texts and the list of servants in P. Brooklyn 35.1446—perhaps because the former identifies the individuals as "ruler of the [foreign] town X" and the latter as "the Asiatic X."

Among lists from New Kingdom times, in *Urk* IV, 11, eleven of the nineteen "male and female servants of booty" given to Ahmose during the Hyksos war have Egyptian names; only two of the eight foreign names have the throwstick, but they are compounded with md^3y and $K^3\check{s}$, words traditionally spelled with this sign. A writing board of the early Eighteenth Dynasty (BM 5647), by contrast, records nine foreign names, eight of which do have the throwstick (see T. E. Peet, "The Egyptian Writing-board B.M. 5647, Bearing Keftiu Names," in *Essays in Aegean Archaeology Presented to Sir Arthur Evans*, ed. S. Casson [Oxford, 1927], pp. 90–99; Jean Vercoutter, *L'Egypte et la monde égéen préhellenique*, BdÉ, vol. 22 [Cairo, 1956], pp. 45–50). An Eighteenth Dynasty ostracon in Leipzig lists twenty-one names of "the new Canaanites," all of which show the throwstick (see Georg Steindorff, "Eine Liste syrischer Sklaven," *ZÄS* 38 [1900]: 15–18). An appendix to the Golenischeff Ritual, a papyrus containing hymns to the royal diadem (Adolph Erman, *Hymnen an das Diadem der Pharaonen* [Berlin, 1911], pp. 55–58), lists fifty-seven non-Egyptian names, all without the throwstick (the list is in a different hand and shows no connection to the main text, but the consonantal structure of the names is un-Egyptian;

Georges Posener, *Syria* 18 [1937]: 186, agrees that they are foreign). Two ostraca of the Nineteenth Dynasty, however (O. Louvre 14354, 14355) preserve fourteen foreign names, thirteen of which do use the throwstick; the remaining name is definitely foreign, so there is evidently a scribal omission at this point. Finally, the war scenes from the various copies of the Battle of Kadesh contain the names of sixteen fallen Hittite leaders, the spellings of which—including some repetitions—show nineteen examples with the throwstick. Five of the six without it are at the Ramesseum, the result of more than one artist working there, though the Ramesseum texs otherwise show a consistent use of the sign in this segment of the Kadesh scenes.

In the broad spectrum of all foreign names found in Egyptian texts, singly or in groups, hieratic texts show a slightly higher tendency to use this sign than hieroglyphic ones (see the collections in Spiegelberg, *ZA* 13 [1898]: 42–56; Max Burchardt, *Die altkanaanäischen Fremdworte und Eigennamen in Aegyptischen* [Leipzig, 1910]; Ranke, *Personennamen*, 2:409–414). But by and large the omission of the throwstick about half the time holds true, no matter what the script or material used (my own files show the same general picture), and a similar scribal variance prevailed at Deir el Medina: e.g., the owner of TT 327 is *Trby,* Hurrian *Tulpiya,* and this name appears both with and without the throwstick on his monuments (Ward, *Essays . . . Kantor,* p. 298; FIFAO 14, 30–34; E. Bogoslovsky, "Monuments and Documents from Deir el-Medina in the Museums of the USSR" (in Russian), *Vestnik Drevnei Istorii,* no. 122 [1972]: 71–73). On this point the village scribes, often rightly accused of careless or corrupt spelling, followed the pattern of scribes at all levels throughout the nation.

10. William C. Hayes, "A Selection of Tuthmoside Ostraca from Dēr El-Baḥri," *JEA* 46 (1960): 32; Ward, *Essays . . . Kantor,* pp. 297 (7), 290 n. 13.

11. For example, *Nh.t,* "Sycamore," a feminine name written *in-iw-ḥ³-y³,* etc., in New Kingdom Texts; see C.A.R. Andrews, "A Family for Anhai?" *JEA* 64 (1978): 88.

12. The complicated subject of group-writing embraces a vast amount of textual material. Briefly stated, group-writing is well attested in Middle Kingdom texts, was most widely used in the New Kingdom, and tapers off thereafter. There has been a long and inconclusive debate as to whether vowels are represented in this orthography. To be fair to the proponents of "vocalization," it should be emphasized that they abstract from the general phenomenon of group-writing what they term the "syllabic orthography," and it is only words spelled in the latter that represent vocalization. But this allows one to sift through the total evidence and pick out what one pleases. For example, Albright, a major supporter of "vocalization," did not "suggest that all 'group' writings in Egyptian had vocalic significance, only those employed in the syllabic orthography" (W. F. Albright and T. O. Lambdin, "New Material for the Egyptian Syllabic

Orthography," *JCS* 2 [1957]: 114 n. 1). This means that it is very much up to the individual as to which word belongs to the syllabic orthography and which does not. Albright and Lambdin solve the matter by refusing to accept as syllabic spelling "those [identifications] which offer phonetic difficulties" (p. 115 n. 3). This approach effectively ignores any spelling that raises questions.

My own view is that a "syllabic orthography" cannot be extrapolated from the wider phenomenon of group-writing and that one should not examine the problem of vocalization using only that part of the evidence which conforms to a theory. Either vocalic principles can explain most of the evidence, or such principles do not exist. It is of no small importance that many words spelled in group-writing thought to be foreign loans are in reality, old native terms dressed up in a new spelling; see William A. Ward, "Late Egyptian *'r.t:* The So-called Upper Room," *JNES* 44 (1985): 329–335. For an overall view of group-writing and the syllabic orthography, see Wolfgang Helck, "Grundsätzliches zur sog. 'Syllabischen Schreibung'," *SAK* 16 (1989): 121–143.

13. BM Stela 290; *HTBM* 9, pl. 48. The name *'kbr* occurs again on a funerary figurine in Zagreb (No. 600, here read *N'kbr*). The name means "mouse"; see Alan R. Schulman, "*Mhr* and *Mškb,* Two Egyptian Military Titles of Semitic origin," *ZÄS* 93 (1966): 125 n. 8.

14. Louvre stela D 19.

15. Ranke, *Personennamen,* 1:44, 10.

16. Kurt Sethe, "Über einige Kurznamen des neuen Reiches," *ZÄS* 44 (1907): 89.

17. Heike Guksch, *Das Grab des Benja, gen. Paheqamen. Theban Nr. 343* (Mainz, 1978), pp. 43–44.

18. John Chadwick, *Documents in Mycenaean Greek,* 2d ed. (Cambridge, 1973), p. 42.

19. Georg Steindorff, "Eine Liste syrischer Sklaven," *ZÄS* 38 (1900): 18.

20. See A. M. Abadallah, "Meroitic Personal Names" (Ph.D. diss., Duke University, 1969); Herbert Donner and Wolfgang Röllig, *Kanaanäische und aramäische Inschriften,* 3 vols. (Wiesbaden, 1962–64); Frank L. Benz, *Personal Names in the Phoenician and Punic Inscriptions* (Rome, 1972), pp. 187–192.

21. Gröndahl, *Personennamen,* collects and studies in Parts I and II, the Semitic and Hurrian names that form the bulk of the personal names at Ugarit; in Parts III–V, names of Anatolian and other origins. It is of interest that this population mix extended to the villages of the Ugaritic city-state; e.g., Text UT 2116, an agreement by several people of the village of Apsuna with regard to a trading venture to Egypt, lists as principals or witnesses to this agreement the foreigners *Tldn* and *Plgn.* See Gröndahl, *Personennamen,* pp. 265, 312; Michael Helzer, *The Rural Community in Ancient Ugarit* (Wiesbaden, 1976), p. 78.

22. Claude F.-A. Schaeffer, *Ugaritica. Études relatives aux découverte des Ras*

Shamra. Première série (Paris, 1939), chap. 2, collects the archaeological evidence for an Aegean presence known at that time. Not all scholars agree that mainland Greeks migrated to Ugarit in Late Bronze times; e.g., P. J. Riis, "The First Greeks in Phoenicia and Their Settlement at Sukas," *Ugaritica VI* (Paris, 1969), p. 435, suggests "a local establishment of half-Mycenaeanized Cypriotes, but not true Greeks."

One must agree with Gröndahl, *Personennamen*, p. 7, that some Aegean personal names ought to be among the repertoire of names from Ugarit. The obvious comparative material consists of the hundreds of personal names in the Linear B texts. The difficultires are formidable, however, because of the peculiarities of representing Greek phonemes in the Linear B script and the problems of identifying Greek cognates to Linear B personal names (see Chadwick, *Documents in Mycenaean Greek*, pp. 42–48 and chap. 4). Even if these drawbacks could be overcome, one would then have to deal with how scribes at Ugarit *heard* Mycenaean names and translated them into the phonemes of Ugaritic and Akkadian.

For a general evaluation of the Canaanite population mix, see G. E. Mendenhall, *The Tenth Generation: The Origins of the Biblical Tradition* (Baltimore, 1973), chap. 5. On names from the Amarna Tablets, see Richard S. Hess, "Personal Names from Amarna: Alternative Readings and Interpretations," *Ugarit Forschungen* 17 (1986): 157–167.

23. One can determine the social stratification of a given society in many ways. In the present volume, B. S. Lesko suggests, on the basis of economic status, that the social strata at Deir el Medina ranged from the upper middle to the lower middle class. This is certainly correct when the village is placed within the economic strata of, say, the whole Theban region. The village had neither the very rich nor the very poor who stood at the upper and lower ends of the economic scale in the Egyptian population as a whole. But I am thinking rather in terms of functional stratification: that is, the relative importance of an individual's place in the functions of the village. In this sense, administrators were the most important. The least important—or the most easily replaced—were the ordinary workmen and the whole range of ancillary workmen. Between these two groups were the artists, physicians, priests, and other specialists who took orders from the administrators but exercised a certain degree of personal initiative and independence in their work. Thus, though in the general economic framework of Egypt the village was indeed middle class, we can speak of upper, middle, and lower functional classes as well. The Canaanites and their near descendants all belonged to the lower *functional* stratum of Deir el Medina and, as far as the present evidence goes, did not rise above that stratum, at least during the first few generations of an originally foreign family's residence in the village.

24. Ward, *Essays . . . Kantor,* p. 299 (17). The word *ḥm.t,* as used in the Deir el Medina archives, is generally translated "slave" (e.g., Bakir, *Slavery,* p. 102; Černý, *Workmen,* chap. 15). This is an unfortunate choice of terminology, since it conjurs up ideas that may not have existed in Egypt. See nn. 1–2 above.

25. A listing of high officials with foreign names is given in Helck, *Beziehungen²,* pp. 353–355, though it must be used with caution (see n. 3 above). No. 17, e.g., (p. 355), though spelled in group-writing, is really Egyptian *Krr,* "frog."

26. Černý, *Workmen,* pp. 126, 146 (Foremen), 223 (Scribes of the Tomb).

27. Peet, *Tomb Robberies;* Alan H. Gardiner, *The Wilbour Papyrus,* 4 vols. (Oxford, 1941–52); B. Menu, *Le régime juridique des terres et du personnel attaché a la terre dans le Papyrus Wilbour* (Lille, 1970). The Tomb Robbery Papyri of the later Twenteith Dynasty are a dozen papyrus manuscripts dealing with the investigation of thefts from both royal and official tombs in the Theban necropolis. The Wilbour Papyrus, also of the Twentieth Dynasty, is a record of land-holdings of both government institutions and private individuals. Hundreds of personal names of ordinary Egyptians are recorded in each, giving a fair cross-section of the population mix in the region of Thebes and in Middle Egypt.

28. Spiegelberg, *Graffiti;* Jaroslav Černý, *Graffiti hiéroglyphiques et hiératiques de la nécropole thébaine.* DFIFAO (1956); Jaroslav Černý and A. A. Sadek, *Graffiti de la montagne thébaine,* 4 vols. (Cairo, 1969–74).

29. In Ward, *Essays . . . Kantor,* 298, this woman is credited with only an offering-table and a funerary figurine. She is actually known from half a dozen funerary figurines listed by Jac. J. Janssen, "An Unusual Donation Stela of the Twentieth Dynasty," *JEA* 49 (1963): 66. She also appears on a late Eighteenth Dynasty family stela of one *St'w,* though her relationship to this official is not stated. Her name is misspelled on the stela with a *Ḥr-* or *wr-*bird in place of the *m,* which led Bogoslovsky ("Monuments and Documents from Deir el-Medina," 90) to read her name as *dy-wry-r'.* But note that other signs on this stela are engraved incorrectly: e.g., the eye determinative in the name *St'w* is engraved as an *r;* a *s'* bird looks like *w,* etc. Photographs are published in Bogoslovsky, *op. cit.,* and in B. Piotrovsky, *Egyptian Antiquities in the Hermitage* (Leningrad, 1974), pls. 49–50. Janssen, in the article cited above, rightly doubts that the Hori named with *Ḏmr* on the offering-table (Cairo Cat. 43586) is the Royal Butler Hori known from several sources. She is not the wife of *St'w* of the Hermitage stela, who is *Pwy,* but may be a sister since she sits with his mother.

30. While Bruyère (MIFAO 88, pp. 8, 50) made out an indirect case for this couple being the parents of Sennedjem himself, I follow Morris L. Bierbrier, *The Late New Kingdom in Egypt (c. 1300–664 B.C.)* (Warminster, 1975), p. 30. The texts of TT I are quite clear on this; Sennedjem's parents are specifically stated to

be Khabekhen and Taheny. The pair $\underline{Tr}$ and ʾ*ti* appear only once in the tomb, in the company of Sennedjem and Iyneferty, so they must be the latter's parents.

31. BM 322 *HTBM*, p. 7, pl. 8. This is the lower part of a rectangular stela with a cavetto cornice, a type common in the New Kingdom. In the top register of such stelae, the deceased and his wife are shown before Osiris; the lower register shows members of the family. The name and titles of the owner and sometimes of his wife are engraved in vertical lines down the sides, e.g.: BM 307, 324, 325; Florence Inv. 2584, 2589; Cairo 34050, 34052, 34054. What remains of BM stela 322 is the lower register portraying family members and part of the vertical side texts, in this case giving the names of both the owner and his wife.

32. Gröndahl, *Personennamen*, p. 46; Huffmon, *APN*, p. 159. The name ʾ*Itnm* occurs several times elsewhere in Egyptian texts: W. Spiegelberg, *ZA* 13 (1898): 48, cites a Third Intermediate Period example; Helck *Beziehungen*², p. 354, quotes W. F. Petrie, *Sedment II* (London, 1924), pl. 53 (Eighteenth Dynasty) but gives no cognate; Ranke, *Personennamen* I p. 52, 2, quotes an example of the New Kingdom from Leiden.

33. *NPN*, p. 112 (the initial signs of the name ʾ*ti* are usually read $T(ʾ)$-, the *t* placed above and behind the ʾ for reasons of space. I do not think this applies in the present case, since both women with this name had husbands with Hurrian names, and there is an excellent cognate for ʾ*ti*; Helck, *Beziehungen*², p. 363 [7], reads this name the same way), 38, 64–65 (the precise relation of Ḥutiya is not stated, and he could as well be a son of *Patta*; however, the other children of *Patta* and *Ataya* have Egyptian nicknames, so I prefer to identify Ḥutiya's wife *Wrnr* as another daughter, since she also has an Egyptian nickname for Tʾ-*wr.t*; see Ward, *Essays . . . Kantor*, p. 291).

34. See n. 30 above.

35. *KRI* 7:390, 2 (Pap. BM 9997): ʾ*nh.t n.t niw.t*, citizeness." Spiegelberg, *ZÄS* 58 (1923): 32–33, lists several examples of the masculine Pʾ-*(n)-irs*. See Ward, *Essays . . . Kantor*, 297 (11); Donald Wiseman, *The Alalakh Tablets* (London, 1953), p. 127; Gröndahl, *Personennamen*, p. 301. The superscript *f* and *m* indicate feminine and masculine names.

36. Koenig, *Catalogue*, no. 6220; Gröndahl, *Personennamen* p. 106; F. V. Winnett and G. Lancaster Harding, *Inscriptions from Fifty Safaitic Cairns* (Toronto, 1978), p. 592, s.r. ʾ*bl*. This is also a South Arabic tribal name; see W. F. Jamme, *Sabaean Inscriptions from Mahram Bilqîs (Mârib)* (Baltimore, 1962), p. 416 (ʾ*blm*).

37. P. Gardiner 7, 4 (*KRI* 7:340, 6–7).

38. E.g., B. Couroyer, "Trois épithètes de Ramsès II," *Orientalia* 33 (1964): 448–453; Hans-Werner Fischer-Elfert, *Die satirische Streitschrift des Papyrus Anastasi I: Übersetzung und Kommentar, Ägyptologische Abhandlungen* 44 (Wiesbaden, 1986), pp. 244–246; Schulman, *ZÄS* 93 (1966): 127–129; *DLE*

1:230–231. Schulman defines the term in Egyptian texts as a military officer responsible for the gathering of intelligence. Anson F. Rainey, "The Military Personnel of Ugarit," *JNES* 24 (1965): 24, and "The Soldier-Scribe in *Papyrus Amastasi I*," *JNES* 26 (1967): 58–60, prefers to identify the *mhr* as a "charioteer" in both Canaanite and Egyptian sources, possibly a Canaanite synonym for the Indo-Aryan *mryn* = *maryannu*, "chariot warrior."

39. See I. Kottsieger, *Ugarit Forschungen* 16 (1984): 101–104. This sense also occurs in Egyptian; see Fischer-Elfert, *Satirische Streitschrift*, pp. 219–222.

40. A. Goetze, *JSS* 4 (1959): 199, a hypocoristicon with the -*anu(m)* ending; Gröndahl, *Personennamen*, p. 156.

41. Greek *Merbalos*, *Maarbal*; Latin *Maharbal*. Cf. Benz, *Personal Names*, pp. 137–38, 340–41. Donner and Röllig, *Kanaanäische und aramäische Inschriften*, p. 80, suggests that the meaning is "Sevant of Baal." The name was popular on Sardinia; see M. Amadasi, *Le iscrizioni fenicie e puniche della colonie in occidente* (Rome, 1967), p. 192.

42. Papyrus juridique Turin 2, 1; 5, 6. Cf. Helck, *Beziehungen²*, p. 353.

43. P. Wilbour A26, 27.

44. Marek Marciniak, *Les inscriptions hiératiques du temple de Thoutmosis III* (Warsaw, 1974), no. 71, 3; Rosalie David, *The Macclesfield Collection of Egyptian Antiquities* (Warminster, 1980), pp. 61–62, stela I6.

45. P. Wilbour A23, 24; Helck, *Beziehungen²*, p. 358.

46. P. Amherst 7, 4.18; P. Wilbour A54, 32 (which spells *B'l* with the recumbent Seth animal only, though this is probably the correct reading as Seth was identified with Ba'al); Helck, *Beziehungen²*, p. 358.

47. This is a fairly common phenomenon: *P³-il*, *P³-ym*, *P³-rwt*, *P³-š'sw*, *P³-ṯpr*, etc. All these names are based on words of Canaanite origin.

48. Koenig, *Catalogue*, no. 6247.

49. TT 359; FIFAO 8–2, 58; Bernadette Letellier, "Autour de la stèle de Qadech; une famille du Deir el-Médineh," *RdE* 27 (1975): 150–163 (names in this family spelled in group-writing such as *Tnr, Wrnr, Tr*, are Egyptian hypocoristica); O. DeM 666, 4 (on the date, see Gutgesell, *Datierung*, p. 410); O. DeM 220, 3; Černý, *LRL*; Wente, *LRL*, 16–17. *Try*'s name occurs more than forty times in nine different spellings, though the throwstick occurs only once; see Černý, *LRL*, 43, 9.

50. O. Turin 57382, v. 7.

51. Laroche, *Noms*, pp. 109, 120; *NPN*, p. 99; Jean Noms, pp. 74, 85.

52. Erman, *Hymnen*, p. 56, nos. b4, e4.

53. Koenig, *Catalogue*, no. 6283.

54. *NPN*, p. 56; Stamm, *Beiträge*, p. 52.

55. Koenig, *Catalogue*, no. 6329; Tallqvist, *APN*, p. 225; Huffmon, *APN*, pp. 135, 248. On *šumu*, "name," see William A. Ward, "Notes on Some Semitic

Loan-words and Personal Names in Late Egyptian," *Orientalia* 32 (1963): 424–425, s.v. *Šm-Bʿl*.

56. Černý, *Workmen*, p. 220 n. 6 (Yvan Koenig, in *Hommages Sauneron I*, BdE 81 [Cairo, 1979], p. 199, follows Černý); Ranke, *Personennamen*, 2:393; 346, 11.

57. Hayes, *JEA* 46 (1960): 32; O. Cairo 25543, r. 2 = Akkadian *Basiya;* Ward, *Essays . . . Kantor,* 297 (7). I render *ḫr* as "Canaanite" rather than the usual "Syrian" since this better reflects the geographical area involved.

58. Bologna 1918 (not in Ranke, *Personennamen*); see, e.g., FIFAO 14, 33, n. 1; MIFAO 86, 52.

59. Although William F. Albright, *Vocalization of the Egyptian Syllabic Orthography* (New Haven, 1934), no. XIX.A.15, considers it a loan from Akkadian *danânu,* "be strong"—a suggestion defended by Manfred Görg, "*ṯnr* ('stark'), ein semitisches Lehnwort?" *GM* 68 (1983): 53–54—the argument is a weak one. *Ṯnr* should rather be considered a native Egyptian word which appears first in the written language of the New Kingdom. The earliest example is of the mid-Eighteenth Dynasty in a "curious and probably corrupt writing" (W. C. Hayes, *Ostraca and Name Stones from the Tomb of Sen-mut (no. 71) at Thebes* [New York, 1942], p. 40).

60. Cf. the list from the Dakhleh stela—Wilhelm Spiegelberg, "Eine Stele aus der Oase Dachel," *RecTrav* 21 (1899): 17—and the variety of spellings for the Libyan name *Mrỉy* (Spiegelberg, "Der Siegeshymnus des Merneptah auf der Flinders Petrie-Stele," *ZÄS* 34 [1896]: 17).

61. Henri Gauthier, *Dictionnaire des noms géographiques contenus dans les textes hiéroglyphiques,* 7 vols. (Cairo, 1925–1931), 5:205–206, and P. Montet, *Géographie de l'Egypte ancienne,* vol. 2 (Paris, 1961), suggest that the term also was used to designate the agricultural region on the west Nile bank which had direct access to the Kharga oasis.

62. Ward, *Essays . . . Kantor,* p. 290 n. 13.

63. Gardiner, *Wilbour Papyrus,* 4:30, 90.

64. Ranke, *Personennamen,* 1:346, 13; Hans D. Schneider, *An Introduction to the History of Ancient Egyptian Funerary Statuettes* (Leiden, 1977), no. 3.2.1.46, 2:70, 3: pl. 25.

65. Louvre stela C 218: Ranke, *Personennamen,* 1:346, 12; Jens Leiblien *Dictonnaire des noms hiéroglyphiques en ordre généalogique et alphabétique: Publié d'après les monuments égyptiens* (Christiana, 1871), no. 2095.

66. E.g., Hittite *Kalli, Kurri;* Babylonian *Kariya;* Hurrian *Kirriya, Keliya.* One must also consider the possibility that this name is Libyan or Nubian. Given such a range of possibilities but no specific information, it is possible to suggest a suitable cognate.

67. The name of the workman *Kr* at Deir el Medina is also spelled *Kry* in

Notes to Page 78

Černý-Gardiner, *HO*, pl. 73, 1. Those from Deir el Medina with this Egyptian name are (1) P^3-*ḥr-n-t*^{3}-*ḥ*^{3}.*t-nḫt*, who is called *Kr* (Spiegelberg, *Graffiti*, no. 1009); (2) the Ship Captain *Kry* (Koenig, *Catalogue,* nos. 6217–18); (3) the Workman *Kr,* mentioned many times (see Gutgesell, *Datierung,* 623, s.v. *Kr;* (4) the Merchant *Kry (Giornale* v. 7, 8).

In the following occurrences of the name found elsewhere, nos. 2, 4, 5, 7, and 10 are women: (1) BM stela 294, *HTBM* 7, pl. 24 (father and son; Eighteenth Dynasty); (2) Wilhelm Spiegelberg and B. Pörtner, *Aegyptische Grabstein und Denkstein aus süddeutschen Sammlungen* (1902), 1: no. 28 (Eighteenth Dynasty); (3) Schneider, *Funerary Statuettes,* no. 3.3.25 (New Kingdom); (4) Leiden V 39, in Pieter Boesser, *Beschreibung der Ägyptischen Sammlung des Niederländischen Reichsmuseums der Altertümer in Leiden. Die Denkmäler des Neuen Reiches,* Part 3. *Stelen.* (Haag, 1913), no. 38 (New Kingdom); (5) Boulaq stela 129, in Lieblein, *Dict. des noms,* no. 757 (New Kingdom); (6) Cairo stela Cat. 34061 (New Kingdom); (7) Spiegelberg and Pörtner, *Aegyptische Grabstein* (1904), 2: no. 19 (New Kingdom); (8) O. Cairo 25738 (Ramesside); (9) Cairo stela Cat. 34122, Abydos (New Kingdom); (10) Florence stela 1636 = 2541; Sergio Bosticco, *Museo archaeologica di Firenze. Le stele egiziane I. Le stele egiziane dall'antico al nuova regno* (Rome, 1959), pl. 51 (later Nineteenth Dynasty); (11) BM stela 1183, in *HTBM* 10, pl. 99 (Twentieth Dynasty); (12) P. Jur. Turin 4, 1, in Théodule Déveria, "Le papyrus judiciaire de Turin," *JA* 6th ser., 8 (1866): pl. 2 (reign of Ramses III); (13) Gardiner, *Wilbour Papyrus,* 4:30 (three individuals); (14) Jules Couyat and Pierre Montet, *Les inscriptions hiéroglyphiques et hiératiques du Ouâdi Hammâmât.* MIFAO, 34. (Cairo, 1913), no. 57 (Saite).

68. Cairo stela JE 30972; and Berlin 8939, menat counterpoise, unpublished. See Jean Yoyotte, "Les principautés du Delta au temps de l'anarchie libyenne," *Mélanges Maspero I,* fasc. 4, 144.

69. TT 339; FIFAO 3/3, 59; Stamm, *Beiträge,* p. 127.

70. Also the Ugaritic masculine *Dll;* Gröndahl, *Personennamen,* p. 124. On *Daliluša,* see Stamm, *Namengebung,* p. 277. Both the masculine and feminine forms are uncommon but widespread geographically.

71. See this chapter's first section and n. 5. His wife, who sits before him, is portrayed as Egyptian but also bears a foreign name, perhaps *'Irbr'*—which might be for *'Ii-Ba'al, 'Ii-Bêlu,* though this is far from certain. The name is actually spelled *'Irbwr'*^{3}.

72. TT 1340. The monuments and family of *Dydy* are discussed in FIFAO 14; and *HTBM,* 10, pp. 26–27. See also KRI 1:402–403 and 3:712–714. He is also (rarely) called a "Deputy in the Place of Truth": O. BM 8494, v.3 (KRI 7:320, 4).

73. KRI 4:2, 13; 3, 16. Note also *Mdydy,* the name of another Libyan chieftain: Ranke, *Personennamen,* 1:167, 30.

74. Ranke, *Personennamen*, 1:104, 3, 4.

75. P. DeM 28, r. 8, v. 11.

76. The name should not be confused with Egyptian $\underline{D}^3 b(.t)$ (Ranke, *Personennamen*, 1:405, 1–3).

77. Tallqvist, *APN*, p. 246; Jean, *Noms*, p. 90; *Zubû* in Old Babylonian, Stephen D. Simmons, "Early Old Babylonian Tablets from Ḥarmel (*Šadappum*) and Elsewhere," *JCS* 14 (1960): 23, text 47:21.

78. *DLE*, 4:156; *Wb*. V. 562, 10: Egyptian $\underline{d}b\hat{\imath}$ = Hebrew *sb'*.

4. *Aspects of Domestic Life and Religion*

I thank Jean Keith-Bennett and Joris F. Borghouts for reading and commenting on early drafts of this paper.

1. See Valbelle, *Ouvriers*, pp. 95, 303.

2. See esp. Jaroslav Černý, "Le culte d'Amenophis Ier chez les ouvriers de la nécropole thébaine," *BIFAO* 27 (1927): 159–203, pls. I–IX; and R. Parker with Jaroslav Černý, *A Saite Oracle Papyrus from Thebes in the Brooklyn Museum* (Providence, R.I., 1962), p. 41.

3. Valbelle, *Ouvriers*, pp. 315, 322–323 (noting that the workers' specific participation in the jubilee festivals is not always clear), 332–335 (attempts to chart the various local festivals that the village celebrated annually). See also p. 315n on the "residence" of Ramses II.

4. Valbelle, *Ouvriers*, pp. 321–322, 319, 326–327, and fig. 3. There may have been some limitations on the villagers' freedom, but for a recent assessment that once more rejects the notion of their strict separation from the Theban community, see Andrea G. McDowell's contribution to this volume and her *Jurisdiction* (reviewed by Morris Bierbrier in *JARCE* 29 [1992]: 210–211).

5. See Joris F. Borghouts in this volume; Valbelle, *Ouvriers*, p. 314 (see especially n. 2). For pre-New Kingdom references, see John Baines, "Practical Religion and Piety," *JEA* 73 (1987), 86–93, and esp. p. 93 for reference to a female seer (t^3 *rḥyt*), "the wise woman" from Deir el Medina. We cannot be sure how much the workers were influenced by the royal texts and illustrations they regularly copied in the tombs. Cathleen Keller, in a December 5, 1990, lecture at Brown University, stated that the workers in a few instances borrowed royal images for their own tomb sites; however, Erik Hornung, *The Valley of the Kings: Horizon of Eternity* (New York: 1990), p. 190, states that there was no borrowing at all, which seems unlikely.

6. See Kenneth A. Kitchen, *Pharaoh Triumphant: The Life and Times of Ramesses II* (Warminster, 1982), p. 190, fig. 60, for an artist's reconstruction of the interior of a typical house.

7. On the cellars, see Bierbrier, *Tomb-builders,* p. 69. On wall paintings, see Bruyère, *Rapport (1934–35),* FIFAO 16, p. 55; Bernard Bruyère, "Un fragment de fresque de Deir el Médineh," *BIFAO* 22 (1923): 121–133.

8. There were also habitations outside the village proper. See Valbelle, *Ouvriers,* pp. 120–121, 252–254.

9. Ibid., pp. 57–58; 61, on the family, esp. pp. 227–247. For general discussion of family issues, see John Baines, "Society, Morality, and Religious Practice," in *Religion in Ancient Egypt,* ed. Byron E. Shafer (Ithaca, 1991), esp. pp. 134, 143–144.

10. See Christopher J. Eyre, "Crime and Adultery in Ancient Egypt," *JEA* 70 (1984): 92–105, esp. p. 100: "The New Kingdom documents from Deir el-Medîna do not give a picture of great marital fidelity within the workmen's community, but the significant texts are few in number, difficult to interpret, and not necessarily representative."

11. Bruyère, *Rapport (1934–35),* pp. 55–57 (but in *CdE* 22 [1936]: 335 he says it is "toujours collé contre un mur et très souvent dans un angle de la chambre" [always close against a wall and often in a corner of the room]), 61, end fig. 18.

12. Bruyère, *Rapport (1934–35),* p. 56 (though in *CdE* 22 [1936]: 335, he gave a length of 1.80 instead of 1.70 meters), p. 57, and fig. 17.

13. Jacques Vandier, *Manuel d'archéologie égyptienne,* vol. 4 (Paris, 1964), pp. 187–193. Compare a ceramic bed model from Deir el Medina, which has plain legs (Bruyère, *Rapport [1934–35],* p. 138, fig. 57). See also H. G. Fishcher, "Bett," *LA* i, pp. 767–768.

14. Bruyère, *Rapport (1934–35),* p. 59 (headrest in House N.O. XII, but see also *CdE* 22 [1936]: 335), 56, 61–64.

15. Bruyère, *Rapport (1934–35),* pp. 57–58 and esp. 255, fig. 131; 257, fig. 133; 259, fig. 136 and pl. 9; 305, fig. 172 (according to Bruyère, Bes is present; for an interpretation of this figure as a child, see Barry J. Kemp, "Wall Paintings from the Workmen's Village at el-'Amarna," *JEA* 65 [1979]: 51 n. 10); 330, fig. 202. See also John Baines, *Fecundity Figures, Egyptian Personification, and the Iconology of a Genre* (Warminster, 1985), p. 128; and Bruyère, *CdE* 22 (1936): 329–340.

16. Bruyère, *Rapport (1934–35),* p. 273, fig. 145; p. 286, fig. 157; p. 311, fig. 182. On the flute player, see also J. Vandier d'Abbadie, "Une fresque civile de Deir el Medina," *RdE* 3 (1938): 27–35; and Lise Manniche, *Sexual Life in Ancient Egypt* (London, 1987), p. 16.

17. Baines, *Fecundity Figures,* p. 332; Kemp, "Wall Paintings," pp. 47–48; Hartwig Altenmueller, "Bes," *LA* i, pp. 720–724; James Romano, *Daily Life of the Ancient Egyptians,* Carnegie Museum of Natural History (Pittsburgh, 1990), pp. 26–27.

18. Christine Hobson, *The World of the Pharaohs* (New York, 1987), p. 117.

19. Edouard Naville, *The Temple of Deir el Bahari,* Part 2, Egypt Exploration Fund (London, 1896), pl. 51, middle colonnade, north wall with Birth of Hatshepsut.

20. O. DeM 2340, 2347, 2344; see J. Vandier d'Abbadie, *Catalogue des ostraca figurés de Deir el Médineh,* DFIFAO 2 (1937), 2: 1–2, p. vii. These are discussed in Emma Brunner-Traut, "Die Wochenlaube," *MIO* 3 (1955): 12–15; and Bruyère, *Rapport (1934—35),* pp. 131–132. See also *Rapport (1948–51),* pp. 62–63, fig. 14, 1.

21. O. DeM 2339. See similar motifs in O. BM 8506, used by Brunner-Traut in "Wochenlaube," p. 14, fig. 4.

22. Kemp, "Wall Paintings," 47–53, pls. 7–8 (on Main Street House 3 and Long Wall Street House 10). See Kemp's more recent comments in "Village in Retrospect," p. 26, on painted fragments with images of convolvulus leaves and papyrus, possibly from a painted panel behind a bed in a second-story bedroom at the Amarna workmen's village. The question of whether or not some of the Amarna and Deir el Medina artisans may have been part of the same population has not been fully determined, but see Barry J. Kemp, "Village in Retrospect," pp. 43–49; and Kemp, *Anatomy,* p. 273. Valbelle, *Ouvriers,* p. 25, opts for "une nette parenté" (a clear relationship) between the two. See most recently A. H. Bowmann, *The Private Chapel in Ancient Egypt: A Study of the Chapels in the Workmen's Village at El Amarna with Special Reference to Deir el Medina and Other Sites* (London and New York, 1991).

23. Kemp, "Wall Paintings," pp. 47–52; (p. 49 cites Peet and Woolley, *The City of Akhenaten,* 1, 184); Rolf Grundlach, "Thoeris," *LA* 6, pp. 494–497.

24. Geraldine Pinch, "Childbirth and Female Figurines at Deir el-Medina and el-'Amarna," *Orientalia* 52 (1983): 405–414, pls. 5, 6, esp. pp. 406, 408. Pinch rejects the earlier designation "concubines" (p. 405; I thank Joris Borghouts for this reference). Cf. Janine Bourriau, *Pharaohs and Mortals: Egyptian Art in the Middle Kingdom* (Fitzwilliam Museum, Cambridge, 1988), p. 125. See also Bruyère, *Rapport (1930),* pp. 12–15, and *Rapport (1934–35),* p. 142.

25. Emma Brunner-Traut, "Wöchnerin," *LA* 6, p. 1284; Pinch, "Childbirth," p. 410; and *Biblical Archaeology Review* 20 (1994): 24.

26. Gay Robins, *Women in Ancient Egypt* (London, 1993), p. 76.

27. Philippe Derchain, "La perruque et le cristal," *SAK* 2 (1975): 55–74, esp. p. 70, though more recent scholarship suggests the wig in Derchain's text was in fact animal fur.

28. Pinch, "Childbirth," pp. 410, 412, esp. a spell from P. Leiden (cited from J. F. Borghouts, *The Magical Texts of Papyrus Leiden I 348,* OMRO 51 [Leiden, 1971], p. 29, pl. 14) which advises "women in childbirth to wear a *nm n sin,*" a "dwarf of clay."

29. Manniche, *Sexual Life*, p. 18. See also Jeanne Bulté, *Talismans égyptiens d'heureuse maternité* (Paris, 1991); Vandier d'Abbadie, "Fresque civile"; and Pinch, "Childbirth," pp. 410, 412.

30. Veronica Wilson, "The Iconography of Bes with a Particular Reference to the Cypriot Evidence," *Levant* 7 (1975): 100, notes Bes's role as patron of music and dance and as guardian of many others besides mothers, including Horus and warriors. See also Kate Bosse-Griffiths, "A Beset Amulet from the Amarna Period," *JEA* 63 (1977): 98–106, esp. 101; Manniche, *Sexual Life*, pp. 17–18. Bes tattoos on the thighs of female dancers and musicians, frequent in New Kingdom material, bore "erotic overtones" (R. S. Bianchi, "Tätowierung," *LA* 6, p. 145).

31. Examples from Vandier d'Abbadie, VA 2344, according to Pinch, "Childbirth," p. 407 (I substitute DeM for Pinch's designation VA). Cf. Pinch, "Childbirth," pp. 407, 410, 412; Kemp, "Wall Paintings," p. 51.

32. Brunner-Traut, "Wochenlaube," pp. 11–30; Bernard Bruyère, "Un fragment de fresque de Deir el Médineh," *BIFAO* 22 (1923): 121–133, esp. p. 132, fig. 5. Brunner-Traut relied on such parallels as O. DeM 2339 and esp. BM 8506.

33. For a cautious discussion of this problem, however, see Kemp, "Village in Retrospect," 43–49; Kemp, "Wall Paintings," 53 and Kemp, *Anatomy*, pp. 304–305, where in discussing the Amarna workers' village, he points to the practice of "domestic femininity," a term that would serve equally well for Deir el Medina.

34. Wolfhart Westendorf, "Geburt," *LA* 2, 459–462, esp. 460; Brunner-Traut, "Wochenlaube," *LA* 6, pp. 1282–1284, esp. 1282.

35. A. T. Sandison, "Frauenheilkunde und -sterblichkeit," *LA* 2, p. 296. A hymn on one votive stela from Deir el Medina, by the artist Neferabu to Meretseger, goddess of the Peak, compares the dedicator's anguish before the deity with sitting on "bricks like a woman in labor" (translated from Turin 102 by Miriam Lichtheim, *AEL*, 2:108).

36. Brunner-Traut, "Wöchnerin," *LA* 6, pp. 1284–1285, esp. 1284. See Kemp, "Wall Paintings," pp. 51–53.

37. As noted in the "Instruction of Any" (*AEL* 2:141), as cited in Catherine H. Roehrig, *The Eighteenth Dynasty Titles Royal Nurse, Royal Tutor . . . ,*" University Microfilms (Ann Arbor, Mich., 1990), p. 336.

38. Kemp, "Wall Paintings," p. 51 and Brunner-Traut, "Wochenlaube," p. 20.

39. On the related deity Meretseger, e.g., see Bruyère, MIFAO 58 (1930).

40. Bruyère, *Rapport (1934–35),* pp. 61–64; Salima Ikram, "Domestic Shrines and the Cult of the Royal Family at El-'Amarna," *JEA* 75 (1989): 89–101.

41. Ikram, "Domestic Shrines," p. 96.

42. Ludwig Borchardt and Herbert Ricke, *Die Wohnhäuser in Tell El-Amarna* (Berlin, 1980), pp. 254–255, with photo on plate 18, B. Depth, not given in the report, is estimated from information on p. 255, fig. 38. Cf. also the shrines found in the humble dwellings of the late Eighteenth Dynasty at Medinet Habu to the south of Deir el Medina, which measure 85 cm × 45 cm × 23 cm (Uvo Hölscher, *The Temples of the Eighteenth Dynasty: The Excavation of Medinet Habu*, vol. 2 (Chicago, 1939), p. 69.

43. See Bruyère, *Rapport (1934–35)*, pp. 61–64, for further discussion of the "bed-altar." See also Ikram, "Domestic Shrines," pp. 96 and 89; and Kemp, "Wall Paintings," p. 52, n. 17 with fuller references.

44. Valbelle, *Ouvriers*, pp. 262, 314.

45. Černý, "Culte d'Amenophis," pp. 162, 172; Parker and Černý, *Saite Oracle*, p. 41.

46. R. J. Demarée, *The ꜣḫ iḳr n Rꜥ-Stelae: On Ancestor Worship in Ancient Egypt* (Leiden, 1983), pp. 7–9 (for detailed description of types and subtypes), chap. 2 (for examples). From Demarée's catalogue I count seven examples of stelae with female dedicatees (A6, 39, 41, 44, 45, 51, 52). Of these, one stela is not illustrated (A39); four of the women on the remaining six wear the tripartite wig.

47. For a rare example of the lotus blossom turned away from the ꜣḫ dedicatee and toward the worshiper, see Alan R. Schulman, "Some Observations on the ꜣḫ iḳr n Rꜥ-Stelae," *BiOr* 43, nos. 3–4 (1986): 334 and 335, C 17, commentary. Cf. Demarée, *Stelae*, p. 174 n. 4.

48. Schulman, "Observations," p. 317, and his "A Birth Scene(?) from Memphis," *JARCE* 22 (1985): 103; Demarée, *Stelae*, pp. 283–284, 286, and esp. n. 26.

49. Demarée, *Stelae*, pp. 53, 129–30 (illus. A49). On the term *sn*, see Morris Bierbrier, "Terms of Relationship at Deir el-Medina," *JEA* 66 (1980): 104–106; and Sheila Whale, *The Family in the Eighteenth Dynasty of Egypt*, Australian Centre for Egyptology Studies, no. 1 (Sydney, 1989), p. 240, citing H. O. Willems, *A Description of Egyptian Kinship Terminology of the Middle Kingdom c. 2000–1650 BC* (Leiden, 1983), p. 159.

50. Demarée, *Stelae*, p. 284. The terms for fathers, brothers, and sons, however, may have had extended kinship meanings; see Detlef Franke, "Verwandtschaftsbezeichnungen," *LA* 6, p. 1033; and Demarée, *Stelae*, pp. 283–286.

51. Demarée, *Stelae*, p. 279; he notes that eleven were found in "official" excavations. Schulman, "Observations," pp. 314 –315, adds to this count another eighteen. For Demarée's additional three examples from Deir el Medina, see "More ꜣḫ iḳr n Rꜥ-stelae," *BiOr* 43, nos. 3–4 (1986): 348–350. See also A. I.Sadek, *Popular Religion in Egypt during the New Kingdom*, Hildesheimer Ägyptologische Beiträge 27 (Hildesheim, 1987), p. 77.

52. Bruyère, *Rapport (1934–35)*, p. 55; Demarée, *Stelae*, pp. 286–287. Baines, however (in "Society," p. 128), asserts that "ancestor cults were not widespread or long-lasting among the non-royal in Egypt, but the recently dead were important to the living in various ways." Also against the idea of an expanded ancestor cult, see Dietrich Wildung, "Ahnenkult," *LA* 1, pp. 111–112; Schafik Allam, "Familie, soziale Funktion," *LA* 2, p. 102. Nevertheless, the geographic distribution of the stelae would seem to oppose the view that private ancestor cults were not widespread. See also Bowmann, *Private Chapel*, pp. 74 ("a developed private ancestor cult existed" in Amarna as well as Deir el Medina) and 68.

53. Distribution of the offering tables is also varied within the site. See Demarée, *Stelae*, pp. 145–153, for discussion of nine (B1–9) limestone offering tables (and two libation basins) dedicated to the *ꜣḫ iḳr*. Demarée stresses that "most of the offering tables/libation basins from our group B, all of which feature the designation as *ꜣḫ iḳr/ꜣḫ iḳr n Rꜥ*, were found in the living-quarters of the Village. These objects evidently also constituted a necessary element in the cultic practices" (p. 287).

54. Demarée, *Stelae*, p. 287; Sadek, *Popular Religion*, pp. 63, 65; Schulman, "Observations," esp. p. 315.

55. Schulman, "Observations," pp. 308, 311, 316, 317, 347; cf. Florence D. Friedman, "On the Meaning of Some Anthropoid Busts from Deir el-Medina," *JEA* 71 (1985): 87–89. A form of *ꜣḫ iḳr n Rꜥ* sculpture in the round (see the discussion of anthropoid busts, below) seems to make an appearance from the Eighteenth Dynasty, the figure being identified by the lotus that he holds. See, e.g., J. R. Ogden, "A Fragmentary New Kingdom Statue at Buenos Aires," *GM* 119 (1960): 69.

56. The fathers, husbands, brothers, or sons found as dedicatees on the *ꜣḫ iḳr n Rꜥ* stelae are similarly found as addressees in the Letters of the Dead. See Demarée, *Stelae*, pp. 282 n. 12, 268 (citing P. Leyden I, 371), and the discussion in Joris F. Borghouts's contribution below.

57. P. of Iouiya 64.19, trans. T. G. Allen, *The Book of the Dead; or, Going Forth by Day*. SAOC, 37 (Chicago, 1974), Spell 64, var. S20.

58. Florence D. Friedman, *On the Meaning of Akh (ꜣḫ) in Egyptian Mortuary Texts*, University Microfilms (Ann Arbor, Mich., 1981), pp. 233–235. On *ꜣḫ* as an earthly individual, see p. 262. On *ꜣḫ iḳr*, see Gertie Englund, *Akh—un notion religieuse dans l'Egypte pharaonique* (Uppsala, 1978), esp. pp. 167–169.

59. A woman whose husband recently survived a serious plane crash was told by a family member that the husband had been spared because the woman's father, dead some ten years at the time, had assuredly helped the man from the burning plane. The belief, or wish, that dead relatives can be efficacious in earthly affairs is a universal and timeless phenomenon.

60. Schulman, "Observations," p. 313 (with references), notes that at both the Amarna workmen's village and at Deir el Medina, funerary and votive types of stelae are equally attested in the house.

61. Demarée, "Remove Your Stela," in *Gleanings from Deir el-Medina*, ed. R. J. Demarée and Jac. J. Janssen (Leiden, 1982), pp. 106–107. See Schulman, "Ex-votos of the Poor," *JARCE* 6 (1967): 153–156, pls. I–II. Mortuary stelae could be reused as ex-votos (objects offered to a god in thanks for a prayer having been answered or in hopes that it will be), as Schulman demonstrated with examples from Memphis.

62. Jean Keith-Bennett, "Anthropoid Busts, II: Not from Deir el Medineh Alone," *BES* 3 (1981): 43–71 (p. 44 for descriptive term "anthropoid busts," p. 48 on the lack of inscriptions, with only two of the Deir el Medina examples and two others of unknown provenance being exceptions).

63. Werner Kaiser, "Zur Büste als einer Darstellungsform ägyptischer Rund-plastik," *MDAIK* 46 (1990): 270. There are also smaller examples in wood, clay, and Nile mud (I thank B. V. Bothmer for this reference). See also Bruyère, *Rapport (1930)*, pp. 10–11. Kaiser, "Zur Büste," esp. p. 271, n. 10 with references; and see B. V. Bothmer, "Ancestral Bust," in *Antiquities from the Collection of Christos G. Bastis*, ed. E. S. Hall (New York, 1987), p. 27, for bust with what was originally a "light brown" face and neck.

64. J. Keith-Bennett (in conversation, July 29, 1992) has noted that twenty-six busts from Deir el Medina—about a third of the known examples from that site—are without heads and therefore, of course, evidence no wig. The tripartite wig that is so common on the busts appears on four of the seven known female dedicatees on the *ꜣḥ iḳr n Rꜥ* stelae from Demarée's study in *Stelae:* A6, 41, 44, and 45. An analysis is needed of the wigs on the *ꜣḥ iḳr* monuments. The origin of the bust form probably cannot be fully determined; suggestions in Friedman, "Meaning," pp. 82–97, while still intriguing, cannot apply to all the busts, which come from so many varied sites. See Keith-Bennett, "Anthropoid Busts," p. 45, on the lotus as perhaps indicative of Deir el Medina exanples. J. Keith-Bennett, *The Anthropoid Busts of Deir el Medineh and Other Sites and Collections: Analysis, Catalogue, and Appendices*, DFIFAO (forthcoming), analyzes the *wsḥ* collars and necklaces.

65. For busts from various sites without hair or with caplike treatment of the head, see Keith-Bennett, "Anthropoid Busts," G1, S1, Ses 1. Five examples of double busts, representing joined figures of a man and a woman, depict the males with caplike hair and the women with tripartite wigs; none of these can be definitely assigned to Deir el Medina, although Louvre E14702 (p. 62) is a possibility. See Kaiser, "Zur Büste," p. 277.

66. Bruyère, *Rapport (1934–35)*, p. 55. See Rudolf Anthes, "Die deutschen

Grabungen auf der Westseite von Theben in den Jahren 1911 und 1913,"
MDAIK 12 (1943): 58–59, pl. 16; Bruyère, *Rapport (1934–35),* p. 171, fig. 66
(now Louvre E 16348); and Keith-Bennett, "Anthropoid Busts," p. 47.

67. Friedman, "Meaning," pp. 85–86; Sadek, *Popular Religion,* p. 78.

68. Keith-Bennett, "Anthropoid Busts," pp. 45, 48. For a recent example
from the Egypt Exploration Society's excavations at Memphis, see Baines, "Practical Religion," p. 87, n. 41.

69. For bust amulets, see Keith-Bennett, "Anthropoid Busts," pp. 52–54.

70. Bothmer, *Antiquities,* p. 29; Valbelle, *Ouvriers,* pp. 313, 315 (also
on Ptah), 324, 332–334. Devotion to Hathor, who had the most important
sanctuary on the site (pp. 168–169), also included worship of Meretseger,
the Peak, who conflated with Hathor. Perhaps Pinch's *New Kingdom Votive
Offerings to Hathor* (still in press at this writing) will clarify these points further.

71. Keith-Bennett, "Anthropoid Busts," p. 44, n. 17; most esp. Keith-Bennett,
"Coiffure, Headdresses, and Beards," Part III, C in DFIFAO publication (forthcoming). Beards in a few cases indicate male gender, however (ibid.). The tripartite wig is also found on shawabtis, anthropoid coffins, and other funerary
equipment: C. H. Roehrig in Sue d'Auria et al., eds., *Mummies and Magic*
(Boston: Museum of Fine Arts, 1988).

72. Berlin bust 20694. See Keith-Bennett, "Anthropoid Busts," p. 48, nn. 32
and 33. See also Kaiser, "Zur Büste," p. 271, for the only other example of a
bust inscription, which is dedicated to the "mistress of the house" but does not
mention Hathor; and n. 12 and p. 272 n. 16: "Apart from these two [inscrip-
tions], only two of the at least 120 known busts which are not pendants, amu-
lettes or other things, show inscriptions" (translation mine).

73. Kaiser, "Zur Büste," p. 273; and Keith-Bennett (in conversation) noted
that Brooklyn Museum 53.246 is, in fact, the only bust of 150 that shows the
carved indication of a cap, which could be interpreted as a shaven head.

74. Keith-Bennett, "Anthropoid Busts," pp. 61–62, also cites five examples of
double busts (plus BM 270, which is a stele representing two wigless busts in
relief). Some objects in this class of busts, which are primarily or entirely non–
Deir el Medina material, do seem to designate gender. See comments in Kaiser,
"Zur Büste," p. 273.

75. J. Vandier d'Abbadie, "A propos des bustes de Laraires," *RdE* 5 (1946):
133–135 and fig. 1; BM 170 in Bierbrier, *Tomb-builders,* p. 95, fig. 69; Demarée, *Stelae,* p. 290 n. 46.

76. Friedman, "Meaning," p. 96.

77. E.g., Valbelle, *Ouvriers,* p. 261. Cf. Bruyère, "La nécropole de Deir el
Médineh," *CdE* 22 (1936): 335.

5. Magical Practices among the Villagers

I thank Professor Leonard Lesko and Barbara Lesko, who invited me to contribute to the symposium during my stay at the Department of Egyptology of Brown University.

1. See John Baines and Christopher J. Eyre, "Four Notes on Literacy," *GM* 67 (1983): 65–96; and Leonard L. Lesko, "Some Comments on Ancient Egyptian Literacy and Literati," in *Studies . . . Lichtheim,* 2:656–667.

2. See P. J. Frandsen, "Editing Reality: The Turin Strike Papyrus," in *Studies . . . Lichtheim,* 1:166–199.

3. E.g., when the crew of workmen was abruptly cut in half, and those laid off were reduced to the status of porters (O. Berlin 12654, r. 1–3).

4. Not that there are no earlier records of thievery. The notorious chief workman Paneb, for instance (discussed on p. 127), took full advantage of his position when there was a collective (re)burial of certain kings; see P. Salt 124, r. 1.4.

5. E.g., "He said to me: 'come on out, let us go get this piece of life sustenance [in order to] have food!' They took me with them and then we opened the place and got a coffin [part], a *deben* worth of silver and gold" (P. BM 10052, 3.4–5 in Peet, *Tomb Robberies*).

6. See the preceding contribution by Florence D. Friedman; Valbelle, *Ouvriers.*

7. See A. I. Sadek, *Popular Religion in Egypt during the New Kingdom,* Hildesheimer Ägyptologische Beiträge 23 (Hildesheim, 1988).

8. R ḥsf ᶜ n ḫpr.y.t, Teaching for Merikareᶜ, 136–137/P.

9. See J. F. Quack, "Zwei Ostrakon-Identifizierungen," *GM* 115 (1990): 83–84; and, on literary evidence from the village, see Leonard H. Lesko's contribution in this volume.

10. O. DeM 1197, 1–2.

11. P. Chester Beatty VII, r. 5.4–5.

12. Cited from P. Turin 1993, v.3.4 (Willem Pleyte and Francisco Rossi, *Papyrus de Turin* [Leiden, 1869–1875], p. 133.4).

13. Cf. Stanley Tambiah, "Form and Meaning of Magical Acts: A Point of View," in *Modes of Thought: Essays on Thinking in Western and Non-Western Societies,* ed. Robin Horton and Ruth Finnegan (London, 1973), pp. 199–229.

14. As its opening words indicate. Moreover, similar phraseology may be met on many a stelophorous statue (perhaps this ostracon was a draft for such an object): e.g., "Herewith I have given free course to the Great Bark and I have repelled the attack of Grimface, so that the course of the bark may take place" (stela Copenhagen/Ny Carlsb. Glypt. 49, 2–4), with a constative ("synchronous") *sḏm.n=f.* Cf. further Jan Assmann, *Ägyptische Hymnen und Gebete*

(Zurich, 1975), pp. 87–94 ("das Performative Element des Hymnus"), although the linguistic basis is not very clear, and some of Assmann's statements—e.g., regarding his no. 20—are at variance with the earlier publication in Assmann's *Der König als Sonnenpriester*, (Glückstadt, 1970), p. 68. Here the descriptive character of this text is noted; see ibid. for some convincing examples of truly "performative" utterances.

15. O. BM 5634 (Černý-Gardiner, *HO*, pp. 83–84). The number of spells against these animals should not distort our picture of the demonic world of ancient Egypt more than necessary. Their frequency in texts from Deir el Medina may simply reflect the working environment among stones and sand.

16. P. Turin 1993, v. 4.1 (Pleyte and Rossi, *Papyrus de Turin*, p. 136.1).

17. See the speech by the god Horus to the drowned ones in the Amduat Netherworld Guide: Erik Hornung, *Das Amduat* (Wiesbaden, 1963), 1:176.6–177.6.

18. The late myth of the origin of the temple of Edfu is a good example.

19. For a modern translation, see my *AEMT*, pp. 51ff.

20. For a translation, see *AEMT*, pp. 74–75. On Nemti, see Erhart Graefe, *Studien zu den Göttern und Kulten im 12. und 10. Oberägyptischen Gau* (Freiburg, 1980).

21. And so is Horus. The contest may reflect some cultic rivalry, a matter too detailed to be discussed here.

22. O. DeM 1212, r., and 1436, as well as P. Chester Beatty VII, r. 5.2–5 and r. 2.5–3.1; XI, r. A.9–12.

23. Two recent English translations are *LAE*, pp. 108–126 (trans. E. F Wente); and *AEL*, 2:214–223.

24. Not just Horus the son of Isis as one would expect (Harsiese) but Horus Hekenu, a name sometimes given to a combative form of this god which certainly well fits the purpose of the spell. Moreover, the god Re῾ attributes the name Atum-Horus-Hekenu to himself (P. Turin 1993, r. 2.10), the text thus perhaps anticipating the transfer of the name at a later point.

25. E.g., the creation myth according to the Heliopolitan version is recited in a late ritual against the chaos-being Apopis (in the late P. Bremner-Rhind) *because* it excludes any mention of this demon in the days of the beginning and so diminishes Apopis's power as compared to that of the primeval gods, thus giving ritual the possibility of dealing with the demon and solving the problem.

26. For an illuminating spell against them, see Ivan Koenig, "Un revenu inconvenant? (Papyrus Deir el-Médineh 37)," *BIFAO* 79 (1979): 103–119.

27. Robert J. Demarée, *The ʾḥ iḳr n R῾-stelae: On Ancestor Worship in Ancient Egypt* (Leiden, 1983); Florence D. Friedman, "On the Meaning of Some Anthropoid Busts from Deir el-Medina," *JEA* 71 (1985): 82–97, and Friedman's contribution to this volume.

28. Alessandro Roccati has proposed the translation "capable spirit" in an article in *Hommages à Serge Sauneron* (Cairo, 1979), 1:281–283. An alternative term *mwt*, simply meaning "dead one," always has a dangerous sense.

29. Several of these ostraca have been edited in Alan H. Gardiner's *Late Egyptian Stories*, Bibliotheca Aegyptiaca 1 (Brussels, 1932), pp. 89–94, and new ones have turned up since. For a translation by Edward Wente, see *LAE*, pp. 137–141.

30. The best-known example is the letter by Butehamun to his wife Iakhtay, in O. Louvre Inv. 698 (Černý-Gardiner, *HO*, 1:80).

31. A large manuscript is P. DeM I, r. (though it does not contain the foregoing passage). For a survey of the other mss., including those from DeM, see Jaroslav Černý and Georges Posener, *Papyrus hiératiques de Deir el Médineh* (Cairo, 1978), 1:2–3; add O. DeM 1658 (Inv. 2752).

32. P. Boulaq IV, 9.1–2. Cf. Georges Posener, "Les 'afārīt dans l'ancienne Egypte," *MDAIK* 37 (1981): 393–401.

33. P. Turin 1995 + 1996, r. 5.8–10 (Pleyte and Rossi, *Papyrus de Turin*, p. 124.8–10).

34. Ibid., v. 1.6 foll. (Pleyte and Rossi, *Papyrus de Turin*, p. 120.6 foll.) For a translation, see *AEMT*, p. 4 foll.

35. See I.E.S. Edwards's masterly edition, *Oracular Amuletic Decrees of the Late New Kingdom* (HPBM[4]), 2 vols. (London, 1960).

36. See, e.g., the text published by Jac. J. Janssen, "Marriage Problems and Public Reactions (P. BM 10416)," in *Pyramid Studies and Other Essays Presented to I.E.S. Edwards* (London, 1988), pp. 134–137.

37. The "qenbet" is dealt with in McDowell, *Jurisdiction*. The usual place to convene this or other representative bodies was a corner of a gate; see Guido van den Boorn, "*Wd'-ryt* and Justice at the Gate," *JNES* 44 (1985): 1–25.

38. Admittedly, this is a matter of speculation in the case of the village oracle. The carriers of the statue may have played an important role here.

39. Jaroslav Černý, "Papyrus Salt 124 (Brit. Mus. 10055)," *JEA* 15 (1929): 243–258, republished in KRI 4:408–414. The *udjat* is a mythical eye, often identified with that of the omnipresent sun god.

40. O. DeM 1057, translated in *AEMT*, p. 1.

41. For discussions, see H.-W. Fischer-Elfert, "Dein Heisser," in Anast. V 7, 5–8 und seine Beziehung zur Lehre des Amenemope, Kap. 2–4, *Die Welt des Orients* 14 (1983): 83–90; and Joris F. Borghouts, "The 'Hot One' (*p' šmw*) in Ostracon Deir el Médineh 1265," *GM* 38 (1980): 21–28.

42. O. Leipzig 8, edited in Černý-Gardiner, *HO* I, pl. 7, no. 5. The "East" is traditionally the place where executions in the netherworld were thought to be carried out; it is obvious what Amenemhat had in mind as the final destination of his opponent.

43. Published as O. DeM 1265.

44. See Borghouts, "The 'Hot One.' "

45. The material in Lucy Mair's well-known *Witchcraft* (London, 1969), for instance, is based mainly on African sources.

46. For a treatment of the dossier, see Borghouts, Divine Intervention, pp. 1–70.

47. Still another term for magic, ˀḫ.w ("akhu"), belongs to the sphere of theology and is thus, as noted earlier, outside the context of popular magic. For its relationship to ḥkˀ, see my article " ˀḫ.w (akhu) and ḥkˀ.w (ḥekau): Two Basic Notions of Ancient Egyptian Magic, and the Concept of the Divine Creative Word," in *La Magia in Egitto ai Tempi dei Faraoni*, ed. Alessandro Roccati and Alberto Siliotti (Milan, 1987), pp. 29–46.

48. Stela DeM with the provisional number 320, now also published in KRI 3:687.

49. O. Gardiner 166, r., published in Allam, *HOP*, 1:46.

50. O. DeM 251.

51. Stela Berlin 20377, 8, republished in KRI 3:654.11.

52. O. Gardiner 149, unpublished, kindly brought to my notice by Robert J. Demarée; quoted from a transcription by Jaroslav Černý with permission of the Griffith Institute, Oxford; translated in full in Borghouts, Divine Intervention, pp. 24–25.

6. Literature, Literacy, and Literati

1. P. Chester Beatty XVIII; Alan H. Gardiner, *HPBM*[3], 1:131.

2. Jaroslav Černý and Georges Posener, *Papyrus hiératiques de Deir el-Medineh*, vol. 1 (Cairo, 1978).

3. Alessandro Roccati, "Tra i papiri torinesi (Scavi nel Museo di Torino, 7)" *Oriens Antiquus* 14 (1975): 243–253.

4. Černý and Posener, *Papyrus hiératiques*, p. viii; P. W. Pestman, "Who Were the Owners in the 'Community of Workmen' of the Chester Beatty Papyri?" in *Gleanings from Deir el-Medina*, ed. R. J. Demarée and Jac. J. Janssen (Leiden, 1982), pp. 155–172.

5. Bierbrier, *Tomb-builders*, p. 80.

6. J.W.B. Barnes, *The Ashmolean Ostracon of Sinuhe* (Oxford, 1952); Bierbrier, *Tomb-builders*, pp. 78–81. Comparatively few ostraca have any corrections at all. Those corrections in black ink (e.g., O. DeM 1253, I, 5) may have been made by the scribe himself before completion, and even the corrections in red (e.g., on O. DeM 1244) could have been noted by the scribe when adding his verse points in red ink; the so-called verse points could indeed have served as collation marks.

7. John Baines, "Literacy and Ancient Egyptian Society," *Man*, n.s. 18 (1983): 585.

8. Georges Posener, *Catalogue des ostraca hiératiques littéraires de Deir el Medineh*, vol. 2 (fasc. 3) (Cairo, 1972), pp. v–viii.

9. These works are commonly found in anthologies of Egyptian literature such as *LAE; AEL;* and John A. Wilson, trans., in J. B. Pritchard's *Ancient Near Eastern Texts Relating to the Old Testament*, 3d ed. (Princeton, 1969).

10. O. Oriental Institue 12074; William K. Simpson, "Allusions to *The Ship-wrecked Sailor* and *The Eloquent Peasant* in a Ramesside Text," *JAOS* 78 (1958): 50–51.

11. See John A. Wilson, "The Language of the Historical Texts Commemorating Ramses III," in *Medinet Habu Studies 1928–29*, Oriental Institute Communication 7 (Chicago, 1930), pp. 24–33.

12. Roccati, "Tra i papiri," pp. 248–253.

13. Černý, *Workmen*, pp. 191–230.

14. Gardiner, *HPBM*³, 1:23.

15. Pestman, "Who Were the Owners?" p. 156.

16. The hymn appears in P. Chester Beatty IV. For the "wild one," see n. 10 above, and Janssen, "Two Personalities," pp. 109–131.

17. Jaroslav Černý, "Papyrus Salt 124 (Brit. Mus. 10055)," *JEA* 15 (1929): 243–258.

18. Baines, "Literacy," pp. 572–599; John Baines and Christopher J. Eyre, "Four Notes on Literacy," *GM* 61 (1983): 65–96; and Herman te Velde, "Scribes and Literacy in Ancient Egypt," in *Scripta Signa Vocis, Studies . . . presented to J. H. Hospers* (Groningen, 1986), pp. 253–264.

19. William C. Hayes, "Inscriptions from the Palace of Amenhotep III," *JNES* 10 (1951): esp. 19; and H. W. Fairman, "The Inscriptions," in *The City of Akhenaton*, ed. J.D.S. Pendlebury (London, 1951), vol. 3, pt. 1, pp. 143–180.

20. "Literacy," p. 572.

21. See Jaroslav Černý, *Catalogue des ostraca hieratiques non litteraires de Deir el Medineh*, 7 vols. (Cairo, 1935–70); Jesus Lopez, *Ostraca ieratici*, Cat. Mus. Eg. Tor., 2d ser. (Milan, 1978–); Serge Sauneron, *Catalogue des ostraca hiératiques non littéraires de Deir el Medineh* (Cairo, 1959–); and Jaroslav Černý and A. A. Sadek, *Graffiti de la montagne thébaine*, 4 vols. (Cairo, 1969–77).

22. Černý, *Workmen*, pp. 319, 334.

23. O. DeM 121, in Wente, *Letters*, p. 162, no. 255.

24. Bierbrier, *Tomb-builders*, pp. 78–80.

25. Jaroslav Černý, "A Stone with an Appeal to the Finder," *Oriens Antiquus*, 6 (1967): 47–50, pls. 16–19.

26. Pestman, "Who Were the Owners?" pp. 158–166; P. Chester Beatty III; Gardiner, *HPBM³*, pp. 26–27.

27. Gardiner, *HPBM³*, p. viii; Pestman, "Who Were the Owners?" pp. 162–163.

28. Jaroslav Černý, "The Will of Naunakhte and the Related Documents," *JEA* 31 (1945): 42–53; Černý, *Workmen*, p. 333; Morris L. Bierbrier, *The Late New Kingdom in Egypt (c. 1300–664 B.C.)* (Warminster, 1975), pp. 26–29; Gardiner, *HPBM³*, p. 78; Pestman, "Who Were the Owners?" p. 156.

29. Černý, *LRL*, pp. 18–19; Wente, *LRL*, pp. 38–40.

30. Pestman, "Who Were the Owners?" p. 171 n. 37.

31. Černý, *Workmen*, pp. 331–332; Bierbrier, *Tomb-builders*, pp. 33–35.

32. Gardiner, *HPBM³*, vol. 2, p. 3, v. lines 5ff.

33. For the "Maxims of Ptahhotep" cf. *LAE*, pp. 159–176, and *AEL*, pp. 61–80. For what survives of the beginning of the "Instruction of Hordedef," cf. *LAE*, p. 340, and *AEL*, pp. 58–59.

34. *LAE*, pp. 177–179; and *AEL*, pp. 59–61.

35. E.g., "Ipuwer" (*AEL*, pp. 149–163; *LAE*, pp. 210–229); "Instruction for King Merikare" (*LAE*, pp. 180–192; *AEL*, pp. 97–107); and "Dispute of a Man and his Ba" (*AEL*, pp. 163–169, *LAE*, pp. 201–209).

36. Alan H. Gardiner, *The Admonitions of an Egyptian Sage* (Leipzig, 1909), pl 17; BM 5645, 1R2–3, 5–6. Cf. Gerald Kadish, in *JEA* 59 (1973): 85; Boyo Ockinga, in *JEA*, 69 (1983): 88–95; *LAE*, p. 231.

37. See E. D. Cruz-Uribe, "The Fall of the Middle Kingdom," *VA* 3 (1987): 107–111.

38. Georges Posener, *Literature et politique dans l'Egypte de la XIIe dynastie* (Paris, 1956), pp. 21–60, 145–157; cf. Alan H. Gardiner, *JEA* 1 (1914): 100–106.

39. *LAE*, pp. 50–56.

40. Gardiner, *HPBM³*, pl. 20; P. Chester Beatty IV, 6v13–14.

41. See Hellmut Brunner, *Die Lehre des Cheti, Sohne des Duauf*, Agyptologische Forschungen 13 (Glückstadt, 1944); Wolfgang Helck, *Die Lehre des Dw³-Htjj* (Wiesbaden 1970); and *LAE*, pp. 329–336.

42. See Posener, *Catalogue;* T.G.H. James, *Pharaoh's People* (London, 1984), pp. 147–149; and Bierbrier, *Tomb-builders*, p. 81.

43. *LAE*, pp. 180–192.

44. Hans Goedicke, *The Report about the Dispute of a Man with His Ba* (*Papyrus Berlin 3024*) (Baltimore, 1970), pp. 5–8.

45. Leonard H. Lesko, "Some Comments on Ancient Egyptian Literacy and Literati," in *Studies . . . Lichtheim,* 2:665–666; cf. also *JAOS* 93 (1973): 78–79.

46. Bierbrier, *Tomb-builders,* p. 81.

47. Georges Posener, *L'enseignement loyaliste* (Geneva, 1976), pp. 14 n. 11, 7–11.

48. See *LAE,* p. 199.

49. Brunner, *Lehre des Cheti,* pp. 95–96 (P. Sallier II, 4, 1); see also *LAE,* p. 330.

50. Lesko, "Some Comments," p. 667.

51. Pestman, "Who Were the Owners?" p. 162.

52. Herodotus *Histories,* 2.102–110; and Diodorus Siculus 1.53–58.

53. E.g., "The Shipwrecked Sailor," "King Khufu and the Magicians," "The Eloquent Peasant," and "The Dispute of a Man with His Ba," all available in English translation in *AEL* and *LAE.*

54. For "Amenemopet," see *LAE,* pp. 241–265, and *AEL,* pp. 146–163. For "Ani," Wilson in Pritchard, *Ancient Near Eastern Texts,* pp. 420–421, and *AEL,* pp. 135–143.

55. See Gardiner, *HPBM³,* p. 38.

56. See Barbara S. Lesko, "True Art in Ancient Egypt," in *Studies . . . Parker,* pp. 85–97.

57. The texts on the walls of Ramesside mortuary temples and in royal tombs were all essentially in Middle Egyptian, though the number of Late Egyptian corruptions and inconsistencies, particularly in the temples, became progressively greater over time.

Acknowledgments

This volume of essays dealing with various aspects of life in the community of artisans at Deir el Medina was an integral part of our original plan for a symposium on the topic that was held at Brown University on February 24, 1990. To all presenters and discussants as well as to the participatory audience I am most grateful. The authors have enhanced their original presentations and patiently endured the queries of several editors. From their point of view the editors, particularly Liz Holmes of Cornell University Press, had a major task in achieving unity with such diversity of approaches and styles. Six authors might not make the job six times as difficult, but nearly so.

We are grateful to all those who have furnished photographs or given permission for illustrations of museum objects as well as reused line drawings, and we trust that these are all properly acknowledged individually above. We thank Mary Winkes for her map and line drawings, and Stephen Thompson for the index as well as for his quick read of the proofs, which prevented a few oversights in each of the chapters. He, of course, cannot be held responsible for any remaining errors. That responsibility falls on the editor and the individual authors.

Again, I thank Bernhard Kendler of Cornell University Press for his enthusiastic support of another difficult project involving multiple authorship. And finally, in addition to Brown University's subvention (which

Acknowledgments

came from the Department of Egyptology's Wilbour Fund) toward the publication specifically of the numerous illustrations in *Pharaoh's Workers*, I also thank Brown University's Lectureship Committee for its support of the original symposium.

L. H. L.

Contributors

Joris F. Borghouts is Professor of Egyptology and Chairman of the Department of Egyptology at the University of Leiden in the Netherlands. He received his Ph.D. from that university in 1971 and has written extensively on Egyptian magic and religion as well as on Egyptian language and literature. He has recently published a grammar of the Middle Egyptian or classical phase of the ancient language.

Florence D. Friedman is Curator of Ancient Art at the Museum of Art, Rhode Island School of Design in Providence, where she both teaches and organizes exhibitions. She received her Ph.D in Egyptology in 1981 from Brandeis University and has written on ancient Egyptian religious concepts as well as art historical topics.

Barbara S. Lesko is the Administrative Research Assistant in the Department of Egyptology at Brown University and an Instructor in the Brown Learning Community, having received her M.A. in Egyptology from the University of Chicago in 1965. She has collaborated with her husband, Leonard H. Lesko, for many years to produce the five-volume *Dictionary of Late Egyptian,* but has specialized in social history, with an emphasis on the women of ancient Egypt.

Contributors

Leonard H. Lesko has been Charles Edwin Wilbour Professor of Egyptology and Chairman of the Department of Egyptology at Brown University since 1982. He received his Ph.D in Egyptology from the University of Chicago in 1969 when teaching for the University of California. His interests span religious and literary texts, ancient oenology, and lexicography and have resulted in a number of publications including the *Dictionary of Late Egyptian* (editor) and *Religion in Ancient Egypt* (co-author).

Andrea G. McDowell received her Ph.D in Ancient History from the University of Pennsylvania in 1987, and her dissertation was later published as *Jurisdiction in the Workman's Communitiy of Deir el Medineh*. After teaching at the University of Leiden and receiving a Research Fellowship at Somerville College, Oxford, she is currently an Assistant Professor of Egyptology in the Department of Near Eastern Studies at the Johns Hopkins University.

William A. Ward, for many years Professor of Ancient Near Eastern History and Languages at the American University of Beirut, is currently Visiting Professor of Egyptology at Brown University and Director of Brown's Ancient Studies Program. He received his Ph.D. from Brandeis University in 1958 and has produced many books including studies of scarabs, Egyptian administrative titles, and intercultural relations in the ancient Eastern Mediterranean world.

Index

Index